GEMSTONES
of the World

Walter Schumann

Translated by Evelyne Stern FGA

Sterling Publishing Co. Inc, New York

Press Ltd, Colchester, Essex

Published (in English) 1977
Reprinted 1979
Reprinted 1986
Reprinted 1990

Translated from the German book "Edelsteine und Schmucksteine"*,
by Evelyne Stern FGA. American consultant: Prof. Anthony C. Tennissen,
Department of Geology, Lamar University, Beaumont, Texas.
*© 1976 BLV Verlagsgesellschaft mbH, Munich.

Library of Congress Catalog Card No.: 77-79503
Sterling: ISBN 0-8069-3088-8 Trade
3089-6 Library

N.A.G. Press: ISBN 7198 0051 X

Typeset in Great Britain at The Grange Press Ltd, Southwick, Sussex,
and printed in West Germany by Druckerei Georg Appl, Wemding

Contents

Preface

Gemstones have always fascinated mankind. In former centuries they were reserved for the ruling classes only. Today everybody can afford beautiful stones for jewelry and adornment. Precious stones for sale, especially if one includes those in so-called costume or fashion jewelry, are so numerous that it is hardly possible for the layman to survey or judge what is available. This little book has been written to help: it shows the many gems of the world in their many varieties, rough and cut, in true-to-nature color photographs. The accompanying text – always adjacent to the photographs – is designed to be of use to both the expert and the layman.

Introductory chapters on formation, properties, deposits, manufacture, synthesis and imitations provide a survey of the world of beautiful stones. Unknown gemstones can be identified with the help of the tables at the end of the book. In order to be able to impart as much information as possible, a telegraphic type of style has been chosen.

In order to avoid any misunderstandings, prices are not mentioned. These can vary considerably from place to place and year to year. The gem expert is in the best position to advise. The properties comprising the quality of a gem are discussed in this book. As practical help for the buyer or collector of gems, there are suggestions on the various possibilities of confusing an individual gemstone with a similar one, a synthetic one or an imitation.

I received valuable help from professional colleagues, friends and acquaintances, institutes, firms and private persons who made stones available for illustration. My thanks are due to all of them with special thanks to Mr. Paul Ruppenthal, Idar-Oberstein. I also thank Mr. Karl Hartmann, Sobernheim, for taking the special photographs.

Walter Schumann

Gemstones for the color plates were made available by:
Carl Friedrich Arnoldi, Idar-Oberstein; Fredrich August Becker, Idar-Oberstein; Ernst A. Bunzel, Idar-Oberstein; Karl A. Bunzel, Idar-Oberstein; Hein Gaertner, Idar-Oberstein; Hans Gordner, Hettenrodt; Karl Hartmann, Sobernheim; Industrie-und Handelskammer, Koblenz, Bezirksstelle Idar-Oberstein; Otto und Dieter Jerusalem GmbH, Herborn; Karl-Otto Kullmann, Hettenrodt; R. Litzenberger, Idar-Oberstein; Hans Walter Lorenz, Idar-Oberstein; Deutsches Edelsteinmuseum, Idar-Oberstein; Erwin Pauly, Veitsrodt; Ulrich Pauly, Veitsrodt; Julius Petsch Jr., Idar-Oberstein; A. Ruppenthal KG, Idar-Oberstein; Dr Walter Schumann, Munich; Curt Stolz, Munich; Christian Weise, Munich; Gebr. Wild, Idar-Oberstein.

Introduction

Gemstones and their influence

Gems have intrigued men for the last 7,000 years. The first known were amethyst, rock crystal, amber, garnet, jade, jasper, coral, lapis lazuli, pearl, serpentine, emerald and turquoise. These stones were reserved for the wealthy and served as status symbols. Rulers sealed documents with jewel-encrusted seals, which were an expression of their wealth and power.

Although sometimes today a gem set in gold or platinum is worn to demonstrate wealth, jewelry is bought increasingly for pleasure, in appreciation of its beauty. Sometimes superstition also plays a part in the purchase of a gemstone.

Formerly, when people were less scientifically knowledgeable, gems always had an aura of mystery, something almost spiritual. That is why they were worn as amulets and talismans. It was thought they offered protection against ghosts, and prejudiced angels and saints in the wearer's favor. They could repulse evil, preserve health, ward off poisons and the plague; they also made princes gracious and led sailors home.

Up to the beginning of the 19th century, gemstones were sometimes used as medicine against illnesses. They could be used in three different ways: the mere presence of the stone was sufficient to effect a cure; the gem was placed on the afflicted part of the body; or the stone was powdered and eaten. Information as to which gem would cure individual illnesses could be found in books. Successes achieved by this lithotherapy were not due to the gems directly, but to the effect of the suggestion on the sufferer. Failures were excused by the explanation that the stone used was not "genuine". Even today calcium tablets made out of powdered pearls are sold for medicinal purposes in Japan.

As a natural consequence of the supposed supernatural powers of gemstones, a link with astrology was formed and gemstones were allocated to the signs of the zodiac. This led to the birthstones: stones which accompany and protect those born under a certain sign of the zodiac. To simplify this, "stones of the month" were created. There are also stones allocated to the sun, the moon and the planets. Over the years, these allocations have often been changed. More recently some states have taken a certain gem which is found within their frontiers as their state emblem.

Gems also have an assured place in modern religion. The breastplate of the high priests of Judea were studded with four rows of gemstones. Precious stones adorn the tiara and miter of the Pope and Bishops as well as the monstrances, reliquaries and icons found in Christian churches.

However, today the gemstone is stripped of all symbolism and aesthetics and is often viewed only as a capital investment. It is a fact that wealth, kept in such small form, has survived the pressures of inflation better than most investments over the last decades.

The English Imperial State Crown with the Black Prince's Ruby and the sparkling Cullinan II.

Terminology

Precious and semi-precious stones All precious and semi-precious stones have something special, something beautiful about them. In the past only a few stones were classed as gems, but today there are many; and new ones are being discovered all the time. Most of them are minerals, some are rocks, some are of organic origin (such as amber, coral and pearl). Even fossils are used as ornamental materials. There is no definite demarcation line and woods, bones, glass and metals can be included. Some materials from these groups are suitable for making ornaments (for instance jet, ivory, moldavite and gold nuggets). By synthesizing precious stones and creating materials not existing in nature (for instance strontium titanate and YAG), the variety of available gemstones has increased considerably.

Harder stones are suitable for jewelry, while softer stones are often sought after by amateur collectors and serious lapidarists. Those which do not quite conform as to color or other structure are called gem varieties.

"Semi-precious" stones refer to softer stones of less value as opposed to precious stones. The designation is still used in the trade but is not a sound expression because many so-called semi-precious stones are more valuable than "precious" ones. A better term for all is gemstones.

Gemstones Collective name for all ornamental stones. There is no real demarcation line between more or less valuable stones and it is therefore a synonym for precious and semi-precious stones.

Minerals A mineral is a natural, inorganic, solid constituent of the earth's crust. Most minerals also have definite crystal forms. Mineralogy is the science of minerals.

Crystals A crystal is a uniform body with a geometric lattice. The varying structures of the lattice are the causes of the varying physical properties of the crystals and therefore also of the minerals and gems. Crystallography is the science of crystals.

Rocks Rocks are aggregates of natural minerals, usually large units. Sand and gravel are also considered as rocks. Petrography is the science of rocks.

Stones Popularly, stones are the collective name for all solid constituents of the earth's crust. For the jeweler a stone is a gem, for the architect the material used for building streets and houses. In the science of the earth, geology, one does not talk of stones, but of rocks and minerals.

Jewels Every personal ornamental piece is a jewel. Generally a jewel refers to a piece of jewelry containing gems set in precious metal. It can also refer to cut, unset gemstones.

The Nomenclature of Gems

The oldest names for gemstones can be traced back to oriental languages, to Greek and to Latin. Greek names especially have left their stamp on modern gem nomenclature. The meaning of the old name is not always certain, especially where the first meaning of the word has been changed.

The original names referred to the special characteristics of the stones: to their color (for instance "prase" to its green color), to their place of discovery ("agate" after a river in Sicily), and lastly to their alleged mysterious powers ("amethyst" protects against drunkenness).

Nomenclature has only been viewed scientifically since the beginning of the modern age. Because of the discovery of many hitherto unknown minerals, new names had to be found. A principle for naming a new mineral was established which is still adhered to today. A new name is devised to refer to some special characteristic of the mineral based on Latin or Greek, to the place of occurrence or after a person.

Mineral names based on occurrences are controversial. The spelling may vary in different languages. It also does not help one's understanding if the most important occurrences of, say, vesuvianite (obviously named after Mount Vesuvius in Italy) are found today in Canada, the U.S. and Russia. Because of this drawback, a new name has been suggested for the stone – idocrase (after its crystal form) – with the result that we now have two names for the same mineral. Additionally a variety of vesuvianite found in Siberia has been named after a local river and is called wiluite, so now we have three different names for the same mineral. There are many other examples of series of synonyms.

Even more questionable is naming them after people. Not only experts who identified or discovered the mineral are honored in this way, but also princes, politicians, economists and others who have little or no connection with mineralogy or gemology.

In addition to the scientific mineral name, the jewelry trade has, in the past, created a profusion of misnomers, mainly to stimulate sales. In some countries they still do. Foreign-sounding names are one way used by large companies to stimulate sales. Two gemstone names invented in this way are tanzanite (blue zoisite) and tsavorite (green grossular garnet).

In order to correct this state of affairs and provide information, the German government has published a legally-binding standard RAL 560 A5. Other countries have similar laws or recommendations. It is questionable whether these established names or any other system of nomenclature will be accepted by the trade internationally. To be fair to the trade, it must be mentioned that it is not always marketing practice or apathy which causes the using of wrong or confusing names; in many cases the expert scientific knowledge is missing. This book might therefore help not only the buyer but also the seller.

Table of Commercial and Mineral Names

Commercial Name	CORRECT Mineralogical Name
Accabar	Black coral
Achrite	Dioptase
African jade	Green grossular garnet
Almandine spinel	Natural purple spinel
Amazon jade	Green microcline feldspar
Arkansas diamond	Rock crystal
Atlas pearls	Beads of white satin spar
Aztec stone	Smithsonite
Beccarite	Green zircon
Bishop's stone	Amethyst
Black amber	Jet
Canary stone	Yellow cornelian
Canary diamond	Yellow diamond
Cape chrysolite or Cape emerald	Prehnite
Cape ruby	Pyrope garnet
Ceruline	Calcite colored with malachite and azurite
Cinnamon stone	Hessonite garnet
Colorado ruby	Pyrope garnet
Coral agate	Agate pseudomorphous after coral
Craquelees	Cracked rock crystal
Cross stone	Staurolite twin crystals and chiastolite
Cymophane	Chrysoberyl cat's eye
Danburite	Synthetic red corundum
Daourite	Red tourmaline
Disthene	Kyanite
Ditroite	Sodalite
Dust pearls	Small seed pearls
Edinite	Prase
Egeran	Idocrase
Enhydrus	Chalcedony with water inclusion
Eye stone	Thomsonite
Feather gypsum	Satin spar
Flame spinel	Natural orange spinel
Flash opal	Opal with one-colored flash
Giogetto	Black pearl
Girasol	Fire opal, water opal or moonstone
Goldfluss	Aventurine glass
Gold opal	Fire opal
Green starstone	Chlorastrolite
Greenstone	Nephrite and chlorastrolite
Hawaiite	Peridot from Hawaii
Heliocite	Aventurine feldspar
Iceland agate	Obsidian
Imperial jade	Fine Chinese jade
Inca stone	Pyrite
Indian jade	Green aventurine quartz

Commercial Name	CORRECT Mineralogical Name
Indian topaz	Yellow sapphire
Jacinth	Red zircon and hessonite garnet
Jet stone	Black tourmaline (schorl)
Kidney stone	Nephrite
Korea jade	Almandine garnet
Lynx eye	Labradorite with green ray
Lynx sapphire	Iolite
Maiden pearl	Untouched pearl
Malacon	Brownish zircon
Manchurian jade	Soapstone
Maori stone	Nephrite
Mexican onyx	Stalagmitic calcite
Montana jet	Obsidian
Montana ruby	Red garnet
Nassau pearl	Pink conch pearl
New Zealand greenstone	Nephrite
Oriental alabaster	Stalagmitic calcite
Oriental amethyst	Violet sapphire
Oriental cat's eye	Chrysoberyl cat's eye
Oriental topaz	Yellow sapphire
Oriental emerald	Green sapphire
Ox-eye	Labradorite feldspar
Paris pearls	Imitation pearls
Paste	Glass imitation
Pigeon-blood agate	Cornelian
Pipe stone	Red siliceous clay
Prase opal	Stained green opal
Rainbow agate	Iridescent agate
Red Sea pearls	Coral beads
River agate	Water-worn agate pebbles
River pearl	Fresh water pearls
Rose kunzite	Synthetic pink sapphire
Rubicelle	Orange-red spinel
Rubolite	Red common opal
Ruby balas, ruby spinel	Red spinel
Schmelye	Glass
Schnide	Blue glassy ordinary opal
Shell marble	Lumachella
Starlite	Blue zircon
Star topaz	Yellow star sapphire
Trainite	Banded variscite
Vesuvian garnet	Leucite
Vienna turquoise	Imitation turquoise
Volcanic glass	Obsidian
Wild pearl	Natural pearl
Yu	Jade
Zunite	Arizona jasper
Zebra stone	Layered jasper

Formation and Structure of Gemstones

As, with a few exceptions, most gemstones are minerals, we must concern ourselves with the origin and structure of these minerals. The formation of the non-mineral gemstones (for instance amber, coral and pearl) will be dealt with in more detail when they are described.

Minerals can be formed in various ways. Some have their origin in the magma and fiery gases of the earth's interior, or in the volcanic lava streams which reach the earth's surface (magmatic minerals). Others crystallize from hydrous solutions or grow with the help of organisms on or near the earth's surface (sedimentary minerals). Lastly, new minerals are formed by re-crystallization of existing minerals under great pressure and high temperatures in the lower regions of the earth's crust (metamorphic minerals).

The chemical composition of the minerals is shown by a formula. Impurities are not included in this formula, even where they cause part or total color change, as with pigmenting substances.

Nearly all minerals grow in certain crystal forms, i.e. they are homogeneous bodies with a regular lattice of atoms, ions and molecules. They are geometrically arranged and their outer shapes are limited mainly by flat surfaces (faces). Most crystals are small, sometimes even microscopically small, but there are also some giant specimens. Such large minerals are usually unsuitable as gems as they normally have numerous inclusions, impurities or various growth marks. The inner structure, the lattice, determines the physical properties of the crystal: its outer shape, hardness, cleavage, type of fracture, specific gravity and optical properties.

In crystallography, crystals are divided into seven systems (isometric (cubic), tetragonal, hexagonal, trigonal, orthorhombic, monoclinic and triclinic). Each system has different crystal axes and different angles at which these axes intersect (see p. 16 and 17).

Isometric system (regular and cubic)   All three axes have the same length and intersect at right angles. Typical crystal shapes are the cube and octahedron (8 faces), rhombic dodecahedron (12 square faces), pentagon dodecahedron (12 pentagon faces), icosi-tetrahedron (24 faces) and hexoctahedron (48 faces).

Tetragonal system (four-sided or tetragonal)   All three axes intersect at right angles, two are of the same length and are in the same plane while the main axis is either longer or shorter. Typical crystal shapes are four-sided prisms and pyramids, trapezohedrons and eight-sided pyramids as well as double pyramids.

Hexagonal system (six-sided)   Three of the four axes are in one plane, are of the same length and intersect each other at an angle of 120° (respectively 60°). The fourth axis is at right angles to the others. Typical crystal shapes are hexagonal prisms and dipyramids as well as dihexagonal dipyramids and double pyramids.

Trigonal system (rhombohedral or three-sided)   Axes and angles are similar to the preceding system, therefore the two systems are often combined as hexagonal. The difference is one of symmetry. In the case of the hexagonal system, the cross-section of the prism base is six-sided; in the trigonal system, it is three-sided. The six-sided hexagonal shape is formed by a cutting-off process of the corners of the triangles. Typical crystal forms of the trigonal system are trigonal prisms and pyramids, rhombohedra and scalenohedra.

Orthorhombic system (orthorhombic or lozenge-shaped)   The three axes of different length are at right angles to each other. Typical crystal shapes are basal pinacoids, rhombic prisms and pyramids as well as rhombic double pyramids.

Monoclinic system (singly inclined)   The three axes are each of different lengths, two are at right angles to each other, the third is inclined. Typical crystal forms are basal pinacoids and prisms with inclined end faces.

Triclinic system (thrice inclined)   All three axes are of different length and inclined to each other. Typical crystal forms are paired faces.

Most crystals are not regularly shaped, but have an irregular form, because some crystal faces have developed better and are more pronounced than others; however the angle between the faces always remains constant. Many minerals occur in a combination of various crystal forms, for instance, octahedron and cube. 80 such combinations are known in calcite.

The arrangement of faces preferred by a mineral is called "habit", for instance pyrite is found in the shape of a pentagon dodecahedron, garnet as a dodecahedron. The habit of a crystal also refers to its type and can be tabular, acicular, foliated, columnar or compact. The technical terms, habit and form, are sometimes called structure for the benefit of the layman. Sometimes minerals occur in unusual, for them, crystal forms. These are called pseudomorphs. They can originate in two ways: they either take up the space vacated by a dissolved mineral or they form a crust around a foreign crystal.

Where two or more crystals are intergrown according to certain laws, one speaks of twins, triplets or quadruplets. Depending on whether the individual crystals are grown together or intergrown, one speaks of contact twins or penetration twins. Triclinic feldspars often occur as contact twins in a foliated form. The lamellae look like striations.

Apart from twinning which adheres to certain laws, many crystals are irregularly intergrown into aggregates. Depending on the growth process, filiform (wire-like), fibrous, shell-like, scaly or grainy aggregates are formed. Well developed, characteristic minerals are formed as druses on the inner walls of rock openings (goedes); these are mainly round hollows created by gas bubbles in magmatic rocks. The best known drusy mineral is amethyst.

Seemingly structureless minerals are called compact. These have a crystalline lattice, but are irregularly grown due to growth restrictions.

Crystal Systems and Shapes

Cubic system

cube

octahedron

rhombic dodecahedron

Tetragonal system

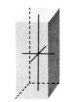

tetragonal prism

dipyramid

pyramid with prism

Hexagonal system

hexagonal prism

hexagonal prism

hexagonal dipyramid

Crystal Systems and Shapes

Trigonal system

dipyramid

rhombohedron

scalenohedron

Orthorhombic system

prism

dipyramid

prism

Monoclinic system

prism

prism

clinopinacoid

Triclinic system

prism

prism

dipyramid

Gemstones in Order of Crystal Systems

Isometric

Almandine
Andradite
Chromite
Cuprite
Demantoid
Diamond
Fluorite
Gahnite
Garnet
Gold
Grossular
Hauynite
Hessonite
Lapis Lazuli
Leucite
Periclase
Pyrite
Pyrope
Rhodizite
Rhodolite
Silver
Sodalite
Spessartite
Sphalerite
Spinel
Strontium titanate
Uvarovite
YAG

Tetragonal

Anatase
Apophyllite
Cassiterite
Chalcopyrite
Idocrase
Leucite
Phosgenite
Rutile
Scapolite
Scheelite
Tugtupite
Wardite
Wulfenite
Zircon

Hexagonal

Apatite
Aquamarine
Beryl

Cancrinite
Coral
Elaeolite
Emerald
Goshenite
Heliodor
Morganite
Painite
Taaffeite
Zincite

Trigonal

Agate
Amethyst
Aventurine
Benitoite
Blue quartz
Calcite
Chalcedony
Chalybite
Chrysoprase
Citrine
Cornelian
Corundum
Dioptase
Dolomite
Fossilized wood
Hawk's eye
Heliotrope
Hematite
Ilmenite
Jasper
Magnesite
Moss agate
Phenacite
Prase
Prasiolite
Proustite
Quartz
Quartz cat's eye
Rhodochrosite
Rock crystal
Rose quartz
Ruby
Sapphire
Sard
Smithsonite
Smoky quartz
Stichtite
Tiger's eye
Tourmaline
Willemite

Orthorhombic

Alexandrite
Andalusite
Anhydrite
Aragonite
Barite
Cat's eye
Celestite
Cerussite
Chrysoberyl
Danburite
Dumortierite
Enstatite
Fibrolite
Hambergite
Hemimorphite
Hypersthene
Iolite
Kornerupine
Meerschaum (?)
Natrolite
Peridot
Prehnite
Psilomelane
Purpurite
Sinhalite
Staurolite
Sulphur
Tanzanite
Tantalite
Thomsonite
Thulite
Topaz
Variscite
Witherite
Zoisite

Monoclinic

Actinolite
Augelite
Azurite
Barytocalcite
Beryllonite
Bowenite
Brazilianite
Chloromelanite
Clinozoisite
Colemanite
Crocoite
Datolite
Diopside
Epidote

Euclase
Garnierite
Gaylussite
Hiddenite
Howlite (?)
Jadeite
Kunzite
Lazulite
Malachite
Moonstone
Nephrite
Orthoclase
Petalite
Pseudophite
Serpentine
Smaragadite
Sphene
Spodumene
Tremolite
Vivianite
Williamsite

Triclinic

Amazonite
Amblygonite
Aventurine feldspar
Axinite
Bytownite
Kurnakovite
Kyanite
Labradorite
Microcline
Rhodonite
Turquoise
Ulexite

Amorphous

Amber
Chrysocolla
Ekanite
Girasol
Glass
Ivory
Jet
Moldavite
Obsidian
Opal
Tektite

Table of Chemical Elements

Symbol	Name	Atomic number	Symbol	Name	Atomic number
Ac	Actinium	89	Mn	Manganese	25
Ag	Silver (Argentum)	47	Mo	Molybdenum	42
Al	Aluminium	13	Mv	Mendelevium	101
Am	Americium	95	N	Nitrogen	7
Ar	Argon	18	Na	Sodium (Natrium)	11
As	Arsenic	33	Nb	Niobium	41
At	Astatine	85	Nd	Neodymium	60
Au	Gold (Aurum)	79	Ne	Neon	10
B	Boron	5	Ni	Nickel	28
Ba	Barium	56	No	Nobelium	102
Be	Beryllium	4	Np	Neptunium	93
Bi	Bismuth	83	O	Oxygen	8
Bk	Berkelium	97	Os	Osmium	76
Br	Bromine	35	P	Phosphorus	15
C	Carbon	6	Pa	Protactinium	91
Ca	Calcium	20	Pb	Lead (Plumbum)	82
Cd	Cadmium	48	Pd	Palladium	46
Ce	Cerium	58	Pm	Promethium	61
Cf	Californium	98	Po	Polonium	84
Cl	Chlorine	17	Pr	Praseodymium	59
Cm	Curium	96	Pt	Platinum	78
Co	Cobalt	27	Pu	Plutonium	94
Cr	Chromium	24	Ra	Radium	88
Cs	Caesium (Cesium)	55	Rb	Rubidium	37
Cu	Copper (Cuprum)	29	Re	Rhenium	75
Dy	Dysprosium	66	Rh	Rhodium	45
Er	Erbium	68	Rn	Radon	86
Es	Einsteinium	99	Ru	Ruthenium	44
Eu	Europium	63	S	Sulphur	16
F	Fluorine	9	Sb	Antimony (Stibium)	51
Fe	Iron (Ferrum)	26	Sc	Scandium	21
Fm	Fermium	100	Se	Selenium	34
Fr	Francium	87	Si	Silicon	14
Ga	Gallium	31	Sm	Samarium	62
Gd	Gadolinium	64	Sn	Tin (Stannium)	50
Ge	Germanium	32	Sr	Strontium	38
H	Hydrogen	1	Ta	Tantalum	73
He	Helium	2	Tb	Terbium	65
Hf	Hafnium	72	Tc	Technetium	43
Hg	Mercury (Hydrargyrum)	80	Te	Tellurium	52
Ho	Holmium	67	Th	Thorium	90
In	Indium	49	Ti	Titanium	22
Ir	Iridium	77	Tl	Thallium	81
I	Iodine	53	Tm	Thulium	69
K	Potassium	19	U	Uranium	92
Kr	Krypton	36	V	Vanadium	23
La	Lanthanum	57	W	Tungsten (Wolfram)	74
Li	Lithium	3	Xe	Xenon	54
Lu	Lutetium	71	Y	Yttrium	39
Lw	Lawrencium	103	Yb	Ytterbium	70
Mg	Magnesium	12	Zn	Zinc	30
			Zr	Zirconium	40

Properties of Gemstones

Hardness

In the case of minerals and gemstones, hardness refers first to scratch hardness, then to cutting resistance. Before the development of optical testing methods, scratch hardness was of great importance in the determination of gemstones. Today the hardness test is only rarely applied to precious stones and then mainly by collectors. It is too imprecise for an expert and the danger of damaging the gem is too great. The advantage of the scratch test is that one can, with simple means, roughly determine the nature of a stone. It is frequently used in mineralogy.

The Viennese mineralogist Friedrich Mohs (1773–1839) invented the scratch hardness test. He defined scratch hardness as the resistance of a mineral when scratched with a pointed testing object. Mohs chose ten minerals of different hardness for comparison and graded these minerals one to ten. Each mineral in this series scratches the previous one, and can be scratched by the following one. Minerals of equal hardness cannot scratch each other. By comparative application of Mohs' hardness scale the hardness (according to Mohs) of every gem can be determined. Stones with scratch hardness 1 and 2 are soft, 3 to 6 medium hard, over 6 hard. Minerals of Mohs' hardness 8 to 10 are also described as "hard gems". This designation is unfortunate, as gems are characterized not only by their hardness, even if that property is valued. The luster and polish of gems of hardness below 7 can be damaged by dust as this may contain small particles of quartz (Mohs' hardness 7). Such stones must be carefully handled when worn or stored so that they do not come into contact with any scratching objects.

When a scratch test is made, care must be taken to employ a sharp-edged test piece on a fresh unbroken mineral face. Imperfect formation, foliated crystals or weathered surfaces can show a lower hardness.

Some gems show different hardness on different faces in different directions. In the case of kyanite (p. 196), Mohs' hardness along the long direction of the crystal is $4\frac{1}{2}$, while across it is 6 or 7. It is therefore also called disthene (double resistance). There are also varying hardnesses in diamond. This makes it possible to work this hardest material (see p. 59). It is important for the gem cutter and lapidary to be familiar with the various hardnesses (scratch as well as cutting resistance) as this is the basis of successful work.

Mohs' scratch hardness is a relative scale. It only shows which mineral scratches another mineral. Nothing is said about increase of hardness within the scale. These differ substantially as can be seen from the following table of absolute hardnesses (cutting hardness in water according to A. Rosiwal).

See also Table of Mohs' hardnesses, p. 22.

In the trade one can buy Mohs' hardness testers as a set in a little box. Specially recommended are hardness test points which are splinters of the mineral set in handy metal holders. The hardness value of the mineral is marked in the metal of the holder to avoid mistakes.

Relative and Absolute Hardness Scale

Scratch hardness (Mohs)	Mineral used for comparison	Simple hardness tester	Cutting hardness (Rosiwal)
1	Talc	Can be scratched with fingernail	0.03
2	Gypsum	Can be scratched with fingernail	1.25
3	Calcite	Can be scratched with copper coin	4.5
4	Fluorite	Easily scratched with knife	5.0
5	Apatite	Can be scratched with knife	6.5
6	Orthoclase	Can be scratched with steel file	37
7	Quartz	Scratches window glass	120
8	Topaz		175
9	Corundum		1,000
10	Diamond		140,000

Cleavage and Fracture

Many gems can be split along certain flat planes, which the expert calls cleavage. Cleavage is related to the lattice of the crystal – the cohesive property of the atoms. Depending on the ease with which a crystal can be cleaved, one differentiates between a very perfect (euclase), a perfect (topaz) and an imperfect cleavage (garnet). Some gems cannot be cleaved at all (quartz). A loosening of contact twins is not cleavage but separation.

Lapidaries and stone setters must take account of the cleavage. Often a small tap or too much pressure when testing for Mohs' hardness is sufficient to split the stone. When soldering, the temperature can cause fissures along the cleavage planes which not only lower the stone's value, but also bring the danger that one day the gem may break completely along these lines. Faceted gemstones with very perfect cleavage, such as euclase (p. 179, No. 4, 5), are small artistic creations.

Cleavage is used to divide large gem crystals or remove faulty pieces. The largest diamond of gem quality ever found, the Cullinan of 3106cts, was cleaved in 1908 into three large pieces which were then cleaved again into numerous smaller pieces. Today small pieces are usually sawn in order to make the best use of the shape of the stone. (See p. 58 and 59).

The breaking of a mineral with a blow producing irregular surfaces is called "fracture". It can be conchoidal (shell-like), uneven, splintery, fibrous, even or grainy. Sometimes the type of fracture helps to identify a mineral. Conchoidal fracture is for instance characteristic of all quartz and glass-like minerals.

Table of Mohs' Hardnesses

Mineral	Hardness	Mineral	Hardness	Mineral	Hardness
Diamond	10	Sillimanite	$6-7\frac{1}{2}$	Thomsonite	$5-5\frac{1}{2}$
Ruby	9	Cassiterite	$6-7$	Apatite	5
Sapphire	9	Epidote	$6-7$	Augelite	5
Alexandrite	$8\frac{1}{2}$	Hiddenite	$6-7$	Dioptase	5
Chrysoberyl	$8\frac{1}{2}$	Kunzite	$6-7$	Glass	5
Rhodozite	8	Amazonite	$6-6\frac{1}{2}$	Hemimorphite	5
Spinel	8	Aventurine		Smithsonite	5
Taaffeite	8	feldspar	$6-6\frac{1}{2}$	Wardite	5
Topaz	8	Benitoite	$6-6\frac{1}{2}$	Kyanite	$4\frac{1}{2}-7$
YAG	8	Ekanite	$6-6\frac{1}{2}$	Apophyllite	$4\frac{1}{2}-5$
Aquamarine	$7\frac{1}{2}-8$	Labradorite	$6-6\frac{1}{2}$	Scheelite	$4\frac{1}{2}-5$
Beryl	$7\frac{1}{2}-8$	Moonstone	$6-6\frac{1}{2}$	Zincite	$4\frac{1}{2}-5$
Emerald	$7\frac{1}{2}-8$	Nephrite	$6-6\frac{1}{2}$	Colemanite	$4\frac{1}{2}$
Gahnite	$7\frac{1}{2}-8$	Orthoclase	$6-6\frac{1}{2}$	Kurnakovite	$4\frac{1}{2}-?$
Painite	$7\frac{1}{2}-8$	Petalite	$6-6\frac{1}{2}$	Purpurite	$4\frac{1}{2}$
Phenacite	$7\frac{1}{2}-8$	Prehnite	$6-6\frac{1}{2}$	Variscite	$4-5$
Almandine	$7\frac{1}{2}$	Pyrite	$6-6\frac{1}{2}$	Fluorite	$4-4\frac{1}{2}$
Andalusite	$7\frac{1}{2}$	Rutile	$6-6\frac{1}{2}$	Barytocalcite	4
Euclase	$7\frac{1}{2}$	Strontium		Magnesite	4
Hambergite	$7\frac{1}{2}$	titanate	$6-6\frac{1}{2}$	Rhodochrosite	4
Uvarovite	$7\frac{1}{2}$	Amblygonite	6	Dolomite	$3\frac{1}{2}-4\frac{1}{2}$
Andradite	$7-7\frac{1}{2}$	Bytownite	6	Chalybite	$3\frac{1}{2}-4\frac{1}{2}$
Cordierite	$7-7\frac{1}{2}$	Sanidine	6	Aragonite	$3\frac{1}{2}-4$
Danburite	$7-7\frac{1}{2}$	Thulite	6	Azurite	$3\frac{1}{2}-4$
Garnet	$7-7\frac{1}{2}$	Tugtupite	6	Cuprite	$3\frac{1}{2}-4$
Iolite	$7-7\frac{1}{2}$	Hematite	$5\frac{1}{2}-6\frac{1}{2}$	Chalcopyrite	$3\frac{1}{2}-4$
Rhodolite	$7-7\frac{1}{2}$	Opal	$5\frac{1}{2}-6\frac{1}{2}$	Malachite	$3\frac{1}{2}-4$
Staurolite	$7-7\frac{1}{2}$	Rhodonite	$5\frac{1}{2}-6\frac{1}{2}$	Sphalerite	$3\frac{1}{2}-4$
Tourmaline	$7-7\frac{1}{2}$	Tremolite	$5\frac{1}{2}-6\frac{1}{2}$	Cerussite	$3\frac{1}{2}$
Amethyst	7	Actinolite	$5\frac{1}{2}-6$	Howlite	$3\frac{1}{2}$
Citrine	7	Anatase	$5\frac{1}{2}-6$	Witherite	$3\frac{1}{2}$
Dumortierite	7	Beryllonite	$5\frac{1}{2}-6$	Coral	$3-4$
Prasiolite	7	Elaeolite	$5\frac{1}{2}-6$	Pearl	$3-4$
Rock Crystal	7	Haüynite	$5\frac{1}{2}-6$	Anhydrite	$3-3\frac{1}{2}$
Smoky quartz	7	Periclase	$5\frac{1}{2}-6$	Celestine	
Rose quartz	7	Psilomelane	$5\frac{1}{2}-6$	(Celestite)	$3-3\frac{1}{2}$
Tiger's eye	7	Sodalite	$5\frac{1}{2}-6$	Barite	3
Zircon	$6\frac{1}{2}-7\frac{1}{2}$	Brazilianite	$5\frac{1}{2}$	Calcite	3
Agate	$6\frac{1}{2}-7$	Chromite	$5\frac{1}{2}$	Wulfenite	3
Axinite	$6\frac{1}{2}-7$	Enstatite	$5\frac{1}{2}$	Jet	$2\frac{1}{2}-4$
Chalcedony	$6\frac{1}{2}-7$	Leucite	$5\frac{1}{2}$	Crocoite	$2\frac{1}{2}-3$
Chloromelanite	$6\frac{1}{2}-7$	Moldavite	$5\frac{1}{2}$	Garnierite	$2\frac{1}{2}-3$
Chrysoprase	$6\frac{1}{2}-7$	Natrolite	$5\frac{1}{2}$	Phosgenite	$2\frac{1}{2}-3$
Demantoid	$6\frac{1}{2}-7$	Willemite	$5\frac{1}{2}$	Gaylussite	$2\frac{1}{2}$
Fossilized wood	$6\frac{1}{2}-7$	Scapolite	$5-6\frac{1}{2}$	Proustite	$2\frac{1}{2}$
Heliotrope	$6\frac{1}{2}-7$	Cancrinite	$5-6$	Pseudophite	$2\frac{1}{2}$
Jadeite	$6\frac{1}{2}-7$	Diopside	$5-6$	Serpentine	$2\frac{1}{2}$
Jasper	$6\frac{1}{2}-7$	Hypersthene	$5-6$	Chrysocolla	$2-5\frac{1}{2}$
Kornerupine	$6\frac{1}{2}-7$	Ilmenite	$5-6$	Ivory	$2-4$
Peridot	$6\frac{1}{2}-7$	Lapis lazuli	$5-6$	Amber	$2-3$
Sard	$6\frac{1}{2}-7$	Lazulite	$5-6$	Meerschaum	$2-2\frac{1}{2}$
Tanzanite	$6\frac{1}{2}-7$	Tantalite	$5-6$	Alabaster	$2-2\frac{1}{2}$
Zoisite	$6\frac{1}{2}-7$	Turquoise	$5-6$	Ulexite	2
Idocrase	$6\frac{1}{2}$	Datolite	$5-5\frac{1}{2}$	Vivianite	$1\frac{1}{2}-3$
Saussurite	$6\frac{1}{2}$	Obsidian	$5-5\frac{1}{2}$	Stichtite	$1\frac{1}{2}-2\frac{1}{2}$
Sinhalite	$6\frac{1}{2}$	Sphene	$5-5\frac{1}{2}$	Sulphur	$1\frac{1}{2}-2$
Smaragdite	$6\frac{1}{2}$				

Specific Gravity

Specific gravity (also called "relative density") is the weight of a specific material compared with the weight of the same volume of water. A gem with the specific gravity of 2.6 is therefore 2.6 times as heavy as the same volume of water.

The specific gravity of gems varies between 1 and 7. Values under 2 are considered light (amber 1.1); those between 2 and 4 normal (quartz 2.6); and those above 4 are heavy (cassiterite 7). The more precious gems (diamond, ruby, sapphire) have specific gravities above that of the rock-forming minerals, especially when these are quartz and feldspar. Therefore they can easily be separated from the quartzoze river sands which form the so-called alluvial deposits (see p. 50). This determination of specific gravity can be very useful in identifying a gemstone (especially for the collector). However, experts make increasing use of optical methods of identification requiring expensive apparatus.

In gemology, where mostly small stones are involved, two methods of determining specific gravity have proved useful: weighing with a hydrostatic balance and the heavy liquid method. The first is time-consuming, but cheap; the second is complicated, can be expensive, but produces good results in a short time with larger lots of unknown gems.

Weighing with a hydrostatic balance works on Archimedes' Principle. The volume of the gem to be tested is established, the specific gravity is then easily worked out.

$$\text{Specific gravity} = \frac{\text{Weight of gem}}{\text{Volume of gem}}$$

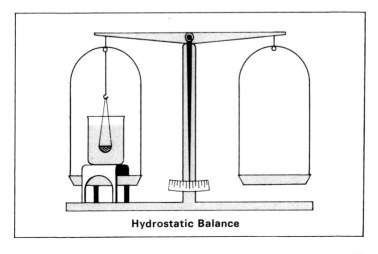

Hydrostatic Balance

A hydrostatic balance can be constructed by anybody (p. 23). The beginner can adapt letter scales. Anyone more advanced should use a precision balance as used by the chemist or pharmacist. The object to be tested is first weighed in air (in the pan under the bridge) and then in water (in the cage in the beaker). The difference in weight corresponds to the weight of the displaced water and therefore the volume of the stone. It is possible by this method for a layman, with practice, to determine the specific gravity correctly to two decimal places. It is important to ensure that the stone is not in contact with a foreign substance, that it is loose and that, when weighed in air, it is dry.

Example:

Weight in air = 5.2
Weight in water = 3.3
Difference = Volume 1.9

$$\text{Specific gravity} = \frac{\text{Weight in air}}{\text{Volume}} = \frac{5.2}{1.9} = 2.7$$

The heavy liquid method requires that the object be suspended in a liquid of the same specific gravity, so that it neither sinks to the bottom nor rises to the surface. The stone to be tested is put into a liquid with a high specific gravity (a heavy liquid), which is diluted and thus lightened until the object has the same specific gravity as the liquid, i.e. until the object is suspended.

There are various heavy liquids available. The ones that can be thinned with distilled water are most suitable for the layman. One of these is Thoulet's Solution (a potassium-mercury-iodide solution) with a specific gravity of 3.2. One can identify most gems with it. For heavier stones one can use Clerici Solution (a thallium-formate-thallium-malonate solution) with a specific gravity of 4.2. This in fact covers the specific gravity of all gems but is expensive and poisonous: laymen should not use it. For specific gravity up to 3.5, one can use Rohrbach's Solution (barium-mercury-iodide solution) but this may be difficult to handle as the mercury iodide tends to separate out. The thinned liquid need not be thrown away; one can recover the original specific weight by evaporation in a steam bath.

The specific gravity of the thinned heavy liquid is determined by the expert with the help of a "Westphal Balance"; laymen are advised to use indicators. These are pieces of glass (available in the trade) or minerals of different known specific gravity. When such an indicator is suspended in the liquid, its specific gravity is the same as that of the liquid and thus of the test object.

The heavy liquid method is complicated but it is recommended when certain gems have to be separated from a lot of unknown stones, or where synthetics or imitations have to be identified.

Table of Specific Gravities

Tantalite	5.18–8.20	Topaz	3.53–3.56	Calcite	2.71
Cassiterite	6.8 –7.1	Diamond	3.47–3.55	Aquamarine	2.67–2.71
Wulfenite	6.7 –7.0	Sphene	3.52–5.54	Tiger's eye	2.64–2.71
Cerussite	6.46–6.57	Hemimorphite	3.4 –3.5	Augelite	2.7
Cuprite	5.85–6.15	Hypersthene	3.4 –3.5	Onyx marble	2.7
Phosgenite	6.13	Sinhalite	3.47–3.49	Labradorite	2.69–2.7
Crocoite	5.9 –6.1	Idocrase	3.32–3.42	Coral	2.6 –2.7
Scheelite	5.1 –6.1	Dumortierite	3.26–3.41	Vivianite	2.6 –2.7
Zincite	5.66	Epidote	3.4	Iolite	2.58–2.66
Proustite	5.57–5.64	Rhodizite	3.4	Aventurine	2.65
Pyrite	5.0 –5.2	Purpurite	3.2 –3.4	Rock crystal	2.65
Hematite	4.95–5.16	Peridot	3.27–3.36	Citrine	2.65
Strontium		Jadeite	3.35	Prasiolite	2.65
titanate	5.13	Tanzanite	3.28–3.35	Rose quartz	2.65
Chromite	4.1 –4.9	Dioptase	3.28–3.35	Smoky quartz	2.65
Ilmenite	4.72	Kornerupine	3.27–3.31	Amethyst	2.63–2.65
Zircon	3.90–4.71	Diopside	3.27–3.31	Aventurine	
YAG	4.6	Axinite	3.27–3.29	feldspar	2.62–2.65
Barite	4.5	Ekanite	3.28	Agate	2.60–2.65
Smithsonite	4.3 –4.5	Enstatite	3.26–3.28	Elaeolite	2.55–2.65
Psilomelane	About 4.35	Tourmaline	3.02–3.26	Chalcedony	2.58–2.64
Witherite	4.27–4.35	Sillimanite	3.25	Chrysoprase	2.58–2.64
Rutile	4.20–4.30	Smaragdite	3.25	Peristerite	2.61–2.63
Chalcopyrite	4.1 –4.3	Apatite	3.17–3.23	Moss agate	2.58–2.62
Spessartite	4.12–4.20	Hiddenite	3.16–3.20	Moonstone	2.56–2.62
Almandine	3.95–4.20	Kunzite	3.16–3.2	Orthoclase	2.56–2.60
Glass	3.15–4.20	Lazulite	3.1 –3.2	Pseudophite	2.5 –2.6
Willemite	3.89–4.18	Fluorite	3.18	Variscite	2.4 –2.6
Painite	4.1	Andalusite	3.12–3.18	Obsidian	2.3 –2.6
Sphalerite	4.08–4.10	Magnesite	3.00–3.12	Howlite	2.53–2.59
Corundum	3.96–4.01	Euclase	3.10	Sanidine	2.57–2.58
Ruby	3.97–4.08	Tremolite	2.9 –3.1	Amazonite	2.56–2.58
Sapphire	3.99–4.00	Actinolite	3.03–3.07	Tugtupite	2.36–2.57
Celestine		Amblygonite	3.01–3.03	Leucite	2.45–2.50
(Celestite)	3.97–4.00	Nephrite	2.90–3.02	Cancrinite	2.4 –2.5
Gahnite	3.58–3.98	Danburite	3.0	Apophyllite	2.30–2.50
Anatase	3.82–3.95	Datolite	2.90–5.00	Colemanite	2.42
Malachite	3.75–3.95	Brazilianite	2.98–2.99	Haüynite	2.4
Azurite	3.7 –3.9	Anhydrite	2.90–2.99	Petalite	2.40
Periclase	3.7 –3.9	Phenacite	2.95–2.97	Thomsonite	2.3 –2.4
Chalybite	3.85	Dolomite	2.85–2.95	Chrysocolla	2.00–2.40
Demantoid	3.82–3.85	Aragonite	2.94	Moldavite	2.32–2.38
Staurolite	3.7 –3.8	Prehnite	2.87–2.93	Hambergite	2.35
Pyrope	3.65–3.80	Jasper	2.58–2.91	Alabaster	2.30–2.33
Uvarovite	3.77	Lapis lazuli	2.4 –2.9	Sodalite	2.13–2.29
Alexandrite	3.70–3.73	Beryllonite	2.80–2.85	Natrolite	2.20–2.25
Chrysoberyl	3.70–3.72	Wardite	2.81	Stichtite	About 2.2
Rhodonite	3.40–3.70	Steatite	2.7 –2.8	Opal	1.98–2.20
Rhodo-		Turquoise	2.60–2.80	Sulphur	2.05–2.08
chrosite	3.30–3.70	Serpentine	2.4 –2.8	Meerschaum	2.00
Kyanite	3.65–3.69	Garnierite	2.3 –2.8	Ulexite	1.9 –2.0
Benitoite	3.65–3.68	Emerald	2.67–2.78	Ivory	1.7 –2.0
Grossular	3.60–3.68	Pearl	2.60–2.78	Gaylussite	1.99
Barytocalcite	3.66	Beryl	2.65–2.75	Kurnakovite	1.86
Spinel	3.58–3.61	Bytownite	2.71–2.74	Jet	1.30–1.35
Taaffeite	3.6	Scapolite	2.57–2.74	Amber	1.05–1.30

Weights used in the gem trades

Carat The weight used in the gem trade since antiquity. The name is derived from the seed (*kuara*) of the African Coraltree or from the kernel (Greek – *kertion*) of the Carob bean. Since 1907 Europe, as well as America, has adopted the metric carat of 200mg or 0.2g. Therefore weights given for famous old diamonds often vary because local carats and not metric carats were used. The carat is subdivided into fractions (1/10ct) or decimals (1.25ct) up to two decimal places. Small diamonds are weighted in "points" = 1/100cts (=0.01cts). The table below illustrates diameter and corresponding carat weight for diamonds cut in the modern brilliant cut (p. 81). Gems with different specific gravity and different cuts obviously have different diameters.

The carat weight of gems is not to be confused with the carat used by the goldsmith. In the case of gold the carat is no weight measure but a designation of quality. The higher the caratage, the higher the content of gold in the piece of jewelry. The weight can be variable.

Gram Weight used in gem trade for less precious stones and for rough stones (for instance quartz).

Grain (Latin – *granum*) Weight measure for pearls. Corresponds to 0.05 grams=0.25 or ¼ carat. Increasingly superceded by carat weights. The old Japanese weight of *Momme* (=3.75 grams=18.75 carats) is hardly used any more in Europe.

Prices in the Gem Trade The price quoted is always the carat price. This has to be multiplied by the actual weight to obtain the price of the particular stone. The price quoted to the final buyer is often the total price. With diamonds the price per carat increases progressively with the size of the gem in very small steps, 10 points with more expensive stones. If, for instance, a one carat stone costs £750/$1275, a two carat stone (of the same quality) does not cost £1500/$2550 per carat, but maybe £2500/$4250 or more. Colored stones have fixed carat prices for much bigger size groups.

Diameters and Weights of Brilliant Diamonds

Diameter in mm	2.2	3.0	4.1	5.2	6.5
Weight in carat	1/25	.10	.25	.50	1.00

7.4	8.2	9.0	9.3	11.0
1.50	2.00	2.50	3.00	5.00

Optical properties

Of all the various properties of a gemstone the optical characteristics are of unsurpassed importance. They produce color and luster, fire and luminescence, play of light and schiller (iridescence). In the examination of gems there is more and more concentration on the optical effects.

Color

Color is the most important characteristic of gems. In the case of most stones, it is not diagnostic in identification, because many have the same color and numerous stones occur in many colors. Color is produced by light; light is electromagnetic vibration at certain wave lengths. The human eye can only perceive wave lengths between 4000Å to 7000Å (p. 36). This visible light falls into six parts, each of a particular color (spectral colors: red, orange, yellow, green, blue, violet). The mixture of all these produces white light. If, however, a certain wavelength is absorbed, the remaining mixture produces a color, but not white. If all wave lengths pass through the stone, it appears colorless; if all light is absorbed the stone appears black. If all wave lengths are absorbed to the same degree, the stone is dull white or gray. If, however, only certain wavelengths are absorbed, the stone will have the color resulting from the remaining spectral mixture.

In the case of gemstones, the metals, mainly chrome, iron, cobalt, copper, manganese, nickel and vanadium, absorb certain wavelengths of white light and so cause coloration. These substances sometimes appear in such small quantities in the stone that they are not indicated in the chemical formula. In the case of zircon and smoky quartz, no foreign substance is responsible for the color; it is caused by the deformation of the internal structure (lattice) and is produced by short wave rays from the atmosphere (ultra-violet rays) resulting in a selective absorption.

The distance the light ray travels through the stone can also influence absorption and thus color. The cutter must therefore use this fact to his advantage. Light colored stones are made thicker and/or are given such an arrangement of facets that the absorption path lengthens and the color deepens, while materials with colors that are too dark are cut thinly. The dark red almandine garnet (p. 104) is therefore often hollowed out on the underside. Artificial light has an influence on the color of a gemstone as it is differently composed from daylight. Artificial light has an unfavorable effect on some stones (for instance sapphire) and a favorable effect on others (emerald and ruby). The most obvious change occurs in alexandrite (p. 98) which is green in daylight and red in artificial light.

Although color is of great importance in gems, with the exception of diamonds, no practical method of objective color determination is known. Color comparison charts are poor substitutes because there is much room for subjective consideration. The measuring methods used in science for color determination are too complicated and expensive for the trade.

Color of streak

The color appearance of gems, even in the same group, can vary greatly. For instance beryl can have all the colors of the spectrum, but can also be colorless. This colorlessness is the true color; it is called "inherent color". All others are produced by coloring substances. The inherent color, as it is constant, can help to identify a stone. The color can be seen by streaking the mineral on a rough porcelain plate, called a "streak plate", because the finely ground powder has the same effect as thin transparent platelets. Steely hematite for instance has a streak color (called streak) which is red. Brass-colored pyrite's streak is black and blue sodalite's is white. In the case of a very hard mineral, it is advisable first to remove a little powder with a steel file and then rub it on the streak plate. These methods of determination are of special interest to collectors. Because of the danger of damaging them, cut gems should not be tested for streak. See Table of Streaks, p. 30.

Color change

The color of some gems is altered by time. Amethyst, rose quartz and kunzite can become paler when exposed to direct sunlight. Generally color changes effected by natural causes are not common. Much more frequently man uses scientific methods to enhance the color of certain gemstones.

Best known is the heat treatment of amethyst. At several hundred degrees, the original violet stone becomes light yellow, red-brown, green or milky white. Most citrines on sale and all prasiolites are amethysts treated in this way. Less attractive colors can be changed to more desirable hues by heating. Greenish aquamarines are heated to a sea-blue color; tourmalines which are too dark can be lightened; and blue tourmalines can be turned green. Diamond-like and aquamarine-colored zircons are produced by heating the red-brown hyacinth variety.

Colors can also be improved by radium and x-ray treatment and, more recently, by bombardment with electrons in an accelerator or with neutrons in an atomic reactor. The resulting colors are sometimes so close to nature that they cannot be detected by the eye; complicated tests are required to unmask them. Some of these resulting colors are not permanent; the stones can become pale, change color or become spotty. In the case of porous gems, such as lapis lazuli, turquoise, pearls and agate, colors are improved by the addition of a pigment. Stone dyeing is a very ancient practice. See coloring of agate, p. 136.

All gems with artificial color changes – with the exception of heat-treated stones and dyed agates – have to be marked as such when offered for sale.

Intergrown azurite and malachite from Arizona, U.S.A. Two of the few gem minerals whose streaks correspond with their appearance.

Table of Streaks

White,
colorless, gray

Agate
Actinolite
Alabaster
Alexandrite
Almandine
Amazonite
Amber
Amblygonite
Amethyst
Amethyst quartz
Anatase
Andalusite
Anhydrite
Apatite
Apophyllite
Aquamarine
Aragonite
Augelite
Aventurine
Aventurine feldspar
Axinite
Barite
Barytocalcite
Benitoite
Beryl
Beryllonite
Brazilianite
Bytownite
Calcite
Cancrinite
Cassiterite
Cerussite
Ceylanite
Chalcedony
Chalybite
Chloromelanite
Chrysoberyl
Chrysocolla
Chrysoprase
Citrine
Celestine
  (Celestite)
Colemanite
Coral
Corundum
Danburite
Datolite
Demantoid
Diopside
Dolomite
Elaeolite
Emerald
Enstatite
Epidote
Euclase

Fluorite
Gahnite
Garnet
Gaylussite
Glass
Grossular
Hambergite
Haüynite
Hemimorphite
Hessonite
Hiddenite
Howlite
Hypersthene
Idocrase
Iolite
Ivory
Jade-albite
Jadeite
Jasper
Kornerupine
Kunzite
Kyanite
Labradorite
Lazulite
Leucite
Magnesite
Meerschaum
Moldavite
Moonstone
Moss agate
Natrolite
Nephrite
Obsidian
Opal
Orthoclase
Peridot
Periclase
Peristerite
Pearl
Petalite
Phenacite
Phosgenite
Prasiolite
Prehnite
Pyrope
Rhodochrosite
Rhodolite
Rhodonite
Rock crystal
Rose quartz
Ruby
Sanidine
Sapphire
Scapolite
Scheelite
Serpentine
Sillimanite
Sinhalite

Smithsonite
Smoky quartz
Sodalite
Spessartite
Spinel
Staurolite
Steatite
Strontium titanate
Tanzanite
Thomsonite
Thulite
Topaz
Tremolite
Turquoise
Tourmaline
Ulexite
Uvarovite
Variscite
Willemite
Witherite
YAG
Zircon
Zoisite

Red, pink,
orange

Crocoite
Cuprite
Hematite
Jasper
Proustite
Rutile
Tantalite
Zincite

Yellow,
orange, brown

Apatite
Cassiterite
Chromite
Cuprite
Crocoite
Hypersthene
Ilmenite
Jasper
Jet
Proustite
Psilomelane
Rutile
Sulphur
Sphalerite
Tantalite
Tiger's Eye

Vivianite
Wulfenite
Zincite

Green,
yellow-green,
blue-green

Chalcopyrite
Chrysocolla
Dioptase
Garnierite
Malachite
Pyrite

Blue,
blue-green,
blue-red

Azurite
Dioptase
Dumortierite
Lapis lazuli

Black, gray

Apatite
Cerussite
Chalcopyrite
Epidote
Gahnite
Hypersthene
Ilmenite
Jet
Psilomelane
Pyrite
Tantalite

Refractive Index

Most of us, when children, noticed that when a stick was partially immersed in water at a slant, it appeared to "break" at water level. The lower part of the stick appeared to be at a different angle from the upper part. What we observed was caused by the refraction of light. It always occurs, when a ray of light leaves one medium (for instance air) and enters obliquely into another (for instance a gem crystal), at the interface between the two materials.

The amount of refraction of crystals is constant in the various types of gems. It can therefore be used in the identification of the type of stone. The amount of the refraction is called the refractive index and is defined as the proportional relation between the speed of light in air to that in the stone. A decrease in the velocity of light in the stone causes a deviation of the light rays.

Example:
Speed of light in air (V_1)   300000 km/sec
Speed of light in diamond (V_2)   125000 km/sec

$$\text{Refractive index} = \frac{V_1 \text{ (AIR)}}{V_2 \text{ (Diamond)}} = \frac{300000}{125000} = 2.4$$

The speed of light in air is 2.4 times faster than the speed of light in diamond. The refractive indices of gems are between 1.2 and 2.6. They vary somewhat with color and occurrence. Doubly refractive gems (see p. 34) have two refractive indices. See Table of refractive indices, p. 32.

The refractive index is measured with a refractometer. The values can be read directly from a scale. However testing is only possible up to a value of 1.86 on a common instrument and only stones with a flat face or facet are suitable, although the expert can find the approximate value of cabochons using his own knowledge. It is fairly easy to measure the refractive index by the immersion method. The gem is viewed after immersing it in a liquid whose refractive index is known. The refractive index of the stone can then be judged according to its brightness and sharpness of its outline or contours.

Immersion method (Becke)

The following data refer to the liquid:

White contour and dark facet edges: gem has lower refractive index.

Black contour and white facet edges: gem has higher refractive index.

Widened contour: refractive index varies considerably.

Uncertain contour (tending to disappear): liquid and gem have same refractive index.

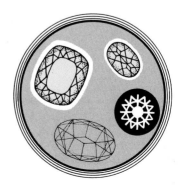

Table of Refractive Indices and Double Refraction

	Refractive index	Double refraction		Refractive index	Double refraction
Hematite	2.94 –3.22	−0.28	Rhodonite	1.733–1.744	+0.011
Proustite	2.792–3.088	−0.296	Periclase	1.74	None
Rutile	2.62 –2.90	+0.28	Spinel	1.712–1.736	None
Cuprite	2.849	None	Clinozoisite	1.724–1.734	+0.010
Crocoite	2.31 –2.66	+0.35	Kyanite	1.715–1.732	−0.017
Anatase	2.49 –2.55	−0.06	Hypersthene	1.67 –1.73	−0.014
Strontium			Diopside	1.671–1.726	+0.028
titanate	2.40 –2.42	None	Dumortierite	1.686–1.723	−0.037
Diamond	2.417–2.419	None	Taaffeite	1.718–1.722	−0.004
Tantalite	2.24 –2.41	+0.17	Idocrase	1.700–1.721	±0.005
Wulfenite	2.30 –2.40	−0.10	Willemite	1.691–1.719	+0.028
Sphalerite	2.368–2.371	None	Magnesite	1.515–1.717	−0.202
Sulphur	1.960–2.248	+0.288	Dioptase	1.644–1.709	+0.053
Phosgenite	2.117–2.145	+0.028	Sinhalite	1.699–1.707	−0.038
Chromite	2.1	None	Tanzanite	1.691–1.700	+0.009
Cassiterite	1.997–2.093	+0.096	Zoisite	1.691–1.700	+0.009
Cerussite	1.804–2.078	−0.274	Rhodizite	1.69	None
Sphene	1.885–2.050	+0.105	Peridot	1.654–1.690	+0.036
		up to +0.135	Pearl	1.52 –1.69	Weak
Zincite	2.013–2.029	+0.016			or none
Zircon	1.777–1.987	+0.059	Axinite	1.675–1.685	−0.010
Scheelite	1.918–1.934	+0.016	Aragonite	1.530–1.685	−0.155
Purpurite	1.84 –1.92	+0.08	Barytocalcite	1.684	None
Malachite	1.655–1.909	−0.254	Kornerupine	1.665–1.682	−0.013
Demantoid	1.888–1.889	None	Dolomite	1.503–1.682	−0.179
Uvarovite	nearly 1.870	None	Hiddenite	1.655–1.680	+0.015
Chalybite	1.63 –1.87	−0.24	Kunzite	1.655–1.680	+0.015
Smithsonite	1.621–1.849	−0.228	Jet	1.64 –1.68	None
Azurite	1.730–1.838	+0.108	Witherite	1.532–1.680	−0.148
YAG	1.83	None	Sillimanite	1.658–1.678	+0.02
Rhodo-			Enstatite	1.663–1.673	+0.010
chrosite	1.600–1.820	−0.22	Euclase	1.652–1.672	+0.020
Painite	1.787–1.816	−0.029	Phenacite	1.654–1.670	+0.016
Spessartite	1.795–1.815	None	Datolite	1.625–1.669	−0.044
Pyrite	over 1.81	None	Jadeite	1.654–1.667	−0.013
Almandine	1.78 –1.81	None			Often none
Benitoite	1.757–1.804	+0.047	Calcite	1.486–1.658	−0.172
Ceylanite	1.77 –1.80	None	Coral	1.486–1.658	−0.172
Corundum	1.766–1.774	−0.008	Onyx marble	1.486–1.658	−0.172
Ruby	1.766–1.774	−0.008	Tourmaline	1.616–1.652	−0.014
Sapphire	1.766–1.774	−0.008			up to −0.044
Epidote	1.733–1.768	+0.035	Turquoise	1.61 –1.65	+0.04
Staurolite	1.739–1.762	+0.015	Andalusite	1.641–1.648	−0.007
Andradite	1.82 –1.89	None	Barite	1.636–1.648	+0.012
Rhodolite	about 1.76	None	Apatite	1.632–1.648	−0.002
Pyrope	1.730–1.760	None			up to −0.004
Alexandrite	1.745–1.759	+0.010	Lazulite	1.615–1.645	−0.030
Chrysoberyl	1.744–1.755	+0.011	Actinolite	1.618–1.641	−0.023
Gahnite	1.715–1.752	None	Prehnite	1.61 –1.64	+0.030
Hessonite	1.742–1.748	None	Topaz	1.610–1.638	+0.008
Grossular	1.738–1.745	None			up to +0.010

Table of Refractive Indices and Double Refraction

	Refractive index	Double refraction		Refractive index	Double refraction
Amblygonite	1.611–1.637	+0.026	Tiger's eye	1.544–1.553	+0.009
Danburite	1.630–1.636	−0.006	Agalmatolite	about 1.55	None
Hemi-morphite	1.614–1.636	+0.022	Moss agate	1.54 –1.55	up to +0.006
Celestine (Celestite)	1.622–1.631	+0.009	Iolite	1.53 –1.55	−0.008 up to −0.012
Hambergite	1.559–1.631	+0.072	Stichtite	1.52 –1.55	−0.027
Smaragdite	1.608–1.630	−0.022	Elaeolite	1.532–1.549	−0.004
Nephrite	1.600–1.627	−0.027 Partly none	Aventurine feldspar	1.532–1.542	+0.01
Vivianite	1.580–1.627	+0.047	Jade-albite	1.525–1.540	+0.015
Brazilianite	1.603–1.623	+0.020	Ivory	1.54	None
Tremolite	1.60 –1.62	−0.02	Fossilized wood	about 1.54	Weak or none
Colemanite	1.586–1.614	+0.028	Jasper	about 1.54	None
Anhydrite	1.571–1.614	+0.043	Thomsonite	1.52 –1.54	+0.028
Howlite	1.586–1.609	−0.019	Chalcedony	1.530–1.539	Up to +0.006
Ekanite	1.60	None	Chrysoprase	1.530–1.539	Up to +0.004
Beryl	1.570–1.600	−0.006 up to −0.009	Apophyllite	1.535–1.537	±0.002
Wardite	1.590–1.599	+0.099	Peristerite	1.525–1.536	+0.011
Variscite	1.55 –1.59	−0.010	Meerschaum	1.53	None
Steatite	1.539–1.589	−0.050	Amazonite	1.522–1.530	−0.008
Augelite	1.574–1.588	+0.014	Alabaster	1.520–1.530	+0.010
Aquamarine	1.577–1.583	−0.006	Moonstone	1.520–1.525	−0.005
Emerald	1.576–1.582	−0.006	Orthoclase	1.519–1.525	−0.006
Bytownite	1.567–1.576	−0.009	Sanidine	1.518–1.524	−0.006
Serpentine	1.560–1.571	None	Cancrinite	1.491–1.524	−0.023
Labradorite	1.560–1.568	+0.008	Ulexite	1.491–1.520	+0.029
Beryllonite	1.553–1.562	−0.009	Petalite	1.502–1.518	+0.016
Scapolite	1.540–1.560	−0.009 up to −0.020	Gaylussite	1.517	None
Agate	1.544–1.553	+0.009	Obsidian	1.48 –1.51	None
Amethyst	1.544–1.553	+0.009	Leucite	1.508–1.509	+0.001
Amethyst quartz	1.544–1.553	+0.009	Haüynite	1.502	None
Aventurine	1.544–1.533	+0.009	Tugtupite	1.496–1.502	+0.006
Rock crystal	1.544–1.553	+0.009	Chrysocolla	about 1.50	None
Citrine	1.544–1.553	+0.009	Lapis lazuli	about 1.50	None
Prase	1.544–1.553	+0.009	Moldavite	1.48 –1.50	None
Prasiolite	1.544–1.553	+0.009	Natrolite	1.480–1.493	+0.013
Quartz	1.544–1.553	+0.009	Sodalite	1.48	None
Rose quartz	1.544–1.553	+0.009	Opal	1.44 –1.46	None
Smoky quartz	1.544–1.553	+0.009	Fluorite	1.434	None

Double Refraction

In all gemstones, except opals, glasses and those belonging to the Isometric (cubic) system, the ray of light enters the crystal and is divided into two rays. This is called double refraction. It can be most easily observed in the case of Iceland spar. It is also easily seen in zircon, sphene and peridot; when looking through the top, one can see the doubling of the edges of the lower facets with the naked eye. In the case of synthetic rutile, the double refraction is so strong that the stone can give a blurred impression. It is up to the lapidary to work the stone in such a way that the double refraction does not appear disturbing. In the case of most gems, double refraction is small and cannot be detected without instruments. Therefore double refraction can help to identify gems. It is expressed as the difference between the highest and lowest refractive indices. The expert also differentiates between positive and negative "optical character". (For data on double refraction, see the table on p. 32.)

Dispersion

White light is split not only when passing through a crystal, but also when it fans out into its spectral colors. The deviation is dependent on the density and on wave lengths of the light. Because the individual spectral colors have different wave lengths, they are also bent differently. (See illustrations p. 36). For instance, in the case of diamond, the refractive index of the red (at a wave length of 6870 Å) is 2.407, of the yellow (5890 Å) is 2.417, of the green (5270 Å) is 2.427 and of the violet (3970 Å) is 2.465. This division of white light into colors of the rainbow is called dispersion.

Color dispersion is particularly large in diamonds where it produces a beautiful play of color, the so-called "fire". Only colorless gems have good dispersion. Natural as well as synthetic gemstones with high dispersion (for instance strontium titanate, rutile, sphalerite, sphene, zircon) are used as substitutes for diamond. See p. 36.

Iceland spar shows double refraction especially clearly.

Table of Dispersion

Rutile	0.280	Hiddenite		0.017
Anatase	0.213 & 0.259	Kunzite		0.017
Strontium titanate	0.190	Scapolite		0.017
Sphalerite	0.156	Tourmaline		0.017
Cassiterite	0.071	Andalusite		0.016
Demantoid	0.057	Apatite		0.016
Melanite (garnet)	0.057	Datolite		0.016
Cerussite	0.051	Euclase		0.016
Sphene	0.051	Alexandrite		0.015
Benitoite	0.039 & 0.046	Chrysoberyl		0.015
Diamond	0.044	Hambergite		0.015
Zircon	0.039	Phenacite		0.015
Benitoite	0.046 & 0.039	Sillimanite		0.015
Smithsonite	0.014 & 0.031	Aquamarine		0.014
Epidote	0.030	Beryl		0.014
Tanzanite	0.030	Brazilianite		0.014
Grossular	0.027	Petalite		0.014
Hessonite	0.027	Emerald		0.014
Spessartite	0.027	Smithsonite	0.031 & 0.014	
Willemite	0.027	Topaz		0.014
Scheelite	0.026	Amethyst		0.013
Spinel	0.026	Amethyst quartz		0.013
Almandine	0.024	Aventurine		0.013
Rhodolite	0.024	Rock crystal		0.013
Staurolite	0.023	Citrine		0.013
Dioptase	0.022	Prasiolite		0.013
Pyrope	0.022	Smoky quartz		0.013
Kyanite	0.020	Rose quartz		0.013
Peridot	0.020	Tiger's eye		0.013
Taaffeite	0.019	Amazonite		0.012
Idocrase	0.019	Moonstone		0.012
Kornerupine	0.018	Orthoclase		0.012
Ruby	0.018	Beryllonite		0.010
Sapphire	0.018	Cancrinite		0.010
Sinhalite	0.018	Leucite		0.010
Calcite	0.008 & 0.017	Obsidian		0.010
Iolite	0.017	Glass		0.010
Danburite	0.017	Calcite	0.017 & 0.008	
		Fluorite		0.007

The dispersion of a stone is expressed in figures as the difference between the red and violet refractive indices. As the color usually comprises a wide spectrum, it is common to measure the Fraunhofer B-line for the red and the G-line for the violet. See Table on p. 35.

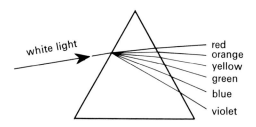

Refraction and dispersion of white light when passing through a prism

Absorption Spectra

The absorption spectrum of a gem is one of the most important aids in identifying it. The absorption spectrum of a stone are the bands of spectral colors of light which have passed through the gem (ill. p. 39). As we know, certain wavelengths (color bands) of the light are absorbed (see p. 27) and the color of the gem is formed from the mixture of the remaining parts of the original white light. The human eye cannot recognize all minute color differences. Red tourmaline, red garnet or even red-colored glass can appear deceivingly like the desirable red ruby. However the absorption spectrum unmasks without any doubt the stone or glass used to imitate the ruby. Most gems have a very characteristic, and even unique, absorption spectrum which is revealed in black vertical lines or broad bands.

The great advantage of the testing method is the ease with which one can differentiate between gems of similar specific gravity and refractive index. One can also use this method for testing rough stones, cabochons and even set stones. An important area where absorption spectroscopy is applied is in differentiating between natural stones, synthetic stones and imitations.

Best results are obtained from strongly colored transparent gemstones. The observation of the absorption spectrum of an opaque stone is only possible when a thin slice of the stone is prepared which may transmit light (as in the case of hematite). Otherwise a translucent edge must be presented, or light must be reflected from the surface.

The testing instrument is the spectroscope, with the help of which one can determine the wavelength of the absorbed light. The wavelength is measured in Ångstrom units (1Å – 1 ten millionth of a millimeter), and more recently also in nanometers (1 NM – 1 millionth millimeter). Because the absorption lines or bands are not always of equal strength, it is usual to note such measured differences. Strong absorption lines are underlined, for instance 6535; weak lines are bracketed, for instance (4327).

Table of Absorption Spectra

All figures are in Ångstrom units (Å).
Strong absorption lines are underlined, weak ones are bracketed.

Agate, artificially dyed yellow : <u>7000</u>, (6650), (6340)
Actinolite : 5030, 4315
Alexandrite, green direction : <u>6805</u>, 6785, 6650, <u>6550</u>, 6490, 6450, <u>6400</u>–<u>5550</u>
Alexandrite, red direction : 6805, <u>6785</u>, 6550, 6450, 6050–5400, (4720)
Almandine : 6170, <u>5760</u>, <u>5260</u>, <u>5050</u>, 4760, 4620, 4380, 4280, 4040, 3930
Amethyst : (5500–5200)
Andalusite : 5535, <u>5505</u>, 5475, (5250), (5180), (5060), (4950), <u>4550</u>, 4475, <u>4360</u>
Apatite, yellow green : 6053, 6025, 5975, <u>5855</u>, <u>5772</u>, <u>5742</u>, 5335, 5295, 5270,
   5250, 5210, 5140, 4690, 4425
Apatite, blue : 6310, 6220, 5250, <u>5120</u>, <u>5070</u>, <u>4910</u>, 4640
Aquamarine : <u>5370</u>, 4560, 4270
Maxixe-Aquamarine : 6540, 6280, 6150, 5810, 5500
Aventurine : 6820, 6490
Axinite : 5320, <u>5120</u>, <u>4920</u>, <u>4660</u>, 4400, 4150
Azurite : 5000
Beryl, artificially dyed blue : 7050–6850, 6450, 6250, 6050, (5870)
Calcite : <u>5820</u>
Chalcedony, artificially dyed blue : 6900–6600, 6270
Chalcedony, artificially dyed green : 7050, 6700, 6450
Chrysoberyl : 5040, 4950, 4850, <u>4450</u>
Chrysoprase, natural : 4439
Chrysoprase, artificially dyed : 6320, 4439
Danburite : 5900, 5860, <u>5845</u>, 5840, 5830, 5820, 5805, 5780, 5760, 5730, 5710,
   5680, 5665, 5645
Demantoid : <u>7010</u>, 6930, <u>6400</u>, <u>6220</u>, 4850, 4640, 4430
Diamond, natural colorless to yellow (Cape) : <u>4780</u>, 4650, 4510, 4350, 4230,
   <u>4155</u>, 4015, 3900
Diamond, natural, brown-green : (5370), <u>5040</u>, (4980)
Diamond, natural, yellow-brown : 5760, 5690, 5640, 5580, 5500, 5480, 5230,
   4935, 4800, 4600
Diamond, artificial color, yellow : <u>5940</u>, 5040, <u>4980</u>, 4780, 4650, 4510, 4350,
   4230, 4155
Diamond, artificial color, green : <u>7410</u>, <u>5040</u>, 4980, 4650, 4510, 4350, 4230, 4155
Diamond, artificial color, brown : (7410), 5940, <u>5040</u>, <u>4980</u>, 4780, 4650, 4510,
   4350, 4230, 4155
Diopside : <u>5470</u>, 5080, <u>5050</u>, <u>4930</u>, 4560
Chrome-Diopside : (6700), (6550), (6350), 5080, 5050, 4900
Dioptase : 5700, 5600, 4650–4000
Ekanite : 6651, (6375)
Emerald, natural : <u>6835</u>, <u>6806</u>, 6620, 6460, <u>6370</u>, (6060), (5940), <u>6300–5800</u>,
   4774, 4725
Emerald, synthetic : <u>6830</u>, <u>6805</u>, 6620, 6460, <u>6375</u>, 6300–5800, 6060, 5940, 4774,
   4725, <u>4300</u>
Enstatite : <u>5475</u>, 5090, <u>5058</u>, 5025, 4830, 4720, 4590, 4490, 4250
Chrome-Enstatite : 6880, 6690, 5060
Epidote : 4750, <u>4550</u>, 4350
Euclase : <u>7065</u>, <u>7040</u>, 6950, 6880, 6600, <u>6500</u>, <u>6390</u>, 4680, 4550
Fluorite, green : 6400, 6006, <u>5850</u>, 5700, 5530, 5500, 4520, 4350
Fluorite, yellow : 5450, 5150, 4900, 4700, 4520
Gahnite : <u>6320</u>, 5920, 5770, 5520, 5080, <u>4800</u>, <u>4590</u>, 4430, 4330
Grossular : 6300
Hematite : (7000), (6400), (5950), (5700), (4800), (4500), (4250), (4000)
Hessonite : 5470, 4900, 4545, <u>4350</u>

Hiddenite : <u>6905</u>, <u>6860</u>, 6690, 6460, <u>6200</u>, <u>4375</u>, 4330
Hypersthene : 5510, <u>5475</u>, <u>5058</u>, 4820, 4485
Idocrase, green : 5300, 4870, <u>4610</u>
Idocrase, brown : 5910, 5880, <u>5845</u>, 5820, 5775, 5745
Idocrase, yellow-green : <u>4650</u>
Iolite : 6450, 5930, 5850, 5350, <u>4920</u>, <u>4560</u>, 4360, 4260
Jadeite, natural green : <u>6915</u>, 6550, 6300, (4950), 4500, <u>4375</u>, 4330
Jadeite, artificial color green : 6650, 6550, 6450
Kornerupine : 5400, <u>5080</u>, 4630, <u>4460</u>, 4300
Kyanite : (7060), (6890), (6710), (6520), <u>4460</u>, 4330
Nephrite : (6890), <u>5090</u>, 4900, 4600
Obsidian, green : 6800, 6700, 6600, 6500, 6350, 5950, 5550, 5000
Opal, fire-opal : 7000–6400, 5900–4000
Orthoclase : 4480, 4200
Peridot : (6530), (5530), 5290, <u>4970</u>, <u>4950</u>, <u>4930</u>, <u>4730</u>, 4530
Petalite : (4540)
Pyrope : <u>6870</u>, <u>6850</u>, 6710, 6500, <u>6200–5200</u>, 5050
Quartz, synthetic, blue : 6450, 5850, 5400, 5000–4900
Rhodochrosite : 5510, 4545, 4100, 3910, 3830, 3780, 3630
Rhodonite : 5480, 5030, 4550, 4120, 4080
Ruby : <u>6912</u>, <u>6928</u>, 6680, 6592, 6100–5000, <u>4765</u>, <u>4750</u>, <u>4685</u>
Sapphire, blue : <u>4710</u>, <u>4600</u>, 4550, <u>4500</u>, 3790
Sapphire, yellow : <u>4710</u>, <u>4600</u>, <u>4500</u>
Sapphire, green : 4710, 4600–4500
Scheelite : <u>5840</u>
Serpentine : 4970, 4640
Sillimanite : 4620, 4410, 4100
Sinhalite : 5260, 4925, 4760, <u>4630</u>, 4520, 4355
Scapolite, pink : 6630, 6520
Spessartite : 4950, <u>4845</u>, 4810, 4750, <u>4620</u>, 4570, 4550, 4400, 4350, 4320, 4240, 4120, 4060, 3940
Sphalerite : 6900, 6650, <u>6510</u>
Sphene : 5900, <u>5860</u>, <u>5820</u>, 5800, 5750, 5340, 5300, 5280
Spinel, natural, red : <u>6855</u>, 6840, <u>6750</u>, <u>6650</u>, 6560, 6500, 6420, 6320, <u>5950–4900</u>, 4650, 4550
Spinel, natural, blue : <u>6350</u>, <u>5850</u>, <u>5550</u>, 5080, <u>4780</u>, <u>4580</u>, 4430, 4330
Spinel, synthetic, blue : 6340, 5800, 5440, 4850, 4490
Spinel, synthetic, green : 6200, 5800, 5700, 5500, 5400
Taaffeite : 5580, 5530, 4780
Tanzanite : 7100, 6910, <u>5950</u>, 5280, 4550
Topaz, pink : <u>6828</u>
Tremolite : <u>6840</u>, 6500, 6280
Turquoise : (4600), 4320, 4220
Tourmaline, red : 5550, 5370, 5250–4610, <u>4560</u>, <u>4510</u>, 4280
Tourmaline, green : <u>4970</u>, <u>4610</u>, 4150
Variscite : 6880, (6500)
Willemite : 5830, 5400, 4900, 4425, 4315, <u>4210</u>
Zircon, normal : 6910, 6890, 6625, 6605, <u>6535</u>, 6210, 6150, 5895, 5620, 5375, 5160, 4840, 4600, 4327
Zircon, low : <u>6530</u>, (5200)

Absorption Spectra

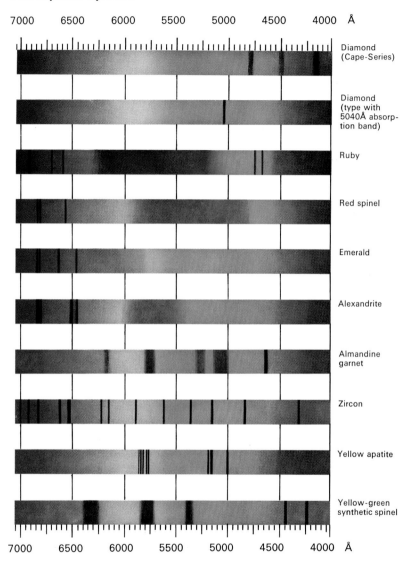

| 7000 | 6500 | 6000 | 5500 | 5000 | 4500 | 4000 | Å |

Diamond (Cape-Series)

Diamond (type with 5040Å absorption band)

Ruby

Red spinel

Emerald

Alexandrite

Almandine garnet

Zircon

Yellow apatite

Yellow-green synthetic spinel

| 7000 | 6500 | 6000 | 5500 | 5000 | 4500 | 4000 | Å |

From *Gemmologists' Compendium* by R. Webster, NAG Press Ltd, London. Taken from *Edelsteinkundliches Handbuch* by Professor Dr Chudoba and Dr Gübelin, Stollfuss Verlag, Bonn.

Transparency

A factor in the evaluation of most gemstones is their transparency. Inclusions of foreign matter and air bubbles or fissures in the interior of the crystal affect the transparency. The path of light through the crystal can also be impaired by strong absorption in the crystal. Grainy, stalky or fibrous aggregates (such as chalcedony, lapis lazuli, turquoise) are opaque because the rays of light are repeatedly refracted or reflected by the many tiny faces until finally they are completely reflected or absorbed. Where the light is only weakened by its passage through a stone, it is said to have translucency.

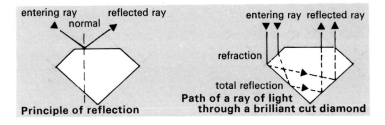

Principle of reflection

Path of a ray of light through a brilliant cut diamond

Luster

The luster of a gem is caused by reflection, i.e. the reflecting of part of the incident light back from the surface. It is dependent on the refractive index and the nature of the surface, but not on the color. The higher the refraction, the higher the luster. Most desirable luster is adamantine, the most common is vitreous. Comparatively rare are the fatty, metallic, pearly, silky and waxy lusters. Stones with no luster are described as dull.

In everyday language, those light effects which are caused by total reflection are also considered as luster. The lower facets of the gem act as a mirror and reflect the entering light more or less completely, so strengthening the lustrous appearance. The phenomenon on the surface of the stone is called brilliance. The ideal complete refraction is found in the diamond cut which thus reaches the highest brilliance.

Pleochroism

Some gems appear to have different colors or depth of color when viewed in different directions. This is caused by the differing absorption of light of doubly refractive crystals. Where two main colors can be observed (only in the tetragonal, hexagonal and trigonal crystal systems), one speaks of dichroism; where three colors can be seen (only in the orthorhombic, monoclinic and triclinic crystal systems), of trichroism or pleochroism. The latter is a collective description for both phenomena. Amorphous gems and those in the isometric (cubic) system show no pleochroism.

Pleochroism can be weak, definite or strong. It must be taken into consideration when cutting in order to avoid poor colors, or shades that are too dark or too light.

Table of Pleochroism

Actinolite:	yellow-green, light green, blue-green
Alexandrite:	green alexandrite viewed in daylight: distinct; pigeon-blood red, orange-yellow, emerald-green
Amethyst:	very weak; purple, gray-purple
Anatase:	distinct; yellow, orange
Andalusite:	strong; yellow, olive, red-brown to dark-red
Apatite:	yellow: weak; golden-yellow, green-yellow
	green: weak; yellow, green
	blue: very strong; blue, colorless
Aquamarine:	blue: distinct; nearly colorless to light blue, blue to sky blue
	green/blue: distinct; yellow-green to colorless, blue-green
Aventurine feldspar:	weak or non-existent
Axinite:	strong; olive green, red brown, yellow brown
Azurite:	distinct; light blue, dark blue
Barite:	blue: weak
Benitoite:	very strong; colorless, green to blue
Beryl:	golden: weak; lemon yellow, yellow
	green: distinct; yellow green, blue green
	heliodor: weak; golden yellow, green yellow
	morganite: distinct; pale pink, blue pink
	purple: distinct; purple, colorless
Brazilianite:	very weak
Cassiterite:	distinct
Chrysoberyl:	very weak; red to yellow, yellow to pale green, green
Citrine:	natural: weak; yellow, light yellow
Chrysocolla:	weak
Corundum:	synthetic: distinct; blue green, yellow green
Danburite:	weak; weak pale yellow, light yellow
Diopside:	weak; yellow green, grass green, olive green
Dioptase:	weak; dark emerald green, light emerald green
Dumortierite:	strong; black, red-brown, brown
Emerald:	natural: distinct; green, blue green to yellow green
	synthetic: yellow green, blue green
Enstatite:	distinct; green, yellow green
Euclase:	very weak; whitish green, yellow green, blue green
Epidote:	strong; green, brown, yellow
Heliodor:	weak; golden yellow, green yellow
Hiddenite:	distinct; blue green, emerald green, yellow green
Hypersthene:	strong; hyacinth red, straw yellow, sky blue
Iolite:	very strong; yellow, dark purple-blue, pale blue
Idocrase:	green: weak; yellow green, yellow brown
	yellow: weak; yellow brown, light brown
	brown: weak; yellow brown, light brown
Jasper:	very weak
Kornerupine:	strong; green, yellow, brown
Kunzite:	distinct; amethyst color, pale red, colorless
Kyanite:	strong; pale blue to colorless, pale blue, dark blue
Lazulite:	strong; colorless, dark blue
Malachite:	very strong; colorless, green
Morganite:	distinct; pale pink, bluish pink
Nephrite:	weak; yellow to brown, green
Orthoclase:	yellow: weak
Painite:	strong; ruby red, brown orange
Peridot:	very weak; colorless to pale green, lively green, oily green
Phenacite:	distinct; colorless, orange yellow
Prasiolite:	very weak; light green, pale green
Pseudophite:	green, yellow
Purpurite:	distinct; brown gray, blood red

Table of Pleochroism Continued

Rhodonite:	distinct; yellow-red, rose red
Rose quartz:	weak; pink, pale pink
Ruby:	strong; yellow-red, deep carmine red
Sanidine:	weak
Sapphire:	orange: strong; yellow brown to orange, nearly colorless
	yellow: weak; yellow, light yellow
	green: weak; green yellow, greenish yellow
	blue: distinct; dark blue, greenish blue
	purple: distinct; purple, light red
	synthetic: dark blue, yellow to blue
Scapolite:	pink: colorless, pink
	yellow: distinct; colorless, yellow
Scheelite:	distinct
Sillimanite:	strong; light green, dark green, blue
Sinhalite:	distinct; green, light brown, dark brown
Smoky quartz:	dark: distinct; brown, red-brown
Sphene:	green: colorless, green
	yellow: strong; colorless, yellow, reddish
Staurolite:	strong; yellowish, yellowish red, red
Tanzanite:	very strong; purple, blue, brown
Thulite:	strong; yellow, pink
Topaz:	red: strong; dark red, yellow, rose red
	pink: distinct; colorless, pale pink, pink
	yellow: distinct; lemon yellow, honey yellow, straw yellow
	brown: distinct; yellow brown, dull yellow brown
	green: distinct; pale green, light blue green, greeny white
	blue: weak; light blue, pink, colorless
	heat-treated: distinct; pink, colorless
Tremolite:	distinct
Turquoise:	weak
Tourmaline:	red: distinct; dark red, light red
	pink: distinct; light red, reddish yellow
	yellow: distinct; dark yellow, light yellow
	brown: distinct; dark brown, light brown
	green: strong; dark green, yellow green
	blue: strong; dark blue, light blue
	purple: strong; purple, light purple
Willemite:	variable
Zircon:	red: weak; red, light yellow
	red brown: very weak; reddish brown, yellowish brown
	yellow: very weak; honey yellow, brown yellow
	brown: very weak; red brown, yellow brown
	brown green: very weak; pink yellow, lemon yellow
	green: very weak; green, brown green
	blue: distinct; blue, yellow gray to colorless

Above: asterism in sapphire and ruby.
Below: play of color in precious opal.

Light and color effects

Many gems show striated light effects or color effects which do not relate to their color and are not caused by impurities or their chemical composition. These effects are caused by reflection, interference and refraction.

Chatoyancy (cat's eye effect)   An effect which resembles the slit eye of a cat (French *chat*=cat, *oeil*=eye): this is caused by the reflection of light by parallel fibers, needles or channels. This phenomenon is most effective when the stone is cut en cabochon in such a way that the base is parallel to the fibers. When the gem is rotated, the cat's eye glides over the surface. The most precious cat's eye is that of chrysoberyl (p. 198). The effect can be found in many gemstones, especially well known are quartz cat's eye, hawk's eye and tiger's eye (p. 124). If one talks simply of cat's eye, one refers to a chrysoberyl cat's eye. All other cat's eye must have an additional designation.

Asterism   This is the effect of light rays forming a star (Greek *aster*=star); the rays meet in one point and enclose definite angles (depending on the symmetry of the stone). It is formed like a cat's eye, but the reflecting fibers lie in various directions. Ruby (p. 82) and sapphire (p. 86) cabochons can show effective six-rayed stars. There are also four-rayed stars and, rarely, twelve-rayed stars. If a piece of rose quartz has been cut as a sphere, the rays move in circles over the whole surface; where included needles are partially destroyed, stunted stars, part circles or light clusters are formed. Asterism also occurs in synthetic gems.

Adularescence   Moonstone, being a variety of adularia (see name, p. 164) shows a blue-whitish opalescence which glides over the surface when the stone is cut en cabochon. Interference phenomena of the layered structure are the cause of this effect.

Aventurization   Colorful play of glittering reflections of small, leaf-like inclusions on an opaque background. The inclusions are hematite or goethite in the case of aventurine feldspar (p. 166); fuchsite or hematite in aventurine quartz (p. 122); and copper scrapings in imitation aventurine glass.

Iridescence   Play of color of some gems caused by dispersion of light in cracks and flaws resulting in the colors of the rainbow (Greek *iris*=rainbow). Commercially this effect is created by artificially producing cracks in rock crystal.

Labradorescence   Play of color in metallic hues, especially in labradorite (hence the name) and spectrolite (p. 166). Blue and green effects are often found, but the whole spectrum is most desirable. The cause of the schillers is most probably interference phenomena of twinned layering.

Opalescence   Milky blue or pearly appearance of common opal (p. 152) caused by reflection of short wave, mainly blue, light. It should not be confused with opalization.

Opalization (often called iridescence)   Play of color of the opal (hence the name, p. 150) which changes with the angle of observation. As recently as the 1960s, this effect was explained as the light refraction of the smallest layered structure. The electron-microscope shows the real cause at a magnification of 20,000x: small spheres of the mineral cristobalite included in a silica gel cause the reflection interference phenomena. The diameter of these spheres is one ten-thousandth of a millimeter. The term should not be confused with opalescence (p. 44).

Silk   Reflection of parallel fibrous inclusions or canals causes a silk-like appearance. Not desirable in faceted rubies and sapphires. Where the included needles are too numerous, the stone becomes opaque and, when cut accordingly, can show a cat's eye.

Luminescence

Luminescence (Latin – light) is a collective definition for the emission of visible light under the influence of certain rays, as well as by some physical or chemical reaction, but not including pure heat radiation. The most important of these phenomena for the testing of gems is the luminescence under ultra-violet light which is called fluorescence. The name fluorescence is derived from the mineral fluorite, which was the substance in which this light phenomenon was first observed. When the substance continues to give out light after irradiation has ceased, the effect is called phosphorescence (named after the well-known light property of phosphorus).

The cause of fluorescence in gems is the incorporation of small metal impurities which often also affect the color, such as chromium, manganese, cobalt and nickel, as well as molybdate, tungsten and some uranium compounds. As various types of gems can contain different trace elements, not all stones within a group necessarily show the same fluorescent colors. Some deposits produce very characteristic fluorescent colors. Iron, if present even in the smallest quantities, prevents any fluorescence.

Gems are tested in ultra-violet light with long waves (4000–3150Å) and short waves (2800–2000Å). This is because some gems react only to one of these wave lengths. The intermediary wave lengths (3150–2800Å) are of no importance in gem testing. It is usual to designate long waves as 3650Å and short waves as 2537Å. Fluorescence can help to identify gems and is particularly useful in recognizing synthetic stones. The strength of fluorescence can vary, and the color can be one of many hues.

Luminescence caused by x-rays can help to differentiate between real and cultured pearls. The mother-of-pearl of the salt-water pearl oyster does not luminesce while that of the fresh-water pearl mussel gives off a strong light. As the inserted nucleus of a cultured pearl has been taken from a piece of fresh-water mother-of-pearl, the cultured pearl shows a luminescence which the real pearls do not have. See Table of Fluorescence of Gems, p. 46.

Table of Fluorescence of Gems

Agate : differs within layers, partly strong ; yellow, blue white
Amazonite : weak ; olive green
Amber : bluish to yellow-green
  Burmite : blue
Amblygonite : very weak ; green
Amethyst : weak ; greenish
Andalusite : weak ; green, yellow-green
Apatite : varies considerably
Aventurine : reddish
Aventurine feldspar : dark red-brown
Axinite : mostly none
Benitoite : strong ; blue
Beryl : pink : weak ; violet
Calcite : red, pink, orange, white, yellow-white
Cerussite : usually yellow, rarely pink, whitish, green or none
Chalcedony : bluish-white
Chrysoberyl : green : weak ; dark red, others : none
Colemanite : white, yellow-white
Coral : weak
Danburite : sky blue
Diamond : varies considerably
  colorless and yellow : usually blue
  brown and green : often green
  synthetic : strong ; yellow
Diopside : strong ; dark violet
Dolomite : pink, orange-red
Dumortierite : weak and variable
Emerald : usually none
Fluorite : usually strong ; blue to violet
Hemimorphite : weak
Hiddenite : very weak ; red-yellow
Ivory : various blues
Jadeite : green : very weak ; gray blue
Kunzite : strong ; yellow red, orange
Kyanite : blue-green : strong ; red
Labradorite : yellow striations
Lapis lazuli : strong ; white
Moonstone : weak ; bluish, orange

Moss agate : varies
Opal : white : bluish, brown, green
  black : usually none
  fire : greenish to brown
Pearls : weak ; not applicable
  Natural black pearls : red to reddish
Petalite : weak, orange
Phosgenite : yellow, orange yellow
Prehnite : weak, orange
Rhodochrosite : weak ; red
Rose quartz : weak ; dark violet
Ruby : strong ; carmine red
Sapphire : blue : violet or none
  yellow : weak ; orange
  colorless : orange yellow or violet blue
Scapolite : pink : orange, pink
  yellow : violet, blue-red
Scheelite : blue, whitish or yellow
Smoky quartz : usually none, rarely weak ; brown yellow
Sodalite : strong ; orange
Sphalerite : usually yellow to orange, sometimes red
Spinel : red : strong ; red
  blue : weak ; reddish or green
  green : weak ; reddish
Topaz : pink : weak ; brown
  red : weak ; brown-yellow
  yellow : weak ; orange-yellow
Tourmaline : colorless : weak ; green-blue
  pale yellow : weak ; dark green
  red : weak ; red-violet
  pink, brown, green, blue : none
Turquoise : weak ; greenish-yellow, light blue
Ulexite : green to yellow, blue
Willemite : green
Witherite : blue, yellow white, white
Zircon : blue : weak ; light orange
  red and brown : weak ; dark yellow

Above : smoky quartz with rutile star.

Below : amber with carbon and insect inclusion.

Inclusions

Only a few gemstones have no optically recognizable marks within them. These are classified in the trade as "clean". Clarity is of special importance for the diamond. The best qualities must show no inclusions under a 10 power hand lens (louche) when examined by an expert in adequate lighting. Only a few years ago irregularities in the crystal were classed as "flaws". As this was not always a fair assessment, the practice is now to speak of inclusions.

Inclusions of minerals are quite common, such as those of the same material (for instance, diamond in diamond) and of a foreign one (for instance, zircon in sapphire). Even if small, they provide a constructive picture of the formation of the surrounding crystal (host crystal). Included minerals can be older than the host crystal, as they were just surrounded. They can also have been formed from a melt at the same time as the host crystal, which surrounded the smaller ones because its growth rate was greater. There are also mineral inclusions which are younger than the host crystal; these were formed out of liquids which entered into the crystal through cracks and fissures.

Organic inclusions are only found in amber (p. 220 and 47). Parts of plants and insects are often preserved in it and bear witness to the life of 50 million years ago.

Irregularities in the crystal structure, marks of the crystallization phases and color striations are classed as inclusions. They can be formed by irregular growth from various crystallizing solutions. Cavities also, when filled with liquid (water, liquid silicic acid) or gases (carbon dioxide or monoxide), are classed as inclusions. Where liquid and gaseous inclusions occur together, they are called two-phase inclusions. Liquid, gaseous and small crystal inclusions are called three-phase inclusions. Completely empty cavities are not known. Air-filled bubbles are frequent in obsidian, glass imitations and synthetic gems, but not in mineral gems.

Even rents or splits (called feathers), whether caused by internal stress or external pressure, are classed as inclusions by the dealer. These types of inclusions can be observed in the interior of a stone and may reach the surface. Air and solutions can enter a stone along such fissures and cause it to change color. If the stone is "heated", the foreign substance can be extruded, but scars show the old crack.

The trade and the layman consider most inclusions as devaluing a stone, because color, optical properties and mechanical resistance can be affected. However, some minerals cause light phenomena which can produce the most valuable properties of some gems: cat's eye effect, asterism and silk (p. 44) and dendrites (p. 130). The golden inclusions of rutile in rock crystal or smoky quartz are most effective, especially when they form a star (p. 47).

Inclusions, next to optical properties, have in recent years become more important for the identification of gemstones. Many types of inclusion are so characteristic that, with their help, one can distinguish between the genuine and any imitation or synthetic stone; sometimes they can even indicate where the gemstone was found.

Deposits and Production of Gemstones

Gemstones are found in many parts of the world, singly or grouped together. Groups large enough to be worked are called "deposits". Single occurrences are referred to as a "find". The word "occurrence" refers to both.

Types of deposits

According to the way the gemstones have been formed, we differentiate between magmatic (formed out of the magma), sedimentary (formed by sedimentation) and metamorphic (re-formed from other rocks) deposits.

It is often more useful to speak of primary and secondary deposits: the former are the gems found in the "original" place, where they were formed; and the latter are those found in "secondary" places to which they were transported.

In the primary deposits the stones still have their original relationship with their host rock. The yield is usually not very large because many tons of non-gem bearing rock have to be handled.

Panning – washing for diamonds with a pan. Prospectors in Angola.

Old type of diamond-recovery plant (washing)

In the case of secondary deposits, the gems have been transported from the place of their formation and deposited somewhere else. During this process harder crystals become rounded and softer ones are made smaller or even destroyed. According to the way the stones have been transported, they are differentiated as fluvial (by river), marine (in the sea) or aeolian (by wind) deposits. Rivers can transport gem-bearing rocks many hundreds of miles. When the current diminishes and with it the transporting energy, the specifically heavier gems are deposited before the lighter quartz-sand. The gems left behind thus enrich certain places. This concentrating process makes mining easier and more productive than working primary deposits.

The gems deposited by the river are called placers or alluvial deposits. In a similar way alluvial deposits can be found in the surf-pounded bays of the sea. In south west Africa (Namibia), such diamond deposits are being worked very successfully. Small gem crystals can even be transported by the wind and enrich a particular place.

Seen genetically, between the primary and secondary deposits there are places where decomposition or weathering takes place. The gems are often found at the foot of steep cliffs or high mountains and have collected in such places as part of the weathered debris, then, because the specifically lighter mother-rock was carried away by rain and wind, the gems were left. These are called eluvial deposits.

Distribution of gems over the earth is irregular. Some regions are more favored than others: South Africa, south and south-east Asia, Brazil, the Urals, Australia and the mountainous zones of the U.S.

Mining Methods

Most gemstone deposits were discovered by accident. Even today systematic prospecting is limited to diamond occurrences. The reason for this is that the price and production of diamond is controlled on a world-wide scale and large capital investment is possible. It is questionable whether greater investment without control of the market would be viable for other gems.

Prospecting for non-diamondiferous deposits is usually accomplished by simple means, without modern techniques or scientific basis. The success of local prospectors in finding new deposits is surprising. A deposit which is being worked is called a mine.

With the exception of diamonds, mining methods in most countries are very primitive. In some districts, they have not changed in the last 2000 years. The simplest method is collecting gems from the surface, from dry river beds or from rock fissures. Crystals grown into the mother-rock are freed with hand tools, compressed air tools or explosives.

The mining of gem from young secondary deposits is comparatively simple. Any overburden is removed; or where the deposits are deeper under the surface, pits or shafts – sometimes to a depth of 30ft/10m – are sunk. Simple roofs protect the entrances against rain, and buckets or electric pumps are used to remove underground water that enters from the bottom of the shaft. Drifts are driven along the gem-bearing layer. Only the larger shafts are supported by timbers.

Even rivers are searched. The water is partly dammed in a certain place to increase the flow, while the worker, standing up to his waist in water, agitates the ground with long sticks and rakes. The specifically lighter clay and sandy material is swept away, while the heavier gems remain. The gem-bearing sands or gravels obtained from the shafts or the river are then washed. Workers agitate baskets which are filled with the gem-bearing gravel and water. Clay and sand are washed away, the specifically heavier gems remain in a concentrate. Lighter gems, such as beryls, feldspars, quartzes and tourmalines, are lost by this method. In some countries hydraulic mining is used, the loose earth being washed downhill by a strong jet of water.

Underground mining with a shaft which has to be hewn out of solid rock is the most expensive method. This is usually only begun after a gem-bearing vein is located.

Various countries have completely different ideas as to mining rights, pay for the workers and sharing of profits. It can generally be said that it is the poor man who mines the gems.

A special problem of gem production is theft, which can threaten every mine by undercutting economically viable prices. There is endless ingenuity employed to smuggle gems out of the mines, but the stringent security methods give protection. Diamond mines are the best protected.

Above left: Gem mining in East Africa. Right: Mining of tourmalines in Brazil
Below: Shaft in a rice field in Sri Lanka

Above: Terrace working and mining arrangements in the Finch diamond mine, South Africa

Below: Diamond mining on the coast of South West Africa (Namibia) at great expense

Cutting and Polishing of Gems

The oldest way of decorating a gemstone is the scratching of figures, symbols and letters on it. From this, the art of stone engraving developed. The origins of gem cutting can be found in India. Up to about 1400, only the natural crystal faces or cleavage planes of transparent stones were polished in order to give them a higher luster and improved transparency. But even before then, opaque stones – mainly agates – were cut and polished with hard sandstone either flat or slightly arched (cabochon).

Stone cutting culminates in the faceted stone. There were reports of a faceted diamond in Venice as early as 800AD, but according to other opinions, the facet cut was only developed around the 15th century. For a long time the technique of faceting was kept a strict secret. Today there are many text-books instructing and helping not only the expert, but also the amateur lapidarist. See also Diamond cutting, p. 80.

Since the beginning of modern times, Amsterdam and Antwerp have developed as diamond cutting centers. Idar-Oberstein became the center of agate and colored stone manufacturing in the 16th century. Nowadays numerous cutting centers are being developed around the world. In order to encourage these centers, many countries have prohibited the export of rough stones.

In the manufacture of gemstones, one differentiates between engraving, working of agates (p. 55), colored stones (p. 55) and diamonds (p. 58). Commercially there is no strict division between the working of agates and colored stones.

Engraving on stones

The art of stone engraving (also called glyptography) refers to the cutting of cameos and of intaglios, as well as to the creation of small objets d'art and other ornamental pieces.

The oldest stone engravings were cylinders engraved with symbols and figures which were used as seals or amulets. They were made in the ancient kingdoms of Sumeria, Babylon and Assyria. The oldest figures are the scarabs of the Egyptians.

Stone engraving was practised in ancient Greece and reached a high standard in ancient Rome. During the Middle Ages, stagnation set in. Today artist craftsmen of international reputation, sometimes using modern techniques, have revived appreciation of the art. The main center of the art is Idar-Oberstein in Germany, where more than 90% of the world's engraved gems are made. In ancient times, agate, amethyst, jasper, cornelian and onyx were used, but today other stones are also engraved, including diamonds. For modern engraving, see p. 142; for technique p. 144.

Cutting and polishing agate

Large stone blocks, sometimes weighing many tons, used to be split with hammer and chisel along fissures or other lines marked in the stone; nowadays they are mostly sawn with diamond-studded circular saws. The blade is cooled with paraffin or a special coolant.

Agate is first roughly shaped on a carborundum wheel. To keep the stone steady, the cutter holds it between his knees. The wheel is cooled with water. The final shaping is obtained on a sandstone wheel. The cutter sits on a chair with a support for his chest. Grooves in the wheel also enable the stone to be cut en cabochon.

The final process is polishing, giving the stone luster and showing up the fine structural lines. Polishing is done on a slowly rotating cylinder or wheel of beech wood, lead, felt, leather, or tin, with the help of a polishing powder such as chromium oxide, tripoli or other pastes. No coolant is used in this process, so special care must be taken otherwise the stone could be damaged by the resultant heat.

Machines have now been developed which cut flat stones automatically. Cabochons can also be cut this way with the aid of a model. Tumbled stones with irregular forms, sometimes called baroque stones, are popular for costume jewelry. For coloring of agates, see p. 136. For history of agate polishing, p. 138.

Cutting and Polishing Colored Stones

In the manufacturing process, the term "colored stones" refers to all gems with the exception of diamonds. (In Germany, they exclude agates as well.) The cutting of the colored stones is called lapidary work; the cutter is known as a lapidary. Most lapidaries specialize in a certain gem or stone group, so that consideration can be best given to the characteristics of the stone, such as depth of color, pleochroism, etc.

Circular saws with edges containing diamond powder instead of teeth, are used first to cut the stone roughly to the required size. The coolant is soapy water, oil or paraffin. The final shape is given to the rough stone on a vertical, roughly-grained carborundum wheel, cooled with water. Opaque stones, or those with inclusions, are cut en cabochon on grooved carborundum wheels.

Transparent stones, once roughly shaped, are faceted on horizontal grinding wheels. For this purpose they are cemented with a special cement or shellac on one end of small 4–6in/10–15cm long holders called "dops". These dops are guided at an angle, related to the facet being cut, by inserting the opposite end of the dop in the appropriate hole of a small board with rows of holes, fixed parallel or at right angles to the grinding wheel. Instead of such a board, a holder with a faceting head is used by amateurs to adjust the angles.

Above: Cutting agate and grinding it on a sandstone wheel
Below: Polishing of agate

Above : Cutting colored stones in a modern factory
Below, left : Shaping. Right : Cutting colored stones in Sri Lanka

The substance from which the cutting wheel was made (lead, bronze, copper, tin etc.) and the type of polishing powder (carborundum, diamond, titanium carbide), as well as the speed of the wheel, varies with the stone to be worked. The coolant is usually water.

The last process is polishing on a horizontally rotating wheel, or wooden cylinder, or on leather straps to remove the last traces of scratches and improve the luster. The polishing compounds for this are usually finely grained materials, such as chromium oxide, diamond powder, diamantine or Tripoli, usually mixed with water. For some gems the compound is mixed with sulphuric or acetic acid.

Because of the specialization in the manufacture of gems, various groups have developed separate skills over the years. For example, the century-old guild of drillers and cutters nowadays only prepares stones for technical purposes such as instrument parts or bearings, and stones for the textile industry.

Cutting and Polishing Diamond

The following processes can be distinguished in the working of diamond: cleaving or sawing, bruting, cutting and polishing.

At one time larger diamonds were cleaved by placing a blade on the stone and tapping it. The best cleavages are octahedral planes. Although the technique of cleaving was common for gem diamonds, it often happened that a stone was broken because inner tensions and hidden cracks had not been recognized. Because of this and the unsuitable stones which cleaving produced, sawing diamonds is the current practice for initial shaping.

The Cullinan diamond, the largest diamond ever found – as large as a fist – was cleaved in 1908 in Amsterdam by the firm of Asscher, in the first stage into three parts, then again, so that finally nine large and 96 smaller brilliants could be cut from it. A special advantage obtained by sawing diamonds is that a higher yield can be obtained from the rough stone. Octahedrons are sawn through the central plane, or just above it, thus yielding two shapes advantageous for cutting brilliant. The sawing plane becomes the table of the brilliant. The disc of a diamond saw (2–2½in/5–7cm diameter) is made of

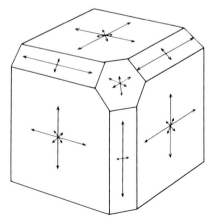

The hardness differences between the various crystal planes of a diamond are shown by the arrows. The shorter the arrow, the harder the resistance in this direction (according to E. M. and J. Wilks).

Diamond cleaving   Diamond polishing

phosphor bronze or another alloy and its edge is impregnated with diamond dust. It is about 1/20mm thick and is rotated at about 5000 r.p.m. The diamond is held in a vice-like arrangement. The sawing process is time-consuming: for a one-carat stone (0.2–0.7in/6–7mm diameter), 5 to 8 hours are needed.

The next process is bruting (or girdling), which gives the diamond its rough shape with girdle, crown and pavilion. Two diamonds are used in bruting. One is fixed in a small lathe; the other is cemented onto a stick and held in the operator's hand. The two stones are ground against each other so that the edges become rounded, corresponding to the double cone of the brilliant shape. Polishing or sawing of diamond is only possible with other diamond, because diamond varies in hardness on different crystal faces and in different directions. (See sketch p. 58).

It is necessary to examine the diamond thoroughly in order to utilize the differences in hardness when cutting it. According to statistical probability, diamond powder must contain grains lying in all directions, so that there are hard directions at all cutting angles. Powder can therefore always be used to grind the less hard facets of a diamond crystal.

The technique of polishing requires much experience. The diamond is held in a dop which places the facet to be polished against a horizontal cast iron wheel which is primed with diamond powder and oil, and rotates at about 1800 to 3000 r.p.m. The corners of all facets and placement of angles are judged by eye and gauged using a loupe. Small full cut brilliants are cut in large numbers in this way with 56 facets and a table. They are only 0.07in/ 1.7mm in diameter with about 50 stones to a carat or about two points each. The loss during cutting amounts to 50–60%. In the case of the Cullinan, it was about 65%. The brilliant is finally polished on the same scaife, but on another ring with finer diamond powder.

For the historic development of the diamond cut, see p. 80.

Sawing of diamonds

Bruting of diamonds

Banks of diamond saws

Drilling pearls

Drilling colored stones

Types of Cuts for Gemstones

Brilliant full cut   Eight cut   Rose   Half dutch rose

Step cut   Scissor cut   Ceylon cut   Emerald cut

Table cut   Cabochon   Cabochon   Mixed cut

Types of Cuts for Gemstones

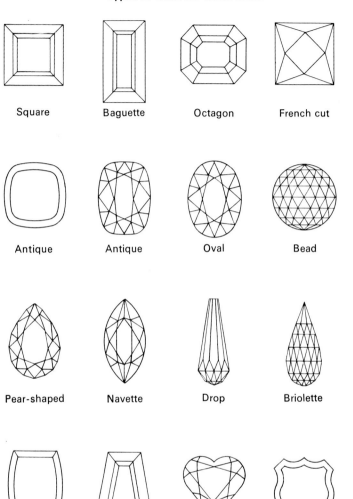

Square	Baguette	Octagon	French cut
Antique	Antique	Oval	Bead
Pear-shaped	Navette	Drop	Briolette
Barrel-shaped	Trapezoid	Heart-shaped	Escutcheon-shaped

Types of cut (pp. 62, 63)

There is no general rule which can be applied to the various cuts. However, three groups or types of cut can be named: faceted cut, plain cut, and mixed cut.

The faceted cut is practically applied only to transparent stones. The number of small even facets gives the gem higher luster and often a better play of color. Most facet cuts are built on two basic types, the brilliant cut and the trap or emerald cut. The plain cut can be level or en cabochon (domed). This is suitable for agates and other opaque stones. In mixed cuts, the upper part is level and the lower part faceted, or vice versa.

Brilliant-full cut   This has at least 32 facets plus the table on the upper part, and 24 facets on the lower part (see p. 80). It has been specially developed for the diamond and is also called the brilliant cut. The word "brilliant" alone refers to a diamond. In the case of other gems, the mineral name must be given. For instance brilliant-cut zircon.

Eight cut   This has 8 facets on the upper and lower parts as well as the table on the upper (see p. 80). It is used for diamonds which are too small for full cut or where this is not advantageous. Up to 300 and sometimes even up to 500 stones per carat are cut in this way.

Rose cut   A facet cut without table or pavilion. It varies in the number and positioning of facets. It is not used today because it does not produce much brilliance.

Step cut   A simple type of facet cut, specially used for colored stones, but also occasionally for diamonds. Several facets are cut parallel to the edges, the facets becoming steeper towards the girdle. The lower part usually has more facets than the upper part.

Scissors cut   A type of step cut. The facets are divided into four sub-facets by the "scissors".

Ceylon cut   This has numerous facets, cut to obtain maximum weight and therefore is not always symmetrical. It is usual to re-cut such stones.

Emerald cut   Step cut with octagon shape, especially used for emerald, but also for longer-shaped diamonds.

Table cut   The simplest type of step cut which is very flat with a large table. It is often used for seals or rings for men.

Cabochon   The main representative of the plain cut. The upper part is domed and the lower part level, or slightly domed. With dark stones the lower part is often hollowed out in order to lighten the color. It is named (French—nail) because of its rounded shape.

Other types   The various types of cut show an abundance of forms: round, spherical, oval, cone, antique (square or rectangular with rounded corners), triangle, square, hexagon, baguette (long rectangle), trapeze, French cut (base and table square, triangular facets), pendeloque or drop (pear-shaped), navette or marquise (pointed elliptical), briolette (pear-shaped with crossed faceted bands), olive (small barrel-shaped) and also many fantasy cuts (hearts, coats of arms, barrels).

Imitations of Gemstones

Attempts to imitate natural gemstones have been made for a very long time. The Egyptians were the first to fake valuable stones with glass and glazing. In 1758 a Viennese, Joseph Strasser, developed a type of glass which could be cut and looked similar to a diamond. Although production and sale of these diamond imitations, called *strass*, was prohibited by the Empress Maria Theresia, they reached the European trade via Paris.

Gablonz and Turnau in Czechoslovakia were important centers for the glass-jewelry industry until 1945. Then this custom was taken over by Neugablonz in Bavaria. For costume jewelry, cheap glass was used. For gem imitations, lead or flint glass with a high refractive index is used. All these imitations had a color similar to that of the gemstone, but other physical properties, especially hardness and fire, could not be satisfactorily imitated. Therefore it became the dream of scientists to fabricate stones that were really the same as the genuine gems. Towards the end of the last century, this hope was realized when the French chemist A. V. Verneuil synthesized rubies at a commercial price.

Synthetically produced crystals are not classed as imitations by the gem trade, but rather as a separate group, in addition to natural gems. In the trade they must be designated as "synthetic". For artificial color changes, see p. 28.

Fabricated Gemstones

These are doublets, consisting of two parts, and triplets, consisting of three parts. There are many combinations: for instance, upper and lower parts of natural gemstone with colored glue between them; or the upper part of colorless gemstone and the lower one of colored glass. Where the doublet has a thin top layer of a hard stone for the protection of the surface, it becomes a triplet. Carefully constructed stones are difficult to recognize, especially when the edges are covered by the setting.

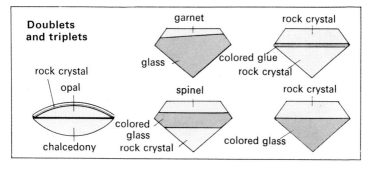

Doublets and triplets

garnet · rock crystal · glass · colored glue · rock crystal · rock crystal · opal · spinel · rock crystal · colored glass · chalcedony · rock crystal · colored glass

Synthetic gemstones

The first synthetics, i.e. man-made gemstones, appeared during the 1830s. They are only of scientific interest, being too small to be used in jewelry. An economically viable synthesis was developed by A. V. Verneuil around the turn of the century with his flame fusion process, a method which is still largely used today. The method is as follows: powdered raw material is melted in a furnace at about 3630°F/2000°C. The molten drops fall on a cradle where they crystallize and form a pear-shaped "boule". Although this boule does not have any crystal faces, the inner structure is the same as that of a natural crystal. The boules grow to about 0.65in/17mm thickness and a height of several inches, they weigh from 200 to 500 carats. The growth time is about 4 hours. In order to release any internal stresses, the boules are split lengthways by a tap before cutting.

Verneuil first produced rubies (red corundum) in 1910, followed by sapphires (blue corundum). Later colorless corundum (called diamondite), then yellow, green and alexandrite-like synthetic corundums were made. In 1947 a rutile substance was added to the melt to produce synthetic star rubies and sapphires. From 1926 synthetic spinels have been produced by the Verneuil process. Their composition is a little different from that of natural spinels and it has not been possible to obtain the genuine color tints of the spinel. But very good colors of other gemstones, such as aquamarines, tourmalines and blue zircons are produced.

Synthetic emeralds of gem size have been produced only since the 1940s, although experiments had been conducted for over a hundred years. In Austria cut stones of pale beryl are given an emerald skin (emerita).

In 1955 a diamond synthesis was successful in both the U.S. and Sweden; it was a high pressure method (50,000–100,000lbs/sq in at 2730–4350°F/ 1500–2400°C). In 1970 diamonds of gem quality and size were produced. However, the production costs are so high that, for the time being, synthetic diamonds are not profitable for the gem-market. However they are indispensable for industrial and scientific purposes. Synthetic rutile has been produced since 1948, it is sometimes called titania or damonite. Its dispersion is six times that of diamond. Synthetic rock crystal is used only for technical purposes, as is synthetic garnet. Synthetic alexandrite and synthetic opal are also produced for gem purposes.

There are some synthetic stones which do not exist in nature, but are used as gem stones because of their optical properties. To this group belong strontium titanate, developed in 1953, and YAG (since 1969 in gem quality), a yttrium aluminium garnet.

An intermediary position between synthetics and doublets is taken by the so-called reconstructed stones. These are melted together from small pieces of genuine gems, but are economically of little importance.

Boules and some gems cut from them

Classification of Gemstones

Mineral classes

As most gems are minerals, it is the scientific custom to classify them according to their mineral class.

1. Element
Diamond, sulphur.

2. Sulphides
Chalcopyrite, proustite, pyrite, sphalerite.

3. Halides
Fluorite

4. Oxides and hydroxides
Agate, alexandrite, amethyst, amethyst quartz, anatase, aventurine, rock crystal, cassiterite, ceylanite, chalcedony, chromite, chrysoberyl, chrysoprase, citrine, cuprite, gahnite, hematite, fossilized wood, jasper, ilmenite, corundum, moss agate, opal, periclase, prasiolite, quartz, smoky quartz, rose quartz, ruby, rutile, sapphire, spinel, taaffeite, tantalite, tiger's eye, zincite.

5. Nitrates, carbonates and borates
Aragonite, azurite, barytocalcite, calcite, cerussite, chalybite, colemanite, dolomite, gaylussite, hambergite, kurnakovite, magnesite, malachite, phosgenite, rhodosite, rhodochrosite, sinhalite, smithsonite, stichtite, ulexite, witherite.

6. Sulphates, chromates, molybdates, tungstates, wolframates
Anhydrite, barite, celestine (celestite), gypsum, crocoite, scheelite, wulfenite.

7. Phosphates, arsenates, vanadates
Amblygonite, apatite, augelite, beryllonite, brazilianite, lazulite, purpurite, turquoise, variscite, vivianite, wardite.

8. Silicates
Actinolite, albite, almandine, amazonite, andalusite, apophyllite, aquamarine, aventurine feldspar, axinite, benitoite, beryl, cancrinite, chloromelanite, chrysocolla, danburite, datolite, demantoid, diopside, dioptase, dumortierite, ekanite, elaeolite, emerald, enstatite, epidote, euclase, feldspar, garnierite, garnet, grossular, haüynite, hemimorphite, hessonite, hiddenite, howlite, hypersthene, idocrase, iolite, jadeite, clinozoisite, kornerupine, kunzite, kyanite, labradorite, lapis lazuli, leucite, meerschaum, microcline, moonstone, natrolite, nephrite, orthoclase, painite, peridot, peristerite, petalite, phenacite, prehnite, pseudophite, pyrope, rhodolite, rhodonite, sanadine, serpentine, sillimanite, scapolite, smaragdite, sodalite, spessartite, sphene, spodumene, staurolite, talc, tanzanite, thomsonite, topaz, tremolite, tugtupite, tourmaline, uvarovite, willemite, zircon, zoisite.

9. Non-minerals
Agalmatolite, alabaster, amber, ivory, jet, coral, moldavite, obsidian, odontolite, onyx marble, pearls, steatite, travertine.

Description of Gemstones

For practical reasons and in order to help the layman, the descriptions of gemstones have not been arranged under the scientific mineral classifications, but rather are separated into five groups with similar characteristics.

The first group contains all the precious stones which are generally known and traditionally traded (with the exception of some newly-discovered varieties). They comprise diamond to malachite, p. 70–177. These stones are worn set in jewelry or are worked into objets d'art. The order of stones within this group is determined by their Mohs' hardness which roughly corresponds with their value.

The second group contains minerals which are cut as collectors' items, and can also be worn in jewelry. (Gems for Collectors p. 178–203). Up to a few years ago, these stones were hardly known in the trade, but they are becoming more popular. The order within this group is determined by Mohs' hardness, which conveys an impression of their practical suitability for gemological use.

The third group contains collectors' gem rarities (p. 204–209). These are minerals which are only cut by collectors, amateur lapidarists and other specialists and have no practical use, apart from collecting and experimenting. In the nature of things, this group will always increase in numbers.

The fourth group contains the rocks (p. 210–215) and is considered in the fringe zone of gems. These are used mainly as decorative stones or in objets d'art. Their importance in the field of costume or fashion jewelry is increasing.

The fifth group contains gems that are of organic or organogenic origin. Called organic gems (p. 216–230) they are not always classed as gems according to the scientific point of view, but they are an important part of the trade.

It should be noted that this suggested classification of gemstones is not without subjective judgment. There is no absolute valid and generally clear-cut classification of gems. Precious gems need no regulations. It seemed important to impart as much information as possible when describing gems. Therefore some of the print used is smaller, abbreviations are used and repetitions avoided.

DIAMOND

Color: Colorless, yellow, brown, sometimes green, blue, reddish, black	Transparency: Transparent
Color of streak: None possible	Refractive index: 2.417–2.419
Mohs' hardness: 10	Double refraction: None, often anomalous
Specific gravity: 3.47–3.55	Dispersion: 0.044
Cleavage: Perfect	Pleochroism: None
Fracture: Conchoidal to splintery	Absorption spectrum: Colorless to
Crystal system: Isometric (cubic); mainly octahedrons, also rhombic dodecahedrons, cubes, twins, plates	yellow: <u>4780</u>, 4650, 4510, 4350, 4015, 4230, <u>4155</u>, 3900
Chemical composition: C, crystallized carbon	Blue-green: (5370), <u>5040</u>, (4980)
	Fluorescence: Variable; Colorless and yellow: mostly blue
	Brown and green: often green

The name diamond refers to its hardness (Greek – *Adamas*, unconquerable). There is nothing comparable to it in hardness; it is therefore nearly imperishable. Its cutting resistance is 140 times greater than that of corundum. However the hardness of a diamond is different in the individual crystal faces. This allows one to cut diamond with diamond (or diamond powder, in which – according to statistical probability – various diamond hardnesses occur). Care has to be taken during mounting because of perfect cleavage. Its very strong luster enables the experienced eye to differentiate between a diamond and its imitations.

Generally it is not very sensitive to chemical attack. Only chromic sulphuric acid can transform it at 392°F/200°C to carbon dioxide. High temperatures induce etchings on the facets and care must be taken during soldering! X rays are not transmitted through diamonds (in contrast to diamond-like minerals and synthetics).

During the last thirty years it has been recognized that there are various types of diamond which differ from each other in their absorption spectra, fluorescence, electric conductivity, and cleavage. Today science differentiates between type Ia, Ib, IIa and IIb. This is of little importance to the trade, but assists the cutter.

The optical properties of diamond are exceptional: they make the stone the king of gems. Diamond has been used for adornment since very early times.
Further details:

Diamond cutting, page 59
Diamond synthesis, page 66
Diamond occurrences, page 72
Diamond production, page 73
Diamond trade, page 75

Diamond valuation, page 76
Famous diamonds, page 78
Development of the brilliant cut, page 80
Diamond world production, page 231

---

1 Diamond, brilliant 0.49cts
2 Diamond, navette 0.68cts
3 Diamond, brilliant 2.22cts
4 Diamond, 3 baguettes, total 0.59cts
5 Diamond, brilliant 0.21cts
6 Diamond, 2 old cut 0.97cts
7 Diamond, 2 brilliants 0.57cts
8 Diamond, brilliant 2.17cts
9 Diamond, roses, total 0.67cts
10 Diamond, 2 navettes, total 0.69cts
11 Diamond, twice sawn, total 1.43cts
12 Diamond, 10 brilliants
13 Diamond, 9 brilliants
14 Diamond, white rough, total 6.37cts
15 Diamond, colored rough, total 10.22cts
16 Diamond aggregate, 8.26cts
17 Diamond crystal on kimberlite
18 Diamond crystal, 8.14cts

Fig. 1–15 twice the original size; Fig. 16–18 reduced by $\frac{1}{3}$ in size.

Diamond Occurrences

Diamonds are found in primary and secondary deposits. Up to 1871 diamonds were only washed out of diamondiferous placers. By chance a primary deposit was discovered in South Africa: volcanic pipes filled with diamond-bearing rock, kimberlite.

Diamond is formed at great depth (maybe 50 miles/80km or more) at 2012–2372°F/1100–1300°C under great pressure by eruption in the volcanic pipes. It is carried with the rising kimberlite to the surface of the earth.

There are diamond deposits in many parts of the world, most occurring in Africa and Siberia. Up to the 18th century a few diamonds came from Borneo, but most from India, where some large stones of historical value were found. Today production in these countries is of little importance.

In 1725 the first diamonds were found in the South American continent in Minas Gerais in Brazil, near the modern town Diamantina. In 1843 a brown-black carbonado was discovered in Bahia; this is a micro-crystalline aggregate which is very tough and therefore in demand for industry. For some time Brazil led the world in diamond production, mainly during the 18th and 19th centuries, then South Africa took over. The main deposits are alluvial, in association with a decomposed rock similar to kimberlite.

South Africa currently has an unsurpassed position as to production and trade. The first diamond find in 1867 was in the region near the source of the Orange River. At first only the alluvial deposits were worked.

In the meantime 250 pipes (geologically formed in the Cretaceous period) were discovered. Only a few are diamondiferous. These contain on top a clay-like rock which is called yellow ground because of its color. This is the weathered product of the blue ground, kimberlite, below. It is an igneous rock rich in olivines, a type of peridot, in a condition of brecciation.

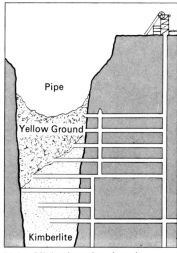

Left: Kimberley mine: The Big Hole.   Right: Mining in a pipe-deposit

Vibrating grease belt with trapped diamonds

The most famous kimberlite pipe, the Kimberley mine, was worked from 1871 to 1908 without any machinery. This produced the largest man-made hole (the Big Hole, see p. 72); the surface hole has a diameter of 1510ft/460m, and the depth is 3510ft/1070m. Today it is half-filled with ground water. Altogether 14.5 million carats of diamonds were found there. Mining was discontinued when it proved not to be economically feasible any more. Today it is mined from underground.

The South African pipe-mines changed from opencast to underground mining to avoid danger from falling rocks. Today a main rock shaft is sunk and then levels are driven into the diamond-bearing rock which is then removed by an automatic block carving method. A cavity is formed by blasting the kimberlite and, as the roof breaks up, the broken rock is extracted. Well known pipe-mines are Bultfontein, De Beers, Dutoitspan, Finch, Jagersfontein and Wesselton.

A great deal of technology is applied in the production of diamonds. The easiest to work is the yellow ground nearer the surface because it breaks up more readily and the diamonds with their higher specific gravity can be washed out. The kimberlite must first be broken up before it is washed in pans. The waste is floated off and the concentrate with the diamonds and other heavy minerals remains. The extraction of diamonds from this concentrate used to be done by hand, but is now mainly automatic using the diamonds' property of adhesion to fatty substances. The concentrate is guided over a vibrating greased belt or table where the diamonds are trapped.

Further sorting of diamonds is done by electrostatic separation, by optical selection with the help of a photo-cell, or increasingly by making use of the fluorescence of diamonds under x-rays.

The amount of diamond present in individual pipes varies. On average one ton of diamond-bearing rock yields half a carat. In some deposits a yield of 0.2 of a carat per ton is still profitable.

Apart from the pipes, there are large alluvial deposits in South Africa. They owe their existence to the fact that the earth's surface was originally maybe 3280ft/1000m higher and was eroded in time, so that the diamond-filled pipes, which had then reached the surface, were weathered.

Diamonds, together with other minerals and rocks, were carried away by water, along the Orange River, some of them into the sea. Therefore one finds secondary deposits in river beds, on old valley terraces and, as known since 1926, along the Atlantic coast on old beaches.

Namibia is an important diamond country. In 1908 the first diamonds were found in Luderitz. Today large alluvial deposits are mined along the Namib Desert coast. With extensive use of machinery, up to 66ft/20m of overburden must first be removed before the diamond-containing gravel underneath can be recovered. From 1961 to 1975 special dredgers also worked the bottom of the sea. The amount of gem diamonds found is large.

A few years ago Russia became the second largest diamond producer. Although diamonds had been found in the Ural Mountains in 1829, these deposits were of no commercial value. In 1949 a new era began. Important alluvial deposits were found in eastern Siberia (Yakutsk), and a few years later numerous pipes. Production is now very extensive. About a quarter of the production is of gem quality.

Diamond Trade

About 80% of world diamond production and trade is managed, i.e. controlled, by agreement with the Diamond Producers Association and the Central Selling Organisation, of which the division dealing with sales of all rough gem diamonds is the Diamond Trading Company (D.T.C.) with its main offices in London.

All diamonds that can be used as gems are sent to the D.T.C. in London and are there sorted and made up into parcels for particular customers. Only a few diamond manufacturers (between 250 and 300) known to the D.T.C. are invited through brokers to buy these lots at fixed prices against cash. It is impossible to buy only part of a parcel. The minimum price of such a parcel is about £25,000 ($42,500).

Further sales and sorting of the parcels are handled by the members of diamond bourses and diamond clubs or by wholesalers. Bourses can be found in Antwerp, Amsterdam, New York, Ramat Gan (Israel), as well as in Johannesburg, London, Milan, Paris, and Vienna, and since 1974, in Idar-Oberstein (West Germany). The most important ones are in Antwerp. Diamond bourses are not exchanges in their usual sense, but are more like diamond wholesale markets. They are internationally federated and submit to strict rules.

Through the Central Selling Organisation, producers control prices of rough diamonds to maintain the value of diamonds.

Weekly production of a diamond mine in Namibia, about 30,000 carats.

It is a fact that diamonds as an investment have weathered all political and economical storms of the last decade. Thus not only was the capital safeguarded, but millions of jobs, which are directly and indirectly linked to diamonds, were preserved. Moreover diamonds account for over 90% of the total gem production.

In the genuine wholesale trade and on the diamond bourses, absolute trust is fundamental although the best selling practices are not always applied towards the eventual customer. It is a fact that purely externally, diamonds can be mistaken for many other gemstones and this can lead to frauds, although not in the legitimate retail trade. A colorless diamond looks similar to rock crystal (p. 116), beryl (p. 96), cassiterite (p. 184), cerussite (p. 200), sapphire (p. 86), scheelite (p. 196), sphalerite (p. 200), topaz (p. 102) and zircon (p. 108). Also many yellowish stones can look like diamonds to a layman (see table p. 244). There are also good glass imitations on the market, for instance strass (p. 65).

Apart from these, there are various synthetic stones which are used to imitate diamonds (see p. 66), strontium titanate (fabulite), synthetic rutile, synthetic sapphire, synthetic spinel, YAG (yttrium aluminium garnet). In 1970 the first gem diamonds were synthesized. However, as the sizes obtained are modest (1 carat) and the production costs extremely high, these synthetics are for the time being mainly of scientific interest. In the trade one also comes across natural diamonds, colored artificially by various irradiation treatments.

Diamond-doublets are made with: upper part – diamond; lower part – synthetic colorless sapphire, rock crystal or glass. Other doublets have synthetic spinel as upper part, fabulite underneath.

Valuation of Diamonds

Only about 20% of all diamonds can be used for jewelry. Most of them are used in industry. These industrial diamonds are indispensable in boring crowns, milling cutters, glass cutters, and grinding wheels, as well as for scientific purposes such as for measuring and hardness testing.

The valuation of gem diamonds requires expertise and experience and considers the color (see below), clarity (p. 77), cut (p. 77) and weight (carat p. 26). These "4 Cs" make up the value of a diamond.

Grading for Color

Diamonds are found in all colors. Mostly they are yellowish to white, or brownish. More rarely they have strong colors (green, red, blue, violet, brown, yellow), which are grouped together as "fancy colors" and, in quality gems, fetch collector's prices.

For commercial purposes, gem diamonds are graded from white to yellowish. At first various terms and definitions were confusing; now international agreements are being reached to deal with color grading of the so-called "yellow series". An early term for better colored diamonds was "River" but this was superseded by "Premier" for stones that looked "whiter than white" because of the bluish stones that came from the mine of that name. Today we know that certain differences are not in color quality but rather in fluorescence.

"River", also called "blue white", is absolutely colorless, although to the unskilled eye it is difficult to detect possible tinges of yellow. Yellow in grading refers only to tinges of color, otherwise the stone would be sorted as "fancy". Another factor is that a larger stone yields more color than a small one. The percentage of River stones is under 1%, of top Wesselton 5%, of Wesselton 10%.

The Gemological Institute of America (G.I.A.), has a rational system of color grading using letters starting at D. In Europe a standardized grading system for eleven countries is being introduced by the jewellers' international organization, C.I.B.J.O.

GIA	Trade terms	Old terms
D	Blue White	River
E	Fine White	Top Wesselton
F		
G	White	Wesselton
H	Commercial White	Top Crystal
I	Top Silver Cape	Crystal
J	Silver Cape	Top Cape
K		
L	Cape	Cape
M		
N		
O	Light Cape	Light Yellow
P		
Q		
R	Dark Cape	Yellow
S–X		

Grading for Clarity

In Germany only the inner cleanliness is understood as "clarity", while in other countries some aspects of finish are taken into consideration. Enclosed minerals, flaws, cleavages and growth lines affect clarity; they are collectively called inclusions, but formerly were called "flaws" or "carbon spots". Polished diamonds without any inclusions under a 10x loupe are considered "flawless". Inclusions visible with larger magnification are not taken into account for grading.

Internally flawless	IF	Free of inclusions under 10x magnification
Very very small inclusions	VVS	Very few, very small inclusions under 10x magnification, difficult to find.
Very small inclusions	VS	Some small inclusions recognizable by an expert under 10x magnification.
Small inclusions	SI	Several small inclusions easily recognized under 10x magnification.
1st pique	PI	Inclusions at once recognizable under 10x magnification, but not diminishing the brilliance appreciably.
2nd pique	P2	Larger and/or many inclusions, slightly diminishing the brilliance recognizable with the naked eye.
3rd pique	P3	Large and/or many inclusions diminishing the brilliance.

Grading for Cut

To grade for cut, the type and shape of cut, proportions and symmetry as well as outer marks are taken into consideration. In Germany the normal cut is the "fine brilliant cut" (p. 81); in the rest of Europe it is the "European cut" which is typified by the proportions in the Scandinavian standard S.C.A.N.D.N. In the U.S., the ideal is considered to be the "Tolkowsky cut", as specified by the American Gemological Association. The following table shows the terms and definitions for grading according to cut of brilliants under 1 carat (RAL 560 A5E).

Term	Definition
Very good	Exceptional brilliance. Few and only minor outer marks.
Good	Good brilliance. Some outer marks.
Medium	Slightly less brilliance. Some larger outer marks.
Poor	Less brilliance. Large and/or many outer marks.

Famous Diamonds

1 **Dresden** 41 carats, most probably from India. Early history not known. Around 1700 in possession of August the Strong, Duke of Saxony. Kept in the Green Hall in Dresden, hence its name.

2 **Hope** 44.50 carats. Appeared 1830 in the trade and was bought by the banker H. T. Hope (hence the name) of London. Probably re-cut from a stone stolen during the French revolution. Changed hands frequently. Since 1958 in the Smithsonian Institution, Washington.

3 **Cullinan I** 530.20 carats. Cut from the largest diamond ever found (3106 carats named after Sir Thomas Cullinan, chairman of the mining company) together with 104 other stones, by the firm of Asscher in Amsterdam in 1908. Adorns the sceptre of King Edward VII; kept in the Tower of London, largest cut diamond, also called "Star of Africa".

4 **Sancy** 55 carats. Said to have been worn by Charles the Brave around 1470. Bought 1570 by Signeur de Sancy (hence the name) from the French Ambassador to Turkey. Since 1906 belonging to the Astor family, London.

5 **Tiffany** 128.51 carats. Found in Kimberley mine, South Africa, in 1878, rough weight 287.42 carat. Bought by the jewellers Tiffany in New York and cut in Paris with 90 facets.

6 **Koh-i-Noor** 108.92 carats. Originally a round stone of 186 carats belonging to the Indian Raj. Bought 1739 by the Shah of Persia, who called it "Mountain of Light" (Koh-i-Noor). Came into possession of the East India Company who presented it to Queen Victoria in 1850. Re-cut, it was set in the crown of Queen Mary, wife of George V, and then in the crown of Queen Elizabeth, now in the Tower of London.

7 **Cullinan IV** 63.60 carats. One of the 105 cut stones from the largest diamond ever found, the Cullinan (see no. 3). Also in the crown of Queen Mary, can be removed from this and worn as a brooch. Kept in the Tower of London.

8 **Nassak** 43.38 carats. Originally over 90 carats and in a Temple of Shiva near Nassak (hence the name) in India. Looted in 1818 by the English, re-cut 1927 in New York. Today in private possession in U.S.

9 **Shah** 88.70 carats. Came from India, shows cleavage planes, partially polished. Has three inscriptions of monarchs' names (amongst them the Shah of Persia's – hence the name). Given in 1829 to Tsar Nicholas I. Kept in the Kremlin, Moscow.

10 **Florentine** 137.27 carats. Early history steeped in legend. 1657 in the possession of the Medici family in Florence (hence the name). During the 18th century in the Habsburg crown, then used as brooch. Whereabouts after First World War unknown.

Other cut diamonds are famous for their size, beauty or sometimes their romantic history, for instance: Cullinan II (p. 9), De Beers, Great Mogul, Jonker I, Nizam, Jubilee, Orlow, Regent, Star of the South, Victoria I.

The greatest rough stones found suitable for gem purposes in carats: Cullinan (3106), Excelsior (995.2), Star of Sierra Leone (968.9), Great Mogul (about 800), Woyie River (770), President Vargas (726.6), Jonker (726), Jubilee (formerly Reitz 650.8), Dutoitspan (616), Baumgold (609).

Development of the Brilliant Cut

Although diamond as a gemstone has been known for over 2,000 years, the first cut to improve the optical effect was developed in the 14th century. Previously, only rough stones were used, perhaps with the rough edges smoothed away. Then the flat surfaces of the octahedron crystal were polished. This "point cut", so called after the shape of the crystal, was the first real diamond cut. It represents the beginning of a series, the final product being the modern brilliant cut.

About 1400 the "table cut" was developed; this was an octahedral crystal with a flat surface on top, the table, and with a smaller facet underneath called the culet. At about the same time the "thin cut" made its appearance. This was the same shape as the table cut but much thinner.

Since the end of the 15th century, a cutting wheel, the scaife, was used to cut additional facets to improve the optical effect of the stone. By about the middle of the 16th century, the table cut had been developed into a faceted stone with a multi-cornered table. This stone, now called the "old single cut", had 18 facets by adding an additional facet above the side edges. The "Mazarin" cut that followed had 34 facets and a rounded instead of a squarish outline from the front. This cut was based on the inspiration of the French Cardinal Mazarin in 1650.

Towards the end of the 17th century, a diamond with 58 facets was developed and was attributed to a Venetian cutter named Vicenzio Peruzzi. This cut had the same number of facets as the modern diamond, although the "rondiste" (girdle or outline) was not round and the facets irregular.

Historic Cut of the Diamond

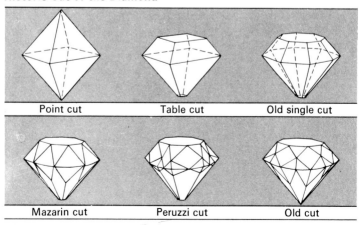

| Point cut | Table cut | Old single cut |
| Mazarin cut | Peruzzi cut | Old cut |

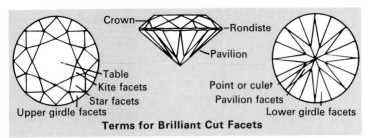

Crown — Rondiste
Table
Kite facets — Point or culet
Star facets — Pavilion facets
Upper girdle facets — Lower girdle facets
Pavilion

Terms for Brilliant Cut Facets

Perfection of the diamond as a gem is only realised by the modern brilliant cut (full brilliant). It was developed around 1910 from the old cuts of the last century. Its characteristics are: round girdle, 32 facets on the crown plus the table, and 24 facets plus, sometimes, a culet on the pavilion. By calculation and experience several variations of the modern brilliant cut have been developed.

Tolkowsky Brilliant (1919, Tolkowsky)   Very good light reflection. Basis of grading according to cut in U.S.

Ideal-Brilliant (1926, Johnson and Rösch)   Not as advantageous as could be assumed from the name. Appears not uniform.

Fine-Cut Brilliant (1939, Eppler)   Proportions were calculated from cut stones with highest brilliance, also developed by experience. Basis of cut grading in Germany.

Parker Brilliant (1951, Parker)   Good reflection, but due to flat crown, has small dispersion and thus little play of colors.

Scandinavian Standard Brilliant (1968)   Basis of polished diamond grading in Scandinavia. Values established from stones cut in Europe.

There are diamonds having more facets: King cut (after 1940) with 86 facets, Magna cut (1949) with 102 facets, Highlight cut (1963) with 74 facets, Princess-144-cut (1965) with 146 facets.

Because of the established proportions of the brilliant cut, further data can be calculated from individual measurements; for instance the weight of a stone can be worked out from the diameter of the girdle or from the total height.

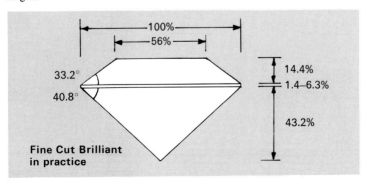

100%
56%
33.2°
40.8°
14.4%
1.4–6.3%
43.2%

Fine Cut Brilliant in practice

RUBY Corundum Group

Color: Varying red	Transparency: Opaque, translucent, transparent
Color of streak: White	
Mohs' hardness: 9	Refractive index: 1.766–1.774
Specific gravity: 3.97–4.05	Double refraction:— 0.008
Cleavage: None	Dispersion: 0.018
Fracture: Small conchoidal, uneven, splintery, brittle	Pleochroism: Strong; yellow-red, deep ruby-red
Crystal system: Hexagonal (trigonal); hexagonal prisms or tablets, rhombohedrons	Absorption spectrum: 6942, 6928, 6680, 6592, 6100–5000, 4765, 4750, 4685
Chemical composition: Al_2O_3, aluminium oxide	Fluorescence: Strong; ruby-red

Ruby is thus named because of its red color (Latin *Rubeus*). It was not until about 1800 that ruby, as well as sapphire, was recognized as belonging to the corundum group. Before that date red spinel and garnet were also designated as ruby.

The coloring pigment is chrome and, for brown hues, some iron additionally. The red color varies with the individual deposits, so it is not possible to determine the source area from the color, as each deposit yields various tones. The designation "Burma-ruby" or "Siam-ruby" is erroneous, and refers more to quality than origin. The most desirable color is "pigeon's blood", pure red with a hint of blue. The distribution of color is often uneven, in stripes or spots. As a rough stone, ruby appears dull and greasy but, when cut, the luster can approach that of diamond.

The hardest mineral after diamond, although only 1/140th as hard, it is seven times as hard as topaz, the next on Mohs' scale. However, the hardness varies in different directions, a fact that is made use of by the lapidary. Because of the great hardness, corundum which is unsuitable for jewelry purposes, is powdered and used as a cutting and polishing medium (i.e. emery).

Ruby has no cleavage, but has certain preferred directions of parting. Because of its brittleness, care must be taken when cutting and setting.

Inclusions are common. They are not indicative of lower quality, but show the difference between a natural and a synthetic stone. The type of inclusion (mineral, canals or other cavities), often indicates the source area. Included rutile needles produce a soft sheen (called silk) or, if cut en cabochon, the effect of a cat's eye (5) or the very desirable asterism – a six-rayed star (4) which moves over the surface when the stone is moved. See also p. 84.

1 Ruby, five facets	6 Ruby, 4 tabular crystals
2 Ruby, 2 drops, 2.51ct, Thailand	7 Ruby, 3 prismatic crystals
3 Ruby, engraved cabochon, 30.97ct	8 Ruby, rolled crystal
4 Star ruby, 2x, Sri Lanka	9 Ruby, tabular crystal
5 Ruby cat's eye, 6.64ct	10 Ruby in host rock, Sri Lanka

The illustrations are 10 times the size of the originals.

The host rock of ruby is mainly a dolomite type marble which has been formed from limestone by contact metamorphism from granite. The yield of rubies from such a primary deposit is not economically profitable. Alluvial deposits are worked because the high specific gravity of rubies allows them to be concentrated (panned) with other heavy minerals from river gravels and then picked out by hand. Production methods are still as primitive as they were hundreds of years ago.

Important deposits are in Burma, Thailand, Sri Lanka and Tanzania; the most important being in upper Burma near Magok. The ruby-bearing layer runs several yards under the surface and is worked by means of pits and shafts. Apparently only 1% of production is of gem quality. The rubies are often of the most valuable pigeon's blood color. Large stones are rare. They are found together with beryls, chrysoberyls, garnets, moonstones, sapphires, spinels, topazes, tourmalines and zircons. Rubies from Thailand often have a brown tint to them. They are found south-east of Bangkok in the district of Chantaburi in clayey gravels. Shafts are sunk to a depth of 26ft/8m.

In Sri Lanka, deposits are situated in the south-west of the island in the district of Ratnapura. Rubies from these deposits (called *illam* by the natives) are usually light red to raspberry red. Some of the rubies are recovered from river sands and gravels.

Since the 1950s Tanzania has produced a decorative green rock (zoisite amphibolite) with quite large but mostly opaque rubies (p. 161, no. 12, 14). Only a few crystals are cuttable. Recently some rubies have been found in the upper Umba River (north west Tanzania). They are purple to brown-red.

There are some unimportant deposits in Afganistan, Queensland (Australia), Brazil, Cambodia, Malagasy Republic, Malawi, Pakistan, Rhodesia and in Montana and North Carolina in the U.S. There are also small ruby and sapphire deposits in Switzerland (Tessin).

Ruby is one of the most expensive gems, large rubies being rarer than comparable diamonds. The largest cuttable ruby weighed 400ct; it was found in Burma and divided into three parts. Famous stones of exceptional beauty are the Edward ruby (167ct) in the British Museum of Natural History in London, the Reeves Star ruby (138.7ct) in the Smithsonian Institution in Washington, the Long Star ruby (100ct) in the American Museum of Natural History (New York), and the Peace ruby (43ct), thus called because it was found in 1919 at the end of World War I. Many rubies are important parts of Royal insignia and other famous jewelry. But some gems, thought to be rubies, have been revealed as spinels, such as the "Black Prince's ruby" in the English State crown and the "Timur ruby" in a necklace among the English crown jewels. The drop-shaped spinels in the crown of the Wittelsbacher of 1830 were also originally thought to be rubies.

Panning for gemstones in a river, Sri Lanka

Today rubies are often cut in the countries where they were found. As the cutters usually aim for maximum weight, the proportions are not always satisfactory, so that many stones have to be re-cut in European lapidary workshops.

There are many imitations on the market, especially glass imitations and doublets. These have a garnet crown and glass underneath, or the upper part of natural sapphire with synthetic ruby underneath. There are many false names, for instance: Balas ruby (spinel), Cape ruby (garnet), and Siberian ruby (tourmaline). Almandine (p. 104), fluorite (p. 198), hyacinth (p. 108), pyrope (p. 104), spinel (p. 100), topaz (p. 102), tourmaline (p. 110) and zircon (p. 108) can be mistaken for ruby.

Since the beginning of this century, synthetic gem rubies have become available; these have the same chemical, physical and optical properties of the natural stones, except that natural rubies transmit short wave ultra-violet light. Only synthetic rubies are used nowadays for watches and bearings, formerly the most important technical application for natural stones.

SAPPHIRE Corundum group

Color: Blue in various hues, colorless, pink, orange, yellow, green, purple, black
Color of streak: White
Mohs' hardness: 9
Specific gravity: 3.99–4.00
Cleavage: None
Fracture: Small conchoidal, uneven, splintery
Crystal system: Hexagonal (trigonal); dipyramidal, barrel-shaped, tabloid-shaped
Chemical composition: Al_2O_3 aluminium oxide
Transparency: Transparent, opaque
Refractive index: 1.766–1.774

Double refraction. —0.008
Dispersion: 0.018
Pleochroism: Blue: definite; dark blue, green-blue
Yellow: weak; yellow, light yellow
Green: weak; green-yellow, yellow
Purple: definite; purple, light red
Absorption spectrum: Blues, from Sri Lanka: 4710, 4600, 4550, 4500, 3790
Yellows: 4710, 4600, 4500
Greens: 4710, 4600–4500
Fluorescence: Blues: (purple) none
Yellows from Sri Lanka: weak; orange
Colorless: orange-yellow or purple

The name sapphire (Greek – blue) used to be applied to various stones. In antiquity and as late as the Middle Ages, the name sapphire was understood to mean what is today described as lapis lazuli. Around 1800 it was recognized that sapphire and ruby are gem varieties of corundum. At first only the blue variety was called sapphire, and corundums of other colors (with the exception of red) were given special, misleading names, such as "Oriental peridot" for the green variety or "Oriental topaz" for the yellow type. Today corundums of all colors except red are called sapphires. Red varieties are called rubies (p. 82). The various colors of sapphire are qualified by description, i.e. yellow sapphire, green sapphire. Sapphire without additional qualification refers to blue corundum. Orange pink sapphire is called Padparadschah (Sinhalese for "Lotus Flower") (7).

There is no definite demarcation between ruby and sapphire. Light red, pink or violet corundums are usually called sapphires, as in this way they have individual values in comparison with other colors. If they were grouped as rubies, they would be stones of inferior quality. Coloring pigment in blue sapphire is iron and titanium; and in violet stones, vanadium. A small iron content results in yellow and green tones; chrome produces pink. The most desired color is pure cornflower blue.

Hardness is the same as ruby and also differs in different directions (an important factor in cutting). There is no fluorescence characteristic for all sapphires. It varies according to color and source area. See also p. 88.

1 Sapphire, oval, 5.73ct, Thailand
2 Star sapphire, 9.46ct, Burma
3 Sapphire, brilliant cut, 2.81ct
4 Sapphire, six faceted stones, together 2.34ct, Tanzania
5 Sapphire, oval, 1.62ct, Sri Lanka
6 Sapphire, drop, 6.09ct
7 Sapphire, yellow, Padparadschah 11.32ct, Sri Lanka
8 Sapphire, antique cut, 5.18ct
9 Sapphire, antique cut, 3.74ct
10 Sapphire, five crystal shapes
The illustrations are 30% larger than the originals.

Inclusions of rutile needles result in a silky sheen or, if the quantities are sufficiently large, in cat's eye or six-rayed star stones: Star sapphire (2). According to some opinions, this asterism is not caused by rutile needles, as is the case with rubies, but by intersecting hollow channels running in three directions.

The main sapphire-bearing rocks are marble, basalt or pegmatite. It is mined mainly from alluvial deposits or deposits formed by weathering, rarely from the primary rock. Production methods are very simple. The underground gem-bearing layer is worked from hand-dug holes and trenches. The yield is separated from clay, sand and pebbles by panning. Washing out the gems is facilitated by their higher specific gravity. Final selection is made by hand. Sapphire is much more common than its brother gem ruby, as the required pigment (iron) is commoner than that needed for ruby (chrome). Today the economically important sapphire deposits are in Australia, Burma, Sri Lanka and Thailand.

The Australian deposits have been known since 1870. The host rock is basalt; the sapphires are washed out of the weathered debris. Quality is modest. Under artificial light the deep blue stones appear inky, blue-green, nearly black; lighter qualities have a green tint. Lately black star sapphires have been found. Accompanying minerals are pyrope, quartz, topaz, tourmaline and zircon. Since 1918 good blue qualities have been found in New South Wales and recently the deposits have become very productive.

The alluvial deposits near Mogok in upper Burma yield rubies and spinels as well as sapphires. The host rock is pegmatite. In 1966 the largest star sapphire was found here, a crystal of 63,000ct (28lb/12.6kg).

Sapphires have been found in Sri Lanka since antiquity. The deposits are in the south west of the island in the region of Ratnapura. The mother rock is a dolomitized limestone, which is enclosed by granite gneiss. They are also found in 10–20in/30–60cm thick river gravel placers from a depth of 3–33ft/1–10m. The deposits are called *illam* by the natives. Sapphires are usually light blue, with a tinge of violet. There are also yellow and orange varieties (like Padparadschah) as well as green, pink, and brown and nearly colorless stones, also star sapphires and cat's eyes. Accompanying minerals are: apatite, iolite, epidote, garnet, moonstone, quartz, ruby, sinhalite, spinel, topaz, tourmaline and zircon.

There are two sapphire deposits in Thailand: one (Bang-Kha-Cha) is near Chantaburi, 138 miles/220km south east of Bangkok, the other (Bo Ploi) is near Kanchanaburi, 75 miles/120km north west of Bangkok. The host rock is veined basalt. Alluvial deposits and deposits formed by weathering are mined; the sapphires are accompanied by garnet, ruby, spinel and zircon. The stones are of good quality in various colors; there is also star sapphire. Blue sapphires have a deep color, and tend to have a tinge of blue-green.

The most desired sapphires used to come from Kashmir (India), where the deposits were situated at a height of 16,500ft/5,000 meters in the Zaskar region, 125 miles/200km south east of Srinagar. Production varied since 1880, and the deposit has apparently been worked out. The host rock is kaolin-rich pegmatite in crystalline schist. The decomposition product yields sapphires of deep cornflower blue color with a silky sheen. Most stones sold today as Kashmir sapphire come from Burma.

Washing of gem-bearing earth

In 1894 sapphire deposits were discovered in Montana (U.S.A.). The host rock is andesite dikes. Mining is carried out on the dike rock, also from weathered material. Color of sapphire varies and is often pale blue or steel blue. There has been no mining since the end of the 1920s. There are deposits in Brazil (Mato Grosso), Cambodia (West), Kenya, Malawi, Rhodesia, and lately Tanzania (North). Isolated star sapphires have been found in Finland (Lapland).

Large sapphires are rare. They are sometimes named in the same way as famous diamonds. The American Museum of Natural History (New York) owns the "Star of India", perhaps the largest cut star sapphire (536ct); also the "Midnight Star", a black star sapphire (116ct). The "Star of Asia", a star sapphire weighing 330ct, is owned by the Smithsonian Institution in Washington. Two famous sapphires (St Edward's and the Stuart sapphire) are part of the English Crown Jewels. In the U.S., heads of the presidents Washington, Lincoln, and Eisenhower have been carved out of three large sapphires, each weighing roughly 2000ct.

They can be confused with various stones. The sapphire looks similar to benitoite (p. 184), iolite (p. 180), kyanite (p. 196), spinel (p. 100), tanzanite (p. 160), topaz (p. 102), tourmaline (p. 112) and zircon (p. 108), as well as blue glass. Many misleading names have been used in the past.

Imitations are made as doublets – blue cobalt glass with a table of thin garnet or a crown of green sapphire and a pavilion of synthetic blue sapphire. Lately doublets have appeared using two small natural sapphires. Star sapphire is imitated by using star rose quartz with blue enamel on a flat back, alternatively the star is engraved on the flat back of a synthetic cabochon or on glass.

Synthetic sapphire was produced with properties identical to the natural stone at the beginning of this century. Since 1947 synthetic star sapphires of gem quality have been sold.

EMERALD Beryl group

Color: Emerald green, light green, yellow-green, dark green	Transparency: Transparent to opaque
Color of streak: White	Refractive index: 1.576–1.582
Mohs' hardness: $7\frac{1}{2}$–8	Double refraction: 0.006
Specific gravity: 2.67–2.78	Dispersion: 0.014
Cleavage: None	Pleochroism: Definite; green, blue-green to yellow-green
Fracture: Small conchoidal, uneven, brittle	Absorption spectrum: <u>6835</u>, <u>6806</u>, 6620, 6460, <u>6370</u>, (6060), (5940), <u>6300–5800</u>, 4774, 4725
Crystal system: Hexagonal (trigonal); hexagonal prisms, columnar	
Chemical composition: Al_2Be_3 (Si_6O_{18}) aluminium beryllium silicate	Fluorescence: Usually none

The name emerald derives from the Greek *Smaragdos*, which in turn came perhaps from the Persian. It means "green stone" and, in ancient times, referred not only to emeralds, but also probably to most green stones.

Emerald, together with aquamarine and beryl, belongs to the beryl group, being the most precious of the group. Its green is incomparable, and is therefore called "emerald green" (not only in mineralogy). The pigment is chrome, sometimes vanadium. The color is very stable against light and heat, and only alters at 1292–1472°F/700–800°C.

Only the finest qualities are transparent. Often the emerald is clouded by inclusions (liquid or gas bubbles, healing cracks and foreign crystals). These are not necessarily classified as faults, but are evidence as to the genuineness of the stone as compared with synthetic and other imitations. The expert refers to these inclusions as a "jardin" (garden).

The most desired color is a deep green which is more valuable, even with inclusions, than a pale and clean quality. Distribution of color is often irregular, in spots or stripes. The luster is usually vitreous.

The physical properties, especially the specific gravity and double refraction as well as pleochroism, vary according to source area. All emeralds are brittle and combined with internal stresses, sensitive to pressure; care must be taken in heating them. They are resistant to chemicals with the exception of fluoric acid.

Emeralds are formed by rising magma and metamorphism. Deposits are therefore found mainly in or near pegmatite veins. Mining is nearly exclusively from host rock, where the emerald has grown into small veins or on walls of cavities. Alluvial mining would hardly be possible as the specific gravity is near that of quartz. Anyway secondary deposits, produced by weathering or other decomposition, are rarely formed. See p. 92.

---

1 Emerald in host rock	6 Emerald, oval, 1.27ct
2 Emerald, oval, 0.91ct, Colombia	7 Emerald, cabochon, 5.24ct
3 Emerald, 2 drops, 1.59ct	8 Emerald, cabochon, 4.26ct
4 Emerald, 2 octagons	9 Emerald, cabochon, 3.11ct
5 Emerald, antique cut, 4.14ct, South Africa	10 Emerald, crystal, Brazil

Emerald Continued from p. 90

The most important deposits are in Colombia, especially the Muzo Mine, 63 miles/100km north west from Bogota. Mined by the Incas, the Muzo deposit was abandoned and rediscovered in the 17th century. The mine yields fine quality stones of a deep green color. Mining, apart from the shafts, is mainly by step-form terraces. The emerald-bearing, soft broken rock is loosened with sticks and the emeralds picked out by hand. The host rock is black carbonaceous limestone. Accompanying minerals are albite, apatite, aragonite, barite, calcite, dolomite, fluorite and pyrite.

The other important deposit, the Chivor Mine, is north east of Bogota, on a hillside 7600ft/2300m in height. Also mined by the Incas, it was then worked intensively by the Spaniards, but closed in 1675. It was then forgotten, and only rediscovered at the turn of the century. The host rock is a gray-black shale and gray limestone. It is mined in terraces, but recently also from shafts.

During the last decades further deposits have been found in Colombia; for instance a secondary deposit (Gachala) near Chivor. The state of Colombia tries to impose a control over the sale of emeralds, but the larger part of the production reaches the trade illegally. Only a third is cuttable. Top qualities are rare. Stones larger than nut-size are usually low quality or broken.

In Brazil there are various deposits in Bahia, also in Goias and Minas Gerais. They are of minor economic importance. Stones are lighter than Colombian ones, mostly yellow-green, but they are often free of inclusions.

Since the second half of the 1950s, emerald deposits have been found in Rhodesia. Most important is the Sandawana mine in the south. Crystals are small, but of good quality. Host rock is a hornblende shale.

In the northern Transvaal (South Africa), emeralds are mined by modern methods using machinery (Cobra and Somerset Mines). Only 5% of production is of good quality. Most stones are light or turbid and only suitable for cabochons.

Emerald deposits were discovered in 1830 in the Urals north of Swerdlowsk. The host rock is a biotite mica shale, interfoliated with talc and chlorite. Good qualities are rare. Most stones are opaque, turbid and slightly yellow-green. At first production was high but deposits are not worked now.

Further emerald deposits without special economic importance are in Zambia, Tanzania, India, Pakistan, Australia (New South Wales, Western Australia) and the U.S. (Connecticut, Maine, North Carolina). The emerald mines of Cleopatra (50 B.C.), east of Asswan in upper Egypt, are of historical interest only.

The Austrian deposits in the Habach Valley near Salzburg are well known. The matrix rock is biotite hornblende shale. The stones are of interest only to mineral collectors, as cuttable material is rare. The stones are mostly turbid, color quality is good. Some individual emeralds have been found in Norway, 31 miles/50km north of Oslo, near Eidsvoll.

Modern emerald mine in South Africa

There are many well-known large emeralds, as famous as diamonds and rubies. Some beautiful specimens of several carats are kept by the British Museum of Natural History in London, by the American Museum of Natural History in New York, in the treasury of Russia and in the Persian crown jewels. In the Viennese treasury is a jug, 4¾in/12cm high and weighing 2205ct, cut from a single emerald crystal.

Because emerald is so sensitive to knocks, the emerald cut (step cut) was developed, the four corners being truncated by facets. Clear, transparent qualities are sometimes brilliant cut. Turbid stones are only used for cabochons or as beads for necklaces. Occasionally emeralds are worn in their natural crystal form, and sometimes engraved.

Possibilities of confusion exist with demantoid (p. 106), diopside (p. 190), dioptase (p. 194), grossular (p. 106), hiddenite (p.114), peridot (p. 158), green tourmaline (p. 110) and uvarovite (p. 106).

Numerous doublets are on the market, mostly two genuine pale stones (rock crystal, aquamarine, beryl or pale emerald) cemented together with emerald-green paste. The pavilion may also be glass or synthetic spinel. The upper parts of natural stones are determined by inclusions and hardness which are features of genuineness. When set, these doublets can be difficult to detect.

The first emerald synthesis was made in 1848 by a Frenchman. Since the turn of the century various methods have been developed and, since the 1950s, commercial products of excellent quality have appeared on the market. An important aid to differentiation is ultra-violet light. Synthetic emerald transmits short ultra-violet light more than natural emerald. There are also stones with synthetic emerald "plating" on colorless beryl, as well as glass imitations on the market.

AQUAMARINE Beryl group

Color: Light blue, blue, blue-green	Refractive index: 1.577–1.583
Color of streak: White	Double refraction: −0.006
Mohs' hardness: $7\frac{1}{2}$–8	Dispersion: 0.014
Specific gravity: 2.67–2.71	Pleochroism: Definite, nearly
Cleavage: None	colorless-light blue
Fracture: Conchoidal, uneven, brittle	Blue: sky blue
Crystal system: Hexagonal (trigonal); long prisms	Absorption spectrum: 5370, 4560, 4270
Chemical composition: $Al_2Be_3(Si_6O_{18})$ aluminium beryllium silicate	Maxixe-aqua: 6540, 6280, 6150, 5810, 5500
Transparency: Transparent to opaque	Fluorescence: None

Aquamarine, together with emerald and beryl, belongs to the beryl group; it is so named (Latin – Water of the Sea) because of its sea water color. It was also a talisman for sailors. A dark blue is the most desired color. Lower qualities are heated to 752°F/400°C to change them to the desired aquamarine blue. It is brittle and sensitive to pressure. It is more frequently transparent than emerald. The pigment is iron. Typical inclusions are fine hollow rods which sometimes reflect white light. Where growth lines are present in larger numbers, a cat's eye effect or even asterism with a six-rayed star is possible.

Because of inclusions of foreign substances, physical properties can vary. The maxixe aquamarine from Brazil has quite different constants. It is rarely used any more because the color apparently fades in daylight.

There are aquamarine deposits in all continents. The most important ones are in Brazil (Minas Gerais, Bahia, Esperito Santo). The host rocks are pegmatite and coarse-grained granite. Numerous finds have been made in the inner highlands of the Malagasy Republic. The well-known deposits in Russia, in the Urals and in Transbaikalia, seem to be worked out.

All other deposits are only of local importance: Australia (New South Wales), Burma, Sri Lanka, India, Kenya, Mozambique, Rhodesia, South Africa, Namibia, Tanzania and the U.S. (Colorado, Connecticut, California, Maine, North Carolina).

Large crystals are comparatively common. The largest aquamarine of cuttable quality was found in 1910 in Marabaya, Minas Gerais (Brazil). It weighed 243lb/110.5kg, was 18in/48.5cm long and $15\frac{1}{2}$in/41–42cm in diameter, and was cut into many stones. There also have been finds weighing a few tons, but the aquamarine was opaque and gray, not suitable for jewelry. The preferred cut is emerald or scissor cut with rectangular or long oval shapes.

Can be confused with euclase (p. 178), kyanite (p. 196), topaz (p. 102), tourmaline (p. 110), zircon (p. 108) and glass imitations.

Synthetic aquamarine can be produced but is uneconomical. The "synthetic aquamarine" sold in the trade is really aquamarine-colored synthetic spinel.

1 Aquamarine, octagon, 72.46ct	5 Aquamarine, antique cut, 18.98ct
2 Aquamarine, octagon, 17.41ct	6 Aquamarine, briolette, 6.65ct
3 Aquamarine, antique cut, 45.38ct	7 Aquamarine, crystal, 68.5mm, 45g
4 Aquamarine, navette, 25.58ct	8 Aquamarine, 3 crystals, together 77g

BERYL Beryl group (also called precious beryl)

Color: Gold, yellow-green, yellow, pink, colorless	Double refraction: —0.006–0.009
Color of streak: White	Dispersion: 0.014
Mohs' hardness: $7\frac{1}{2}$–8	Pleochroism: Golden: Weak; lemon yellow, yellow
Specific gravity: 2.65–2.75	Heliodor: Weak; golden yellow, green-yellow
Cleavage: None	Morganite: Definite; pale pink, bluish-pink
Fracture: Conchoidal, brittle	Green: Definite; yellow-green, blue-green
Crystal system: Hexagonal (trigonal); long prisms	Absorption spectrum: Not usable
Chemical composition: $Al_2Be_3(Si_6O_{18})$ aluminium beryllium silicate	Fluorescence: Morganite: weak; violet
Transparency: Transparent to opaque	
Refractive index: 1.570–1.600	

Beryl as a gemstone refers to all varieties of the beryl group which are not emerald-green (p. 90) or aquamarine blue (p. 94). The name is derived from the Greek *beryllos*, possibly of Indian origin, although the meaning is not known. The German word *brille* (spectacle glasses) is derived from it as, in antiquity, eye glasses were made from colorless beryl. Precious beryl refers to all the above beryls, and is also used for all precious stones from the beryl group. Many color varieties have special names in the trade. All are resistant to chemicals with the exception of fluoric acid. They are brittle and therefore easily damaged by knocks, have a vitreous luster, and they occur with aquamarine.

Bixbite (3) Strawberry-red beryl. Meaning of word unknown. Scientists do not accept this as separate variety.

Golden Beryl (1) Yellow beryl. Color varies between lemon yellow and golden yellow. Pigment is probably iron. Inclusions are rare. Decolorization at 482°F/250°C. Most important deposits: Sri Lanka, Namibia.

Goshenite (5) Colorless beryl, named after a find in Goshen, Massachusetts (U.S.). Used as imitation for diamond and emerald, by foiling the cut stone with silver or green metal foil.

Heliodor (2, 6) Color varies between lemon yellow and gold ("Present of the sun"). Apparently discovered in 1910 in Namibia, but similar stones had previously been known in Brazil and Malagasy Republic. Pigment is uranium oxide, radioactive.

Morganite (4) Soft pink to violet beryl, also called pink beryl. Named after mineral collector J. P. Morgan in U.S. Specific gravity between 2.80 and 2.90. Lower color qualities can be improved by heating above 752°F/400°C. Important deposits are in Brazil (Minas Gerais), Malagasy Republic, Mozambique, Rhodesia, Namibia, and the U.S. (California).

Green beryl is designated in the trade as aquamarine (p. 94), as the color can be heat treated at 752–842°F/400–450°C and improved into aquamarine. Beryls are usually emerald cut. Opaque varieties can have a cat's eye effect or asterism. Because of the richness of the color, confusion is possible with many gems. Doublets are known.

---

1 Golden beryl, antique cut, 28.36ct	5 Goshenite, navette, 25.58ct
2 Heliodor, antique cut, 45.24ct	6 Heliodor, oval, 29.79ct
3 Bixbite, antique cut, 49.73ct	7 Beryl, two crystals, together 32.5g
4 Morganite, antique cut, 23.94ct	8 Morganite, rough, 24.5g

CHRYSOBERYL

Color: Golden yellow, green-yellow, brown
Color of streak: White
Mohs' hardness: $8\frac{1}{2}$
Specific gravity: 3.70–3.72
Cleavage: Imperfect
Fracture: Weak; conchoidal
Crystal system: Orthorhombic; long prismatic crystals, intergrown triplets
Chemical composition: $Al_2(BeO_4)$ beryllium aluminium oxide

Transparency: Transparent
Refractive index: 1.744–1.755
Double refraction: +0.011
Dispersion: 0.015
Pleochroism: Very weak; reddish-yellow, yellow, light green, green
Absorption spectrum: 5040, 4950, 4850, 4450
Fluorescence: Usually none
Green: Weak; dark red

Chrysoberyl (Greek – gold) has been known since very early times. Today the varieties alexandrite and chrysoberyl cat's eye are especially valued. Deposits of chrysoberyl (3, 9, 10) are found in Brazil (Minas Gerais, Minas Novas) and Sri Lanka; also in Upper Burma, Malagasy Republic, Rhodesia and Russia (Urals). Stones are fashioned mainly in emerald, Ceylon and brilliant cuts. The famous Hope chrysoberyl, a light green, faceted stone of 45ct is completely clean. Can be confused with andalusite (p. 178), brazilianite (p. 190), golden beryl (p. 96), hiddenite (p. 114), peridot (p. 158), sapphire (p. 86), sinhalite (p. 186), scapolite (p. 188), spinel (p. 100), synthetic spinel (p. 66), topaz (p. 102), tourmaline (p. 110) and zircon (p. 108).

Alexandrite (5–8) (Named after Czar Alexander II) is one of the most desired gems. It is green in daylight, and light red in artificial light. This color change is seen best in thicker stones. Alexandrite cat's eye is a great rarity. Care must be taken when working with it as it is sensitive to knocks, not resistant to alkalies, and the color changes under great heat.

The deposits in the Urals are worked out. Today it is mainly mined in Sri Lanka and Rhodesia. Further deposits are in Burma, Brazil, Malagasy Republic, Tasmania and the U.S. The largest stone of 1876ct was found in Sri Lanka. The largest cut stone weighs 66ct and is in the Smithsonian Institution in Washington. Can be confused with synthetic corundum, which shows a poor green in daylight, but good strawberry red under artificial light. There are also doublets with a good color change on the market: red garnet on top, red glass underneath.

Chrysoberyl cat's eye (2, 4), also called cymophane (Greek – waving light), is an attractive variety. Fine, parallel inclusions produce a silver-white line which appears as a moving light ray in a cabochon-cut stone. The name chrysoberyl cat's eye is derived from this effect, which reminds one of the pupil of a cat. "Cat's eye" by itself always refers to chrysoberyl, all other cat's eye must be designated by an additional name. There are deposits in Sri Lanka and Brazil, also in China. Can be confused with quartz cat's eyes (p. 124).

SPINEL

Color: Red, pink, violet, yellow, orange, blue, dark green, black	Transparency: Transparent
Color of streak: White	Refractive index: 1.712–1.736
Mohs' hardness: 8	Double refraction: None
Specific gravity: 3.58–3.61	Dispersion: 0.026
Cleavage: Imperfect	Pleochroism: None
Fracture: Conchoidal, uneven	Absorption spectrum: Red: 6855,
Crystal system: Isometric; octahedron, twins, rhombic, dodecahedron	6840, 6750, 6650, 6560, 6500, 6420, 6320, 5950–4900, 4650, 4550
Chemical composition: Mg(Al₂O₄) magnesium aluminium oxide	Fluorescence: Red: Strong; red Blue: Weak; reddish or green Green: Weak; reddish

The derivation of the name "spinel" is uncertain. It may mean "spark" (Greek) or "point" (Latin). Spinel occurs in all colors, the favorite being a ruby-like red. The pigments are chrome and iron. Large stones are rare and star spinels very rare.

The blue variety is sensitive to high temperatures. The dark green to black opaque spinel is called Ceylonite, also pleonaste (Greek – surfeit, because of its numerous crystal faces). The brown variety is called Piconite (French), yellow is known as Rubicelle (diminutive of French word for ruby) and the pale red is known as balas ruby (after a region of Afghanistan).

Spinel was recognized as an individual mineral only 150 years ago. Before then it was classed as ruby, because it also occurs with it. Some well-known "rubies" are really spinels, such as the 1.9in/5cm long, oval "Black Prince's Ruby" and also the 361ct "Timur ruby" in a diamond set necklace; both are in the English Crown Jewels. Both are uncut and only polished. The drop-shaped spinels in the Wittelsbacher's crown of 1830 were also originally thought to be rubies.

Main deposits in Burma (near Mogok) and in Sri Lanka (near Ratnapura). Less important deposits are in Anatolia, Afghanistan, Brazil, Thailand and the U.S. (New Jersey). The two largest spinels (formed as roundish octahedrons) weigh 520ct each and are in the British Geological Museum in London.

Synthetic spinels have been on the market since the 1920s (p. 66) and are increasing in importance. They imitate natural spinel, and also many other gems. Further chances of confusion are with amethyst (p. 118), chrysoberyl (p. 98), garnet (p. 104), ruby (p. 82), sapphire (p. 86) and topaz (p. 102). An expert can easily recognize spinel because of the absence of the double refraction. A collector's rarity is zinc spinel, i.e. gahnite (p. 204).

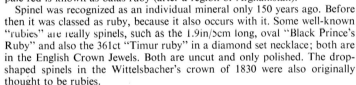

1 Pleonaste crystals in mother rock	7 Spinel, blue, 15.08 and 30.11ct
2 Spinel, 28.47 and 4.16ct	8 Spinel, 12 different reds
3 Spinel, 3 faceted stones	9 Spinel, rubicelle, 3.14 and 5.07ct
4 Spinel, so-called balas ruby 17.13ct	10 Spinel, crystals and other rough stones
5 Spinel, antique cut, 5.05ct	
6 Spinel, two ovals, 7.96 and 5.32ct	

TOPAZ Precious topaz

Color: Colorless, yellow, red-brown, light blue, pinky red, pale green	Transparency: Transparent
Color of streak: White	Refractive index: 1.610–1.638
Mohs' hardness: 8	Double refraction: +0.008–+0.010
Specific gravity: 3.53–3.56	Dispersion: 0.014
Cleavage: Perfect	Pleochroism: Yellow: Definite; lemon-honey-straw yellow
Fracture: Conchoidal, uneven	Blue: Weak; light blue, pink, colorless
Crystal system: Orthorhombic, prisms with multi-faceted ends, often 8-sided in cross-section striations along length	Red: Definite; dark red, yellow, pink red
Chemical composition: $Al_2(SiO_4)$ $(F,OH)_2$ fluor containing aluminium silicate	Absorption spectrum: Pink: <u>6828</u>
	Fluorescence: Pink: Weak; brown Red: Weak; yellow-brown Yellow: Weak; orange-yellow

In antiquity all yellow and brown gemstones, even green ones, were called "topaz". The name most probably derived from the name of an island in the Red Sea, now Zebirget, formerly *Topazos*.

Colored stones are rarely vivid. The most common color is yellow with a red tint. The most valuable is pink. Siberian topazes lose some color in sunlight. The rough stones should not be scratch tested because of the danger of cleavage. Care must be taken during polishing and setting for the same reason. They are not resistant to sulphuric acid.

Deposits are associated with pegmatites or secondary placers. During the 18th century, there was a famous mine at Schneckenstein in the Ore Mountains in Saxony. Today's most important suppliers are Brazil (Minas Gerais, Esperito Santo), Sri Lanka, Burma and Russia (Urals, Transbaikalia). Further deposits throughout the world are in Australia, Japan, Malagasy Republic, Mexico, Nigeria, Rhodesia, Namibia and the U.S. Light blue topazes are also found in Northern Ireland, Scotland and Cornwall, England.

Topazes weighing several pounds are known. In 1965 a blue topaz of nearly 220lb/100kg was said to have been found in the Ukraine. The Smithsonian Institution in Washington has cut topazes of several thousand carats.

Colored stones are usually emerald or scissor cut, and colorless ones are brilliant cut. Topazes with disordered inclusions are cut en cabochon.

There are many possibilities for confusion: apatite (p. 194), aquamarine (p. 94), beryl (p. 96), brazilianite (p. 190), chrysoberyl (p. 98), citrine (p. 120), diamond (p. 70), fluorite (p. 198), golden beryl (p. 96), kunzite (p. 114), orthoclase (p. 164), phenacite (p. 180), ruby (p. 82), sapphire (p. 86), spinel (p. 100), tourmaline (p. 110) and zircon (p. 108). The Braganza, a famous stone of 1640ct in the Portuguese crown, is a colorless topaz and not a diamond as was believed for a long time.

Further difficulties in identification are created by heat-treatment: yellow topazes become pink, colorless or blue.

The quartz variety citrine (p. 120) and yellow heat-treated amethyst (p. 118) are falsely called "gold topaz" or "Madeira topaz", so real topaz is sometimes referred to as "precious topaz".

GARNET

This is a group of differently colored minerals (1) with similar chemical composition. The name derives from the Latin for grain because cf the rounded crystals. Garnet, in the popular sense, is understood to mean red "garnets", almandine and pyrope. Data common to all garnets:

Color of streak: White	Double refraction: Only rhodolite
Cleavage: Imperfect	Pleochroism: None
Fracture: Conchoidal, splintery, brittle	Fluorescence: None
Crystal system: Isometric; rhombic, dodecahedron, icositetrahedron	Transparency: Transparent, translucent

PYROPE (4, 5) Sometimes mistakenly called "cape ruby", garnet group

Color: Red with brown tint	Refractive index: 1.730–1.760
Mohs' hardness: 7–7$\frac{1}{2}$	Dispersion: 0.022
Specific gravity: 3.65–3.80	Absorption spectrum: 6870, 6850,
Chemical composition: $Mg_3Al_2(SiO_4)_3$ magnesium aluminium silicate	6710, 6500, 6200–5200, 5050

Pyrope (Greek – fiery) is so-called because of its red color. It was the fashion stone of the 18th and 19th centuries. Main deposits are in Czechoslovakia, South Africa, Australia. Confused with almandine, spinel (p. 100), ruby (p. 82). **Rhodolite** (6, 7, 8): rose-red or pale violet type of pyrope. Found in the U.S. (North Carolina), Sri Lanka, Brazil, Zambia and Tanzania.

ALMANDINE (9, 10) Garnet group

Color: Red with a violet tint	Refractive index: 1.78–1.81
Mohs' hardness: 7$\frac{1}{2}$	Dispersion: 0.024
Specific gravity: 3.95–4.20	Absorption spectrum: 6170, 5760,
Chemical composition: $Fe_3Al_2(SiO_4)_3$ iron aluminium silicate	5260, 5050, 4760, 4620, 4380, 4280, 4040, 3930

Its name is derived from the town in Asia Minor. In order to lighten the color, the underside of some cut stones is hollowed out. Main deposits are in Sri Lanka, India, Afghanistan and Brazil, Austria and Czechoslovakia. Can be confused with pyrope (p. 104), ruby (p. 82) and spinel (p. 100).

SPESSARTITE (2, 3) Garnet group

Color: Orange to red-brown	Refractive index: 1.795–1.815
Mohs' hardness: 7–7$\frac{1}{2}$	Dispersion: 0.027
Specific gravity: 4.12–4.20	Absorption spectrum: 4950, 4845,
Chemical composition: $Mn_3Al_2(SiO_4)_3$ manganese aluminium silicate	4810, 4750, 4620, 4570, 4550, 4400, 4350, 4320, 4240, 4120, 4060, 3940

Its name is derived from a former occurrence in Spessart, Germany. Now found in Sri Lanka, Brazil, U.S., Malagasy Republic and Sweden. Can be confused with hessonite (p. 106).

1 Range of garnet colors	6 Rhodolite, brilliant cut, 4.02ct
2 Spessartite crystal in mother rock	7 Rhodolite, navette, 2 ovals
3 Spessartite, 3 cabochons	8 Rhodolite crystal, rolled
4 Pyrope crystal, icositetrahedron	9 Almandine in mica
5 Pyrope, 3 faceted stones	10 Almandine, 3 faceted stones

GROSSULAR (4, 5) garnet group

Color: Green, yellow, copper-brown	Transparency: Transparent, translucent
Mohs' hardness: 7–7½	Refractive index: 1.738–1.745
Specific gravity: 3.60–3.68	Dispersion: 0.027
Chemical composition: $Ca_3Al_2(SiO_4)_3$	Absorption spectrum: 6300
calcium aluminium silicate	Further data: Garnet, p. 104

The name derives from the Latin for gooseberry. Since the 1960s, has been found in gem quality, mainly green. Deposits are in Sri Lanka, Canada, Pakistan, South Africa, Tanzania, Russia and the U.S. Can be confused with emerald (p. 90) and demantoid (p. 106).

Hessonite (1, 2, 3) brown-orange variety (Greek – less) of grossular. Also called "cinnamon stone". Found especially in Sri Lanka. Can be confused with spessartite (p. 104) and hyacinth (p. 108).

Leuco garnet (6) is a colorless garnet. Deposits are in Canada and Mexico.

Hydrogrossular is opaque or green grossular; found in South Africa. Also called "Transvaal jade" because of its similarity to jade (p. 154).

Andradite is usually not suitable for jewelry. Varieties such as demantoid, melanite and topazolite have gem qualities.

DEMANTOID (7) garnet group, andradite variety

Color: Green, emerald green	Transparency: Transparent
Mohs' hardness: 6½–7	Refractive index: 1.888–1.889
Specific gravity: 3.82–3.85	Dispersion: 0.057
Chemical composition: $Ca_3Fe_2(SiO_4)_3$	Absorption spectrum: 7010, 6930,
calcium iron silicate	6400, 6220, 4850, 4640, 4430

Demantoid (diamond-like luster) is the most valuable garnet. Found in the Urals, it can be confused with grossular (p. 106), peridot (p. 158), emerald (p. 90), spinel (p. 100), tourmaline (p. 110) and idocrase (p. 186).

Melanite (9) is opaque, a black variety (Greek – black) of andradite. Found in Germany (Kaiserstuhl), France and Italy. Used for mourning jewelry.

Topazolite (10) is a lemon-yellow variety (similar to topaz) of andradite. Only small crystals are found in Switzerland (Zermatt) and the Italian Alps.

UVAROVITE (8) garnet group

Color: Emerald green	Transparency: Transparent to
Mohs' hardness: 7½	translucent
Specific gravity: 3.77	Refractive index: about 1.870
Chemical composition: $Ca_3Cr_2(SiO_4)_3$	Dispersion: None
calcium chromium silicate	

Named after Russian statesman. Deposits are in Urals, Finland, Poland, India, the U.S. and Canada. Can be confused with emerald (p. 90).

1 Hessonite crystal in host rock	7 Demantoid, 3 rough and 3 cut
2 Hessonite, 2 cabochons	stones
3 Hessonite, 3 faceted stones	8 Uvarovite crystals, partly rolled
4 Grossular, rhombic dodecahedron	9 Melanite, 2 crystals
5 Grossular, green and copper-brown	10 Topazolite, rough and faceted
6 Leuco garnet, navette, 1.97ct	

ZIRCON

Color: Colorless, yellow, brown, orange, red, violet, blue, green
Color of streak: White
Mohs' hardness: $6\frac{1}{2}$–$7\frac{1}{2}$
Specific gravity: 3.90–4.71
Cleavage: Imperfect
Fracture: Conchoidal, very brittle
Crystal system: Tetragonal; short, four-sided prisms with pyramidal ends
Chemical composition: $Zr(SiO_4)$ zirconium silicate
Transparency: Translucent
Refractive index: 1.777–1.987
Double refraction: +0.059 (none in green stones)

Dispersion: 0.039
Pleochroism: Yellow: Very weak; honey, yellow-brown, yellow
Red: Very weak; red, light brown
Blue: Definite; blue, yellow, gray, colorless
Absorption spectrum: (Normal) 6910, 6890, 6625, 6605, 6535, 6210, 6150, 5895, 5620, 5375, 5160, 4840, 4600, 4327
Fluorescence: Blue: Very weak; light orange
Red and brown: Weak; dark yellow

Zircon has been known since antiquity. The derivation of its name is uncertain. Because of its high refractive index and strong dispersion, it has great brilliance and intense fire. It is brittle and therefore sensitive to knocks and pressure. The edges are easily damaged (pack singly – care needed during cutting). Relatively high content of radioactive elements (uranium, thorium) cause large variations of physical properties. Zircons with the highest values in optical properties and specific gravity are scientifically designated as normal or high zircons. Those with lower values are low zircons. The alteration caused by radioactive elements in green zircons is so advanced that these stones can be nearly amorphous.

Hyacinth: yellow-red to red-brown variety.

Starlite: blue variety (heat-treated).

Deposits are mostly alluvial and are found in Cambodia, Burma, Thailand and Sri Lanka; also in Australia, Malagasy Republic, Tanzania, Vietnam and France (Haute Loire).

In nature the gray-brown and red-brown zircons are the most common. Colorless specimens are rare. In the South Asiatic countries where found, the brown varieties are heat-treated at temperatures of 1472–1832°F/800–1000°C, producing colorless and blue zircons. These colors do not necessarily remain constant, ultra-violet rays or sunlight can produce changes. Colorless stones are brilliant cut; colored ones are given a brilliant or emerald cut. Synthetic zircons are scientifically of great interest. Green zircons are rare in the trade, and are in demand by collectors.

Can be confused with aquamarine (p. 94), cassiterite (p. 184), chrysoberyl (p. 98), hessonite (p. 106), sapphire (p. 86), sinhalite (p. 186), synthetic spinel (p. 66), sphene (p. 195), topaz (p. 102), tourmaline (p. 110) and idocrase (p. 186). Colorless heat-treated zircon has been fraudulently offered for diamond (p. 70) as "matara diamond". All zircons (except the green) have strong double refraction, which can readily be seen under the loupe at the facet edges, an important identification mark.

1 Zircon, rectangular, 9.81ct	6 Zircon, octagon, 7.92ct
2 Zircon, drop and brilliant	7 Zircon, octagon, 4.02ct
2 Zircon, brilliant, 14.35ct	8 Zircon, 4 brilliants
4 Zircon, two brilliants	9 Zircon, 3 faceted stones
5 Zircon, oval, 5.11ct	10 Zircon, rough stones

TOURMALINE

Color: Colorless, pink, red, yellow, brown, green, blue, violet, black, multi-colored
Color of streak: White
Mohs' hardness: $7-7\frac{1}{2}$
Specific gravity: 3.02–3.26
Cleavage: None
Fracture: Uneven, small conchoidal, brittle
Crystal system: Hexagonal (trigonal); usually long crystals with triangular cross section and rounded sides, definite striation parallel to main axis, often several prisms grown together
Chemical composition: (NaLiCa) $(Fe_{11}Mg\ Mn\ Al)_3\ Al_6((OH)_4$ $(BO_3)_3Si_6O_{18})$ aluminium borate silicate, complicated and changeable composition

Transparency: Transparent, opaque
Refractive index: 1.616–1.652
Double refraction: -0.014 to -0.044
Dispersion: 0.017
Pleochroism: Red: Dark red-light red
Yellow: Definite; dark yellow–light yellow
Brown: Definite; dark brown–light brown
Green: Strong; dark green–light green
Blue: Strong; dark blue–light blue
Absorption spectrum: Red: 5550, 5370, 5250–4610, <u>4560</u>, <u>4510</u>, 4280
Green: <u>4970</u>, <u>4610</u>, 4150
Fluorescence: Colorless: Weak; green-blue
Pale yellow: Weak; green-blue
Red: Weak; red-violet
Pink, brown, green, blue: none

No gemstone has such richness in color variation as tourmaline. Known in antiquity in the Mediterranean area, the Dutch imported it in 1703 from Sri Lanka into Europe. They gave the new stone a Sinhalese name *Turamali*, the original meaning of which is not known.

According to color, the following varieties are recognized:

Achroite (Greek – without color) colorless or nearly so. Rare.

Rubellite (p. 113 nos. 2, 4) (Latin – reddish) pink to red, sometimes with a violet tint; ruby color most valuable.

Dravite (p. 113 nos. 1, 7, 8) (after Drave in Austria) yellow brown to dark brown.

Verdelite (p. 113 nos. 6, 13) (Italian/Greek – greenstone) green in all shades, most common of all tourmalines. Emerald green most valuable.

Indigolite or Indicolite (p. 113 nos. 3, 5, 10–12, 15) blue in all shades.

Siberite (after finds in Urals) lilac to violet blue. Sometimes used as synonym for rubellite.

Schorl (4, 5) black, very common. Rarely used for jewelry. Name derived from old mining term.

Uni-colored tourmalines are quite rare. Most crystals have various color shades or even different colors (6, 8). Often there is some layered color. Brazil produces stones with a red interior, inner "skin" white, outer "skin" green. The South African tourmalines are green inside and the outer layer is red. A tourmaline with a red inside and a green "skin" is sometimes called a "watermelon" (6). The nuances and colors are particularly effectively shown when slices of cross-section are polished (1). See p. 112.

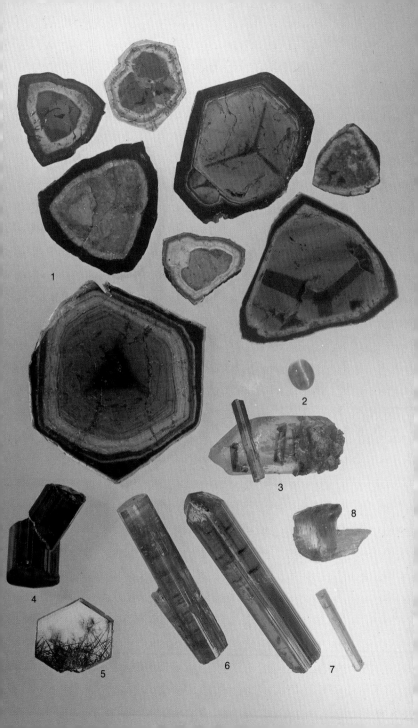

Tourmaline cat's eyes exist in various colors, but only in the pink and green varieties (p. 110 no. 2) is the chatoyancy strong, caused by inclusions of foreign crystals. Some tourmalines show a slight change of color in artificial light.

In recent times the color designation is often added instead of the name of the variety, e.g.: yellow tourmaline, green tourmaline, pink tourmaline. Science differentiates between tourmalines of different compositions and has names for special groups: Buergerite=iron tourmaline; Dravite=magnesium tourmaline; Elbaite=Lithium tourmaline; Schorl=iron tourmaline; Tsilaisite =manganese tourmaline; Uvite=magnesium tourmaline.

By heating and subsequent cooling, as well as by applying pressure, i.e. by rubbing, a tourmaline crystal will become electrically charged. One end becomes negative, the other positive, and it will attract dust particles as well as small pieces of paper (pyro- and piezo-electricity). The Dutch who first imported tourmaline into Europe knew of this effect. They used a heated stone to pull ash out of their meerschaum pipes and thus called it *aschentrekker* (ash puller). For a long time this was the proper name for a tourmaline.

Deposits are found in pegmatites and alluvial deposits. The most productive deposits, apart from Sri Lanka and the Malagasy Republic, are in Brazil (Minas Gerais, Bahia). Mozambique supplies good red and two-colored stones. Further deposits are in Angola, Australia, Burma, India, Rhodesia, Namibia, Tanzania, Thailand, Russia (Ural, Transbaikalia) and the U.S. (California, Maine, New York, Connecticut, Colorado). In Europe, the collector finds tourmaline on Elba and in Switzerland (Tessin).

The most desired colors are pink, intense red and green. Because of the strong pleochroism, the stone must be cut so that the table lies parallel to the main axis. In the case of pale stones, the table should be perpendicular to the long axis in order to obtain the deeper color.

By heating to 842–1202°F/450–650°C, small color changes can be produced: green tourmaline becomes emerald green, red-brown ones a fiery red. There are no synthetic tourmalines for commercial uses.

Because of the variety of color, tourmaline can be confused with many gems: especially amethyst (p. 118), andalusite (p. 178), chrysoberyl (p. 98), citrine (p. 120), demantoid (p. 106), hiddenite (p. 114), peridot (p. 158), prasiolite (p. 120), smoky quartz (p. 116), ruby (p. 82), emerald (p. 90), synthetic green spinel (p. 66), pink topaz (p. 102), idocrase (p. 186), zircon (p. 108) and some glass imitations. Important identification marks for tourmaline are high double refraction and strong pleochroism.

The illustrations are 20% larger than the originals.

SPODUMENE (Augite group, pyroxene group)

Most probably the name refers to the gray unassuming color (Greek – burnt to ashes) of the common spodumene. Since 1879, gem varieties have been known as hiddenite and kunzite.

HIDDENITE (1–3, 8) spodumene group

Color: Yellow-green, green-yellow, emerald green
Color of streak: White
Mohs' hardness: 6–7
Specific gravity: 3.16–3.20
Cleavage: Perfect
Fracture: Uneven
Crystal system: Monoclinic; prismatic, tabular
Chemical composition: LiAl (Si$_2$O$_6$) lithium aluminium silicate

Transparency: Transparent
Refractive index: 1.655–1.680
Double refraction: +0.015
Dispersion: 0.017
Pleochroism: Definite; blue-green, emerald green, yellow-green
Absorption spectrum: <u>6905</u>, <u>6860</u>, 6690, 6460, <u>6200</u>, <u>4375</u>, 4330
Fluorescence: Very weak; red-yellow

Named after W. E. Hidden who discovered this stone in 1879 in North Carolina (U.S.); not found much on European markets but very popular in the U.S. Colors are not always constant. Deposits found in pegmatite veins, especially in Brazil, Malagasy Republic, the U.S. (North Carolina, California) and Burma. Working is very difficult because of perfect cleavage (sensitive to pressure). Note pleochroism: table must be perpendicular to main axis. Mostly the emerald cut is used, sometimes the brilliant cut. Can be confused with beryl (p. 96), chrysoberyl (p. 98), diopside (p. 190), euclase (p. 178), pale emerald (p. 90) and green tourmaline (p. 110).

KUNZITE (4–7) spodumene group

Color: Pink-violet, light violet
Color of streak: White
Mohs' hardness: 6–7
Specific gravity: 3.16–3.20
Cleavage: Perfect
Fracture: Uneven
Crystal system: Monoclinic; prismatic, tabular
Chemical composition: LiAl(Si$_2$O$_6$) lithium aluminium silicate

Transparency: Transparent
Refractive index: 1.655–1.680
Double refraction: +0.015
Dispersion: 0.017
Pleochroism: Definite; amethyst-color, pale red, colorless
Absorption spectrum: Negligible
Fluorescence: Strong; yellow-red, orange

Named after G. F. Kunz who first described this gem in 1902. Colors can become faded. Often found in a large crystal. Working is difficult because of the perfect cleavage (sensitive to pressure). Occurs in pegmatites; main deposits are in Malagasy Republic, the U.S. (California, Maine), Brazil and Burma. Because of strong pleochroism, table must be perpendicular to main axis. Brown and green-violet colors can be improved by heat-treatment. Can be confused with several pink stones, especially amethyst (p. 118), beryl (p. 96), topaz (p. 102) and colored glass.

1 Hiddenite, octagon, 22.03ct
2 Hiddenite, pear-shaped, 9.30ct
3 Hiddenite, octagon, 19.14ct
4 Kunzite, octagon, 16.32ct
5 Kunzite, oval, 3.13ct
6 Kunzite, antique cut, 6.11ct
7 Kunzite, 2 crystals
8 Hiddenite, crystal and broken piece

QUARTZ

Minerals of the same or similar chemical composition are included under the single group of Quartz (SiO_2 resp. $SiO_2.nH_2O$) silicon dioxide:
Macrocrystalline quartz includes amethyst, aventurine, rock crystal, citrine, prase, hawk's eye, quartz cat's eye, smoky quartz, rose quartz and tiger's eye. Microcrystalline quartz includes chalcedony group – agate, fossilized wood, chrysoprase, heliotrope, jasper, cornelian, moss agate, onyx, sard.
Amorphous quartz includes opal group–precious opal, fire opal, common opal.

ROCK CRYSTAL (8–10) quartz group

Color: Colorless	Transparency: Transparent
Color of streak: White	Refractive index: 1.544–1.553
Mohs' hardness: 7	Double refraction: +0.009
Specific gravity: 2.65	Dispersion: 0.013
Cleavage: None	Pleochroism: None
Fracture: Conchoidal, very brittle	Absorption spectrum: Not usable
Crystal system: Hexagonal (trigonal); hexagonal prisms	Fluorescence: None

The name crystal comes from the Greek for "ice", as it was believed that rock crystal was eternally frozen. Rock crystals weighing many tons have been found. Cuttable material is rare. Inclusions are of goethite (star quartz, no. 12), gold, pyrite, rutile and tourmaline (p. 111 no. 5). They are found all over the world and are mainly used as costume jewelry and to imitate diamonds. Can be confused with all colorless gems and glass. It becomes smoky when treated with radium and x-ray. Synthesized for industrial purposes only. Rhinestones, formerly rock crystal pebbles from the Rhine, are today multi-colored glass imitations.

SMOKY QUARTZ (1–7) quartz group, falsely called smoky topaz

Color: Brown to black, smoky gray	Transparency: Transparent
Color of streak: White	Refractive index: 1.544–1.553
Mohs' hardness: 7	Double refraction: +0.009
Specific gravity: 2.65	Dispersion: 0.013
Cleavage: None	Pleochroism: Dark: Definite; brown, reddish brown
Fracture: Conchoidal, very brittle	
Crystal system: Hexagonal (trigonal); hexagonal prisms	Absorption spectrum: Not usable
	Fluorescence: Usually none

Named after its smoky color. Very dark stones are called "morion". Pales when heated to 572–752°F/300–400°C; there are frequent inclusions of rutile needles (1, 2). Found worldwide; Scottish variety is called "cairngorm". Can be confused with andalusite, axinite, sanidine, tourmaline and idocrase.

---

1 Smoky quartz with rutile inclusions
2 Smoky quartz with rutile, cabochon
3 Smoky quartz, oval, 3.8g
4 Smoky quartz, two crystals
5 Smoky quartz, octagon, 5.6g
6 Smoky quartz, oval, 6.2g
7 Smoky quartz crystal

8 Rock crystal, 4 stones, faceted and cabochon
9 Rock crystal, crystals and twins
10 Rock crystal, brilliant cut, 5g
11 Rock crystal, baguette, 1.8g
12 Star quartz, 15g

AMETHYST (4–8) quartz group

Color: Violet, pale red-violet	Transparency: Transparent
Color of streak: White	Refractive index: 1.544–1.553
Mohs' hardness: 7	Double refraction: $+0.009$
Specific gravity: 2.63–2.65	Dispersion: 0.013
Cleavage: None	Pleochroism: Very weak; violet,
Fracture: Conchoidal, very brittle	gray-violet
Crystal system: Hexagonal (trigonal);	Absorption spectrum: (5500–5200)
hexagonal prisms	Fluorescence: Weak; greenish
Chemical composition: SiO_2 silicon	
dioxide	

Amethyst is the most highly valued stone in the quartz group. It is said to have many supernatural powers: it brings luck, ensures constancy, protects against magic and home-sickness. The name (Greek) probably means "not drunken" as amethyst was also worn as an amulet against drunkenness. Crystals are always grown onto a base. Pyramids are not well developed, therefore are often found as "crystal points" with deepest color. These crystals are broken off the base.

Heat treatment between 878–1382°F/470–750°C produces light yellow, red brown, green or colorless varieties (be careful when soldering). See also p. 120. There are some amethysts that lose some color in daylight. The original color can be restored by x-ray radiation.

Found in geodes in alluvial deposits. The most important deposits are in Brazil, Uruguay and the Malagasy Republic. The best stones are faceted, others are tumbled or worked into ornaments. Can be confused with beryl (p. 96), fluorite (p. 198), glass, synthetic corundum (p. 66), kunzite (p. 114), spinel (p. 100), topaz (p. 102) and tourmaline (p. 110). Amethyst is synthesized but not for the jewelry market.

AMETHYST QUARTZ (1–3) quartz group

Color: Violet with whitish stripes	Transparency: Translucent
Color of streak: White	Refractive index: 1.54–1.55
Mohs' hardness: 7	Double refraction: $+0.009$
Specific gravity: 2.65	Dispersion: 0.013
Cleavage: None	Pleochroism: None
Fracture: Conchoidal, brittle	Absorption spectrum: Not usable
Crystal system: Hexagonal (trigonal);	Fluorescence: None
compact	
Chemical composition: SiO_2 silicon	
dioxide	

Amethyst quartz is the rougher, more compact formation of amethyst, layered and striped with milky quartz. Occurs together with amethyst. It is mostly found in Brazil, Malagasy Republic, Namibia and the U.S. Former deposits were in Meuglitz Valley, Saxony, Germany and the Auvergne (France). Used for beads, cabochons, ornaments and objets d'art. Can be confused with striped fluorite (p. 198).

1 Amethyst quartz, rough	5 Amethyst, 4 faceted stones
2 Amethyst quartz, seven cabochons	6 Amethyst, double-ended crystal
3 Amethyst quartz, polished slice	7 Amethyst, brilliant cut, 4.16ct
4 Amethyst, navette, 3.94ct	8 Amethyst, geode on agate

CITRINE (1–6) quartz group

Color: Light yellow to gold-brown
Color of streak: White
Mohs' hardness: 7
Specific gravity: 2.65
Cleavage: None
Fracture: Conchoidal, very brittle
Crystal system: Hexagonal (trigonal);
  hexagonal prisms with pyramids
Chemical composition: SiO_2 silicon
  dioxide

Transparency: Transparent
Refractive index: 1.544–1.553
Double refraction: +0.009
Dispersion: 0.013
Pleochroism: Natural: Weak; yellow-
  light yellow
  Heat-treated: none
Absorption spectrum: Not usable
Fluorescence: None

The name is derived from its lemon-yellow color. Most commercial citrines are heat-treated amethysts (p. 118) or smoky quartzes (p. 116). Brazilian amethyst turns light yellow at 878°F/470°C and dark yellow to red brown at 1022–1040°F/550–560°C. Some smoky quartzes turn yellow earlier, at 572–752°F/300–400°C (be careful when soldering). All heat-treated stones have a red tint. The natural citrines are mostly pale yellow. Treated citrines show no pleochroism, natural ones weak pleochroism. The trade often calls citrines "topazes". This is incorrect, even when qualified as Bahia-topaz, gold topaz, Madeira topaz, etc.

Natural citrine is rare. Deposits are in Brazil (Bahia, Goyez, Minas Gerais), Malagasy Republic, the U.S. (Pikes Peak, Colorado), Spain (Cordoba, Salamanca), Russia (Mursinska/Ural), France and Scotland. Well-colored, transparent specimens are used as ringstones and pendants. Less attractive stones are made into necklaces or ornaments.

Can be confused with all yellow gemstones, especially yellow beryl (p. 96), orthoclase (p. 164), yellow topaz (p. 102) and yellow tourmaline (p. 110).

PRASIOLITE (7, 8) quartz group

Color: Leek-green
Color of streak: White
Mohs' hardness: 7
Specific gravity: 2.65
Cleavage: None
Fracture: Conchoidal, very brittle
Crystal system: Hexagonal (trigonal);
  hexagonal prisms
Chemical composition: SiO_2 silicon
  dioxide

Transparency: Transparent
Refractive index: 1.544–1.553
Double refraction: +0.009
Dispersion: 0.013
Pleochroism: Very weak; light green,
  pale green
Absorption spectrum: Not usable
Fluorescence: None

This leek-green quartz (Greek – leek) is not found in nature but since 1950 has been produced by heating amethyst and yellow quartzes from the Montezuma deposit in Minas Gerais, Brazil, to a temperature of 932°F/500°C. Arizona is also said to supply cuttable material. Can be confused with beryl (p. 96), peridot (p. 158) and tourmaline (p. 110).

1 Citrine, heat-treated, rough
2 Citrine, heat-treated, faceted
3 Citrine, heat-treated, rectangle
4 Citrine, natural, rough

5 Citrine, natural, oval
6 Citrine, two octagons
7 Prasiolite, rough
8 Prasiolite, 2 faceted stones

ROSE QUARTZ (3–7) quartz group

Color: Strong pink, pale pink	Chemical comp.: SiO_2 silicon dioxide
Color of streak: White	Transparency: Transparent, translucent
Mohs' hardness: 7	Refractive index: 1.544–1.553
Specific gravity: 2.65	Double refraction: +0.009
Cleavage: None	Dispersion: 0.013
Fracture: Conchoidal, very brittle	Pleochroism: Weak; pink, pale pink
Crystal system: Hexagonal (trigonal); prisms, mostly compact	Absorption spectrum: Not usable
	Fluorescence: Weak; dark violet

Named after its color, it is often crackled, usually a little turbid. Crystals with flat faces have been found only in the last few years. Color can fade. Traces of included rutile needles cause six-rayed stars when cut en cabochon (4). Brazil is the largest supplier. The best quality comes from the Malagasy Republic. Worked into cabochons, bead necklaces and ornamental pieces, only the larger clear pieces can be faceted (5).

AVENTURINE (1, 2) quartz group. Also aventurine quartz

Color: Green, gold-brown, iridescent	Chemical comp.: SiO_2 silicon dioxide
Color of streak: White	Transparency: Translucent, opaque
Mohs' hardness: 7	Refractive index: 1.544–1.553
Specific gravity: 2.65	Double refraction: +0.009
Cleavage: None	Dispersion: 0.013
Fracture: Conchoidal, brittle	Pleochroism: None
Crystal system: Hexagonal (trigonal); crypto-crystalline	Absorption spectrum: 6820, 6490
	Fluorescence: Reddish

A type of glass discovered by chance about 1700 (Italian – *a ventura*) gave the name to the similar-looking stone. Dark green with metallic iridescence caused by fuchsite (green mica) inclusions, the red and brown are caused by iron-mica inclusions. Important deposits are in India, Brazil and Russia. Used for cabochons and ornamental objects, it is very popular in South East Asia. Can be confused with aventurine feldspar (p. 166) and jade (p. 154).

PRASE (8, 9)

Compact quartz aggregate, it is leek-green in color (Greek – leek, hence the name!) with actinolite inclusions. European deposits are in East Germany (Ore mountains), Finland, Austria (near Salzburg) and Scotland. Sometimes green jasper is called prase (p. 146). Can be confused with jade (p. 154).

BLUE QUARTZ (10) Also called siderite

Coarse-grained quartz aggregate; the inclusions of crocidolite fibers (or rutile needles) cause the dull blue color. Found in Salzburg in Austria, Scandinavia, South Africa and Brazil. Used for ornaments.

1 Aventurine, 5 cabochons	6 Rose quartz, 6 cabochons
2 Aventurine, rough, partly polished	7 Rose quartz
3 Rose quartz, rough	8 Prase, rough, partly polished
4 Star rose quartz, 20.23ct	9 Prase, 2 cabochons
5 Rose quartz, octagon, 8.16ct	10 Blue quartz, rough, partly polished

QUARTZ CAT'S EYE (1, 2) quartz group

Color: White, gray, green, yellow, brown	Chemical composition: SiO_2 silicon dioxide
Color of streak: White	Transparency: Translucent, opaque
Mohs' hardness: 7	Refractive index: 1.544–1.553
Specific gravity: 2.65	Double refraction: $+0.009$
Cleavage: None	Dispersion: 0.013
Fracture: Irregular	Pleochroism: None
Crystal system: Hexagonal (trigonal); fibrous aggregate	Absorption spectrum: Not usable
	Fluorescence: None

Compact quartz with fibrous, parallel hornblende. Not to be called "cat's eye" without the prefix of quartz, as that term refers to chrysoberyl cat's eye (cymophane p. 98). Sensitive to acids. Found in Sri Lanka, also in India and Brazil. Cut en cabochon, shows chatoyancy like a cat's eye. Can be confused with chrysoberyl cat's eye (p. 98). Sometimes de-colored hawk's eyes or tiger's eyes are substituted.

HAWK'S EYE (3, 4) quartz group, also called Falcon's Eye

Finely fibrous quartz aggregate with crocidolite (type of hornblende), blue-gray to blue-green. Iridescence of planes; fractures have silky luster. It is sensitive to acids. Found in South Africa together with tiger's eye. Used for ornamental objects, rings, pendants. Cabochons show chatoyancy (small ray of light on surface) which is reminiscent of the eye of a bird of prey.

TIGER'S EYE (5, 6) quartz group

Color: Gold-yellow, gold-brown	Transparency: Opaque
Color of streak: Yellow-brown	Refractive index: 1.544–1.553
Mohs' hardness: 7	Double refraction: $+0.009$
Specific gravity: 2.64–2.71	Dispersion: 0.013
Cleavage: None	Pleochroism: None
Fracture: Fibrous	Absorption spectrum: Not usable
Crystal system: Hexagonal (trigonal); fibrous aggregate	Fluorescence: None
Chemical composition: SiO_2 silicon dioxide	

Formed from hawk's eye through pseudomorphism of crocidolite in quartz, keeping the fibrous structure. Brown iron produces the golden-yellow color. There is chatoyancy on the fractures and a silky luster. It is sensitive to acids. Found together with hawk's eye in slabs of a few inches thickness, the fibers being perpendicular to the slab. The most important deposit is in South Africa; also found in Western Australia, Burma, India and the U.S. (California). Used for pendants and objets d'art. When cut en cabochon, the surface shows chatoyancy reminiscent of the eyes of a cat. For tiger's eye matrix, see p. 202.

1 Quartz cat's eye, rough	4 Hawk's eye, 2 cabochons
2 Quartz, cat's eye, cabochon 3.96ct	5 Tiger's eye, rough, partly polished
3 Hawk's eye, rough	6 Tiger's eye, 7 cabochons

CHALCEDONY quartz group

Chalcedony describes a group of micro-crystalline quartzes (p. 116): agate, dendritic agate, chalcedony, chrysoprase, heliotrope, fossilized wood, jasper, cornelian, moss agate, onyx and sard, as well as a bluish variety of chalcedony. Some scientists describe chalcedony as the fibrous variety and classify the grainy jasper in a separate group. The nomenclature in the trade is even more confusing. The name chalcedony is derived from an ancient town on the Bosphorus. While the crystal quartzes (rock crystal, amethyst) have a vitreous luster, chalcedonies are waxy or dull.

CHALCEDONY (4–6) quartz group

Color: Bluish, white, gray	Transparency: Dull, translucent
Color of streak: White	Refractive index: 1.530–1.539
Mohs' hardness: $6\frac{1}{2}$–7	Double refraction: up to $+0.006$
Specific gravity: 2.58–2.64	Dispersion: None
Cleavage: None	Pleochroism: None
Fracture: Uneven, shell-like	Absorption spectrum: Dyed blue:
Crystal system: Hexagonal (trigonal);	6900–6600,6270
fibrous aggregates	Fluorescence: Blue-white
Chemical comp.: SiO_2 silicon dioxide	

While the microscopic fibers are parallel and perpendicular to the surface, chalcedony shows macroscopically radiating stalactitic, grape-like or kidney shapes (4). Always porous; can therefore be dyed. Natural chalcedony has no layering or banding. The trade also offers parallel layered, artificial blue-colored agate as chalcedony (5). There is a wide distribution of deposits, especially in Brazil, India, the Malagasy Republic and Uruguay. In ancient times used for cameos and as a talisman against idiocy and depression. Today used for ornamental objects, in gem engraving and as cabochons.

CORNELIAN (2, 3) quartz group

The name is derived from the Kornel type of cherry because of its color. It is the flesh-red to brown-red variety of chalcedony. The best qualities come from India, where the brown tints are enhanced to red by exposure to the sun. Most cornelians are agates from Brazil and Uruguay, colored with ferrous nitrate solution. When held against the light, the colored variety shows stripes, the natural variety has a cloudy distribution of color. In antiquity it was thought to still the blood and soften anger. Use and additional data as with chalcedony.

SARD (1) quartz group

Red-brown variety of chalcedony (named after town in Asia Minor). No strict separation from cornelian, with common deposits and uses. Artificially colored sard is produced from chalcedony by saturation with sugar solution.

---

1 Sard, 8 faceted and cabochon stones
2 Cornelian, rough
3 Cornelian, 7 faceted and cabochon stones
4 Chalcedony nodule, partly polished
5 Chalcedony, 3 banded stones
6 Chalcedony, 7 cabochons

CHRYSOPRASE (1–4) quartz group

Color: Green, apple green	Transparency: Translucent, opaque
Color of streak: White	Refractive index: 1.530–1.539
Mohs' hardness: $6\frac{1}{2}$–7	Double refraction: up to $+0.004$
Specific gravity: 2.58–2.64	Dispersion: None
Cleavage: None	Pleochroism: None
Fracture: Rough, brittle	Absorption spectrum: Natural: 4439
Crystal system: Hexagonal (trigonal);	Dyed with nickel: 6320, 4439
microcrystalline aggregates	Fluorescence: None
Chemical comp.: SiO_2 silicon dioxide	

The Greek name (gold-leek) seems unsuitable. Chrysoprase is the most valuable stone in the chaldedony group. The microscopic quartz fibers have a radial structure. The pigment is nickel. Large broken pieces are often full of fissures with irregular colors. Color can fade in sunlight and when heated (be careful when soldering). Colors may recover under moist storage.

Occurs as nodules in weathered materials of nickel ore deposits and in the crevices. It is comparatively rare. Since the 14th century it has been mined in Frankenstein, Upper Silesia (Poland) but is now worked out. Since 1960, the best qualities have come from Queensland, Australia. Other deposits are in Brazil, India, Malagasy Republic, South Africa, Russia (Urals) and the U.S. (Arizona, California, Oregon).

Used as cabochons and for ornamental objects. Best qualities sometimes given a cut named after Frederick the Great of Prussia 1712–86 (a single row of facets along the edges of a large table). Used in earlier centuries as interior decoration for Wenceslaus Chapel in Prague and Sanssouci Castle in Potsdam (near Berlin). Can be confused with jade (p. 154), prehnite (p. 188), smithsonite (p. 198), variscite (p. 196), and artificially colored green chalcedony.

CHRYSOPRASE MATRIX (3, 4)

Chrysoprase with brown or white matrix rock (3). Used for ornamental objects and in jewelry when cut en cabochon.

HELIOTROPE (5, 6) quartz group

Heliotrope is an opaque, dark green chalcedony with red spots (Greek – sunturner, derivation not known). It is also known as Bloodstone. During the Middle Ages, special magic powers were ascribed to it, as the red spots were thought to be drops of Christ's blood. The colors are not always constant. The most important deposits are in India, also in Australia, Brazil, China and the U.S. Used as seals for men's rings and other ornamental objects.

In the trade, the synonym "blue jasper" is used when scattered red spots are present. Actually heliotrope is not jasper (p. 146), even if a radial structure with spherical aggregates simulates a grainy appearance. The Germans call it "bluestone", because "bloodstone" refers to hematite (p. 162) in German.

---

1 Chrysoprase, partly polished	5 Heliotrope, rough, partly polished
2 Chrysoprase, 4 cabochons	6 Heliotrope, 7 faceted and cabochon
3 Chrysoprase, 2 stones with matrix	stones
4 Chrysoprase-matrix, partly polished	

MOSS AGATE (5, 6) quartz group

Color: Colorless with green inclusions	Transparency: Translucent
Color of streak: White	Refractive index: 1.54–1.55
Mohs' hardness: $6\frac{1}{2}$–7	Double refraction: up to $+0.006$
Specific gravity: 2.58–2.62	Dispersion: None
Cleavage: None	Pleochroism: None
Fracture: Rough	Absorption spectrum: Not usable
Crystal system: Hexagonal (trigonal); microcrystalline	Fluorescence: Variable
Chemical composition: SiO_2 silicon dioxide	

Moss agate is a colorless, translucent chalcedony (scientifically not an agate) with moss-like green, stem-like hornblende. When there are numerous hornblende inclusions, it is known as moss jasper in the trade (scientifically not true jasper, p. 146). Moss agate colors are brown and red through oxidation of the hornblende.

It occurs as filler in fissures and as pebbles. The best qualities come from India. Further deposits are in China and the U.S. (Colorado, Michigan, Oregon, Utah, Washington, Wyoming).

It is used in thin slabs so that the moss-like image can be seen effectively; also used as plates, cabochons for rings, brooches and pendants, and other ornamental objects; a very popular gemstone.

Can be well imitated by doublets. Two translucent gray chalcedony plates are glued together after an iron and manganese compound between them has crystallized showing moss-like markings.

DENDRITIC AGATE (1–4) quartz group

This is colorless or white-gray translucent chalcedony (scientifically not strictly an agate) with tree-like or fern-like images called dendrites (Greek – tree-like). These dendrites are iron or manganese inclusions of dark brown or black color. They are not organic and resemble ice crystals on windows in the winter. They are formed from the finest cleavage plates by the crystallization of decomposing solutions of neighboring rock.

Occur together with other chalcedonies. Most important deposits are in Brazil (Rio Grande do Sul); also in India and the U.S. Because the Indian stones used to reach Europe via the Arabian harbor of Mocha, these stones are also called Mocha stones.

Scenic Agate A dendritic agate with brown or reddish color tint and includes dendrites resembling landscape-like images (2).

Mosquito Agate or Midge Stone. A dendritic agate where the included dendrites resemble swarms of mosquitoes (4).

Used in rings, brooches, pendants. When cutting, the dendritic inclusions must remain near the surface. Imitations were attempted with silver nitrate, but were not successful.

---

1 Dendritic agate, fern-like
2 Scenic agate
3 Dendritic agate, two pieces, radial inclusions

4 Mosquito agate
5 Moss agate, ten cabochons
6 Moss agate, two pieces, partly polished

AGATE quartz group

Color: Various, banded or layered	Transparency: Translucent, opaque
Color of streak: White	Refractive index: 1.544–1.553
Mohs' hardness: $6\frac{1}{2}$–7	Double refraction: $+0.009$
Specific gravity: 2.60–2.65	Dispersion: None
Cleavage: None	Pleochroism: None
Fracture: Uneven	Absorption spectrum: Dyed yellow:
Crystal system: Hexagonal (trigonal);	7000, (6650), (6340)
microcrystalline aggregates	Fluorescence: Varies with bands:
Chemical composition: SiO_2 silicon	partly strong; yellow, blue-white
dioxide	

The name agate is derived from the Sicilian river Achates where agates were probably found in antiquity. It is not certain whether or not this is the river Dirillo in the south-east of the island.

Agate is a banded chalcedony, sometimes containing opal substance. The individual bands can be multi-colored, or more or less of the same color. The agates of the exhausted German mines were red, pink and brown, separated by gray bands. The South American agates are usually dull gray without special markings; therefore they are usually treated (p. 136). Transparency varies from nearly transparent to opaque.

Agates are found as nodules or geodes in siliceous volcanic rocks (melaphyre, porphyry) with sizes varying from a fraction of an inch to a circumference of several yards. The bands are formed by rhythmic crystallization, but scientific opinions vary as to how. It was thought that the agate bands crystallize gradually in the hollows formed by gas bubbles from a siliceous solution. Now the theory that their formation is simultaneous with that of the matrix rock, has won support. According to this idea, the liquid drops of the silicic acid cool with the cooling rock and produce a layered crystallization from the outside. The various bands – especially those close to the outer wall – may vary in thickness, but normally their thicknesses remain constant throughout the nodule. The outer wall and the outermost layer may form a white crust due to weathering.

Where the inner cavity of the nodule is not filled with an agate mass, well-developed crystals can form in the remaining spaces: rock crystal (p. 116), amethyst (p. 118) or smoky quartz (p. 116); sometimes accompanied by calcite (p. 206), hematite (p. 162), chalybite and zeolite. A nodule with crystals in the central cavity is called a geode (5). See also p. 134.

1 Agate nodule in cross section, banded agate, $\frac{1}{3}$ natural size, Uruguay
2 Agate nodule in cross section, orbicular agate with concentric eye (eye agate), $\frac{2}{3}$ natural size, India
3 Agate nodule in cross section, orbicular, $\frac{2}{3}$ natural size, India
4 Agate nodule in cross section, orbicular agate with eccentric eye (eye agate), $\frac{2}{3}$ natural size, India
5 Agate geode, $\frac{2}{3}$ natural size, Brazil

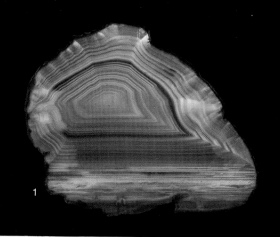

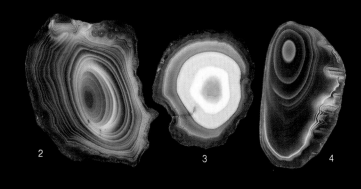

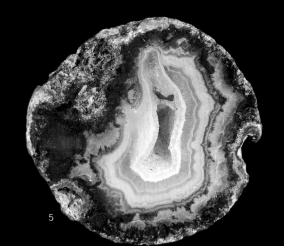

Varieties: According to sample, design or structure of the agate layer, trade and science have given various names to the agates.

Eye agate: ring shaped design with point in center (p. 133 no. 2, 4).

Layer agate: layers parallel to skin (p. 133 no. 1).

Dendritic agate: colorless or gray-white translucent chalcedony with dendrites (p. 131 nos. 1–4). Not layered, not real agate.

Enhydritic agate: agate or chalcedony nodule, partly filled with water which can be seen through the walls. After the agate is taken from surrounding rock, the water often dries out.

Fortification agate: patterned like the ground-plan of an old-fashioned fortress (2).

Orbicular agate: circular layer (p. 133 no. 3) group: eye agate.

Moss agate: colorless, translucent chalcedony with moss-like inclusions of hornblende (p. 131 nos. 5, 6). Is not layered and not really agate.

Scenic agate: shows scenery-like image by brown or reddish coloring and included dendrites (p. 131 no. 2).

Pseudo-agate: interior similar to agate with layering and geode opening, although outside not nodule-like, but geometric shape (p. 137 no. 2). As they are not symmetrical, these forms are not crystals and not derived from such. It is not known how these were formed. Found in Brazil. Length of individual piece can measure up to 28in/75cm. Deposits discovered only recently. Also called polyhedric quartz.

Tubular agate: full of feeding canals (3).

Sard stone: agate with parallel layers (1).

Brecciated agate: broken agate pieces held together with quartz (p. 137 no. 3).

Deposits: The most important agate deposits at the beginning of the 19th century were in the neighborhood of Idar-Oberstein, Germany. Today these have been worked out. Rarely larger than the human head, they have beautiful colors such as gray, red, pink, yellow, brown and pale blue. These could not be dyed.

Today's most important deposits, discovered in 1827 by emigrants from Idar-Oberstein, are in the south of Brazil and the north of Uruguay. The deposits are layered in weathered materials and river sediments and are derived from melaphyric rocks. They are found together with amethyst, chalcedony, citrine and cornelian. Nodules of several hundredweights are found. The color is generally gray; the striations are hardly recognizable. They can be given an attractive appearance by dyeing (p. 136). Brazilian agates are in great demand as layer stones for engraving. There are further deposits in China, India, Malagasy Republic, Mexico and various states of the U.S. In Oregon are found the so-called "thunder eggs", layered with a grooved surface, sometimes with star-shaped interiors. See also p. 136.

---

1 Cross section of agate nodule with even layers. $\frac{1}{3}$ natural size. Found in Brazil
2 Cross section of agate nodule (with bastion-like edges). $\frac{1}{3}$ natural size. Found in Brazil
3 Cross section of canal agate nodule. $\frac{1}{2}$ natural size. Found in Idar-Oberstein

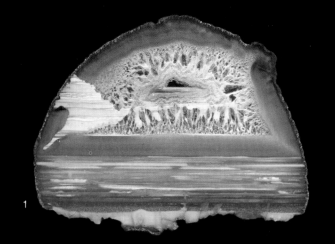

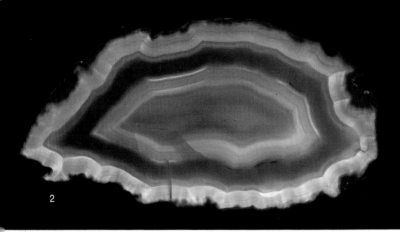

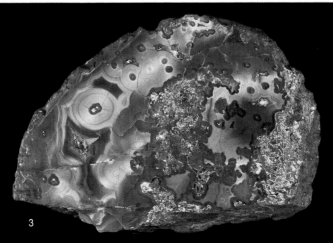

Coloring: The South American deposits produce agates which normally appear gray and without markings. Only when dyed do they obtain their coloring and lively structure. The art of dyeing was known to the Romans. In Idar-Oberstein, Germany, it has been practiced since the 1820s and has been brought to a perfection not achieved anywhere else. This is the reason why this town has developed into the most important center for the cutting of agate and other stones. The absorption of the dye varies with the porosity and water content of the individual layer of the agate. White layers, consisting of dense quartz aggregates, absorb little or no color. Layers which are easily dyed are called soft, the others hard.

Details of the process are a commercial secret. Generally inorganic pigments are used, as the organic ones tend to fade in light and are less intense. Before the process, the agates are cleaned in warm acid or lye, cut into the final shape and sometimes even polished.

Coloring red: imitation of cornelian or sard (1b). The pigment used is iron oxide. The agate is laid into a solution of iron nitrate, then heated. By altering techniques, various reds can be obtained. The yellow layer turns red by heating alone.

Coloring yellow: the pigment is iron oxide. The agate is saturated with hydrochloric acid, then slightly warmed, producing a lemon yellow color.

Coloring black: imitation of onyx (1c). Pigment is carbon. Use of concentrated sugar solution, following treatment with heated sulphuric acid, produces a dark black color in agate. By certain variations, browns can be produced. Recently cobalt nitrate has also been used.

Coloring brown: imitation of sard (1b). By treatment with sugar solution and heating, or by use of cobalt nitrate (see Black), browns are produced in agate.

Coloring green: imitation of chrysoprase (1d). Pigment is bi-valent iron. Saturation with chromium salt solution and subsequent heat treatment produces green. The same result can be obtained by the use of nickel nitrate solution and heat.

Coloring blue: imitation of chalcedony (1e). Pigment is bi-valent iron. Agates are first placed in a solution of potassium ferro-cyanide and subsequently boiled in hydrous iron sulphate.

See also p. 138.

---

1 Agate plate, a—natural, b–e—colored, $\frac{1}{3}$ natural size, Brazil
2 Pseudo-agate, $\frac{1}{2}$ natural size, Brazil
3 Brecciated agate, partly polished, $\frac{1}{2}$ natural size, U.S.

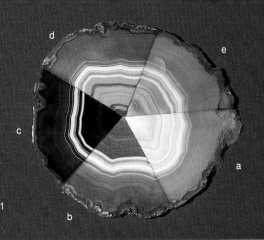

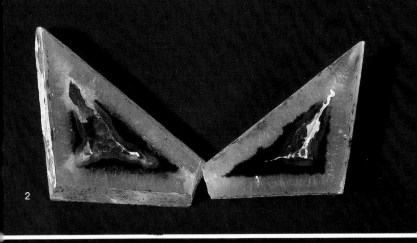

Old agate mill with waterwheel, Idar-Oberstein

Agate Continued from p. 136

The development of the agate industry in Idar-Oberstein. Agate has a special position amongst stones; there is a unique industry centered around it in Idar-Oberstein, Germany. The bases for this development were deposits of agate and jasper, good local sandstone for the production of cutting and polishing wheels, and water power to work the wheels.

Gemstones have been worked in and near Idar-Oberstein since the first part of the 16th century. Agate polishing was first mentioned in documents in 1548, but it is known that, 100 years before that, agate, jasper and quartz were locally mined, but possibly worked somewhere else.

Toward the end of the 17th century, there were about 15 workshops; and around 1800, 30 workshops cutting agate and using the river for energy. Toward the beginning of the 19th century, local agate deposits were beginning to be worked out and many experts left the area. However new life was brought to the industry when, by chance, some emigrants who were wandering around as musicians, discovered large deposits in Brazil.

By 1834 the first supply of Brazilian agate had reached Idar-Oberstein and by 1867 there were 153 polishing shops. With the emergence of steam power and especially since the advent of electric energy, the industry has been decentralized. Today there are numerous workshops in the district.

See also p. 140.

1 Bowl of Brazilian agate, diameter 4.2in/11.2cm, height 2.6in/6.8cm
2 Bowl of Brazilian agate, diameter 5¼in/14cm, height 1½in/4cm

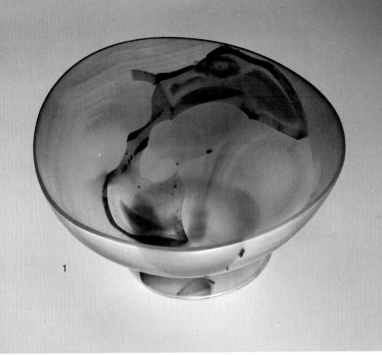

Agate polishers of the last century at work.

Agate Continued from p. 138

The History of Agate Polishing: The oldest way to polish agate was to rub it against a horizontal sandstone. Polishing against a vertically rotating sandstone probably became common during the 14th century. A waterwheel outside the house was turned by a river or dammed pond to drive the axle inside the house. Several sandstone grinding wheels were mounted vertically on to this axle. These wheels were about 56in/150cm high and 15–19in/40–50cm wide. The polishers lay on their stomachs on special chairs and pushed the agate hard against the rotating wheels, which were sprinkled with water constantly. Because the sandstone wheel had an obtuse angle in the middle of its working surface, two workers could share one wheel.

With the increasing use of steam and, later, electricity and also the new method of polishing using carborundum, a sitting posture was adopted. See further, modern polishing, page 55.

Uses: At least 3000 years ago, the Egyptians used agate for cylinder seals, ring stones, cameos and vessels. As a talisman, it was supposed to protect the wearer from storm and lightning, to quench his thirst and to bestow the power of oratory. Today it is used for objets d'art, rings, brooches, pendants and as layer stones for cameos (p. 142). It is also used by industry because of its toughness and resistance to chemicals.

1 Agate, decorative egg	7 Agate, handle for a letter opener
2 Agate, pendant	8 Agate, brooch
3 Agate, ring	9 Agate, seal
4 Agate, mortar	10 Agate, pill box
5 Agate, handles for knives and forks	11 Agate, dentist's instrument
6 Agate, handles for a manicure set	12 Agate, letter opener

LAYER STONES

Layer stones are multi-layered materials used in the art of gem carving and engraving, also called glyptography. Usually this material is cut from agates with even parallel layers, a lighter layer above a darker one. Brazil supplies the best raw material, usually two-layered, but sometimes three-layered ones are seen. Some masterpieces are cut out of five-layered material. Engravings in multi-layered and curved agates are rare.

The combination of a black base and a white upper layer is called Onyx (Greek – fingernail, because of its translucence). In the case of Sard-onyx, the base is brown; Cornelian-onyx has a red base. Onyx is the name also given to uni-colored chalcedony (for example, black onyx). This must not be confused with onyx marble, which is not true onyx though it is called so (p. 210).

The bluish-gray tint is produced by the use of the thin white upper layer, i.e. by distribution of the light and translucency of the black background. Such layer stones are sometimes called "niccolo". These stones are in demand for seal rings and for engravings of coats-of-arms and initials (p. 145 nos. 6, 8). Engravings which have a negative picture, as used for a seal, are called "intaglios"; those with solid, raised images are called "cameos".

Layers in agate, as required for this work, are not often found in nature in the colors of onyx, cornelian, or sard. Therefore such stones are mostly dyed, as described on p. 136. The dyed and natural stones have the same names.

Recently onyx layer stones have been produced from unlayered, uni-colored gray chalcedony. A square block is saturated with a solution of cobalt chlorate and chlorammonium, and is thus dyed black. With the help of hydrochloric acid, this color is then removed up to a depth of 0.04in/1mm. When the block is sawn in half, the sawn surfaces are black and the reverse sides are white; however it is said that the dark color tends to fade.

There are also doublets on the market with a white chalcedony plate glued on to a piece of black chalcedony.

Creation of a Cameo

1 A layer stone with different colors in even parallel layers is cut out of a block of agate, as seen in the background
2 Several two-layered stones can be cut out of the first piece
3 The lower layer is dyed black or red-brown. The upper layer remains white because it does not absorb the pigment
4 The main features of the cameo are indicated. In mass production, a template is used
5–8 These illustrate the art of the engraver: his experience, knowledge of the stone, and his technical perfection lend the personal touch
9 The final result is an example of the masterly precision of the engraver's art in colored onyx

---

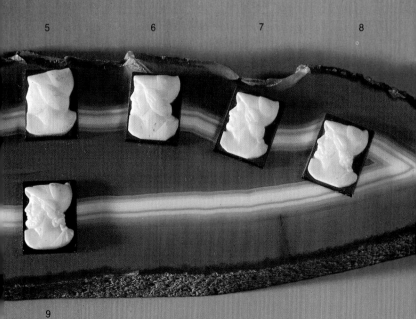

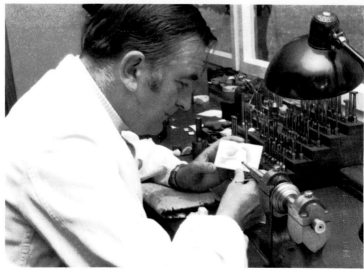

A gem engraver at work

The Technique of Stone Engraving

The main tool of the engraver is a small lathe with a horizontal spindle, to which various instruments can be attached. These can be wheels, spheres, cones or needles which are kept handy on a rack nearby. The spindle is driven by an electric motor at 3000–5000 r.p.m. The spindle is rigid and the engraver guides the stone by hand. This requires great precision and knowledge of the particular stone.

The rotating tips are prepared with diamond polishing powder and oil; by this means, they are cooled and given an abrasive surface because the tiny diamond particles are pressed into the softer iron during the engraving process.

The polishing is performed with wood, leather or another softer material using water and special polishing pastes. This process also removes any marks made by a metal pencil during preliminary sketching.

A flexible spindle can also be used. However this is usually only used for larger sculptures, where the stone is too heavy to be guided by hand.

See also Engraving on Stones, p. 54.

1

3

2

4

5

7

8

JASPER quartz group, sometimes called hornstone

Color: All colors, mostly striped or spotted	Chemical composition: SiO_2 silicon dioxide
Color of streak: White, yellow, brown, red	Transparency: Opaque
Mohs' hardness: $6\frac{1}{2}$–7	Refractive index: About 1.54
Specific gravity: 2.58–2.91	Double refraction: None
Cleavage: None	Dispersion: None
Fracture: Splintery	Pleochroism: None
Crystal system: Hexagonal (trigonal); microcrystalline, grainy aggregates	Absorption spectrum: Not usable
	Fluorescence: None

Jasper is usually considered as chalcedony (p. 126). Some scientists, however, put it in a group by itself within the quartz group. The name is derived from the Greek and means "spotted stone" because the name then referred to its green transparent qualities. Sometimes it is called hornstone, but usually this only refers to the gray variety. The finely grained, dense jasper contains up to 20% foreign materials which determine the color, streak and appearance. Uniformly colored jasper is rare; usually it is multi-colored, striped or spotted. According to foreign materials included, the streak can be yellow, brown to red, otherwise it is white. Petrified material is often jasper (p. 148).

Occurs as fillings in fissures or in nodules. Deposits are found all over the world: in India (Dekkan), Russia (Ural), the U.S. (numerous states), France (Dauphine), West Germany (Baden) and East Germany (Saxony). In antiquity, it was used for cylinder seals and as amulets against sight disturbances and drought.

Today it is popular for ornamental objects, cabochons and for stone mosaics. Care must be taken during cutting and polishing: banded jasper tends to separate along the layers.

Varieties: According to appearance, occurrence or composition, there are many names used in the trade: agate jasper, Egyptian jasper, riband jasper (usable as layer stone for engraving), basanite (black, fine-grained jasper from North Carolina (U.S.) used by jewellers and goldsmiths for streak tests of precious metals), blood-jasper (misleading name for heliotrope, p. 128), scenic jasper (scenic image caused by inclusions), nunkirchner jasper (gray-brown, very fine-grained, named after occurrence in Hunsruck near Idar-Oberstein). This is colored with prussian blue and is then called "Swiss lapis" and used as a substitute for lapis lazuli (p. 172). Other names include plasma (dark green, uniformly finely grained), prase (green colored jasper or stone of the compact quartz group, p. 122) and silex (brown and red spots).

1 Jasper breccia, Australia	8 Yellow jasper, cabochon, Australia
2 Pop jasper, 2 stones, South Africa	9 Yellow jasper, Australia
3 Pop jasper, 2 stones, Australia	10 Multi-colored jasper, India
4 Moukaite, Australia	11 Striped jasper, South Africa
5 Multi-colored jasper, 2 stones, India	12 Multi-colored jasper, India
6 Multi-colored jasper, cabochon, Australia	13 Banded jasper, Australia
7 Zebra jasper, South Africa	14 Silex, Egypt
	15 Multi-colored jasper, India
	16 Multi-colored jasper, rough, India

FOSSILIZED WOOD quartz group, also called agatized wood, petrified wood

Color: Brown, gray, red	Chemical composition: SiO_2 silicon
Color of streak: White, partly colored	dioxide
Mohs' hardness: $6\frac{1}{2}$–7	Transparency: Opaque
Specific gravity: 2.60–2.65	Refractive index: About 1.54
Cleavage: None	Double refraction: Weak or none
Fracture: Uneven, splintery	Dispersion: None
Crystal system: Hexagonal (trigonal);	Pleochroism: None
microcrystalline aggregate, rarely	Absorption spectrum: Not usable
amorphous	Fluorescence: None

Fossilized wood is petrified wood with the mineral composition of jasper, chalcedony and, less frequently, opal; it consists of silicon dioxide only. The wood has not actually become stone as is usually understood by the layman. The organic wood is not changed into stone, only the shape and structural elements of the wood are preserved. The expert speaks of a pseudomorphosis of chalcedony (or jasper or opal) after wood.

Well preserved petrification occurs only where trees after their death are quickly covered with fine-grained sedimentary rock. Thus the outer structure of the wood is preserved in a negative form among the enclosing rock. It is not a change that takes place, but an exchange. Sometimes this process is so slow that the inner structure of the wood, the annual rings (5), the structure of the cells, even wormholes, are preserved. It can also happen that the appearance is totally changed by the crystallization process.

The colors are mostly dull gray or brown, sometimes also red, pink, light brown, yellow and even blue to violet. The colors become stronger with cutting and polishing.

The most important occurrence is the "petrified wood" near Holbrook in Arizona (U.S.). There are fossilized tree trunks of up to 213ft/65m long and 10ft/3m thick belonging to the araucaria variety of plants. The tree trunks were deposited there from various parts by water about 200 million years ago, and then covered by several hundred yards of sediment. In the course of time, part of the fossilized wood was exposed by weathering from the enclosing sandstone. Nowhere is the fossilized wood as splendidly colored as in Arizona. In order to preserve this unique natural beauty spot, the "Petrified Forest" was declared a national park in 1962.

There are smaller deposits of petrified wood on all the continents. Egypt supplies good quality (Dschel Moka Ham near Cairo), as does Argentina (Patagonia). In Nevada (Virgin Valley), the fossilized wood shows the beautiful iridescence of opal.

It is used mostly for ornamental objects and decorative pieces (table tops, ashtrays, bookends, paper weights), less frequently for jewelry purposes.

1 Fossilized wood, ashtray	4 Fossilized wood, partly polished
2 Fossilized wood, bottle cork holder	5 Fossilized wood, with year rings
3 Fossilized wood, five fern tree	6 Fossilized wood, two sections of
pieces	tree trunk

The illustrations are 50% smaller than the originals.

1 2 3 4 5 6

OPAL quartz group

The name is derived from an Indian word for "stone". It is divided into three groups: the opalescent precious opals, the yellow-red fire opals and the common opals. Their physical properties vary considerably.

Color: White, gray, blue, green, orange	Transparency: Transparent, opaque
Color of streak: White	Refractive index: 1.44–1.46
Mohs' hardness: $5\frac{1}{2}$–$6\frac{1}{2}$	Double refraction: None
Specific gravity: 1.98–2.20	Dispersion: None
Cleavage: None	Pleochroism: None
Fracture: Conchoidal, splintery, brittle	Absorption spectrum: Fire opal:
Crystal system: Amorphous; kidney	7000–6400, 5900–4000
or grape-shaped aggregates	Fluorescence: White: white, bluish,
Chemical composition: $SiO_2.nH_2O$	brownish, greenish
hydrous silicon dioxide	Black: usually none
	Fire: greenish to brown

PRECIOUS OPAL

The special characteristic of these gems is their opalescence, a rainbow-like iridescence which changes with the angle of observation. Until the 1960s, this was thought to be caused by the refraction of light from the thin surface layers. The real cause was discovered under the electron microscope using a magnification of 20,000: tiny spheres (0.001 of a millimeter in diameter) of the mineral cristobalite layered in siliceous jelly cause the reflection or interference appearances. Strictly speaking, precious opal is not really amorphous.

Opal always contains water; the content varies but it can be as much as 30%. It can happen that in the course of the time, the stone loses water, cracks and the opalescence diminishes. This can, at least temporarily, be restored by saturation with oil or water. The aging process is avoided and the opalescence increased when stored in moist absorbent cotton (cotton wool). Care must be taken during setting. A little heat can evaporate the water. Opal is also sensitive to pressure and knocks as well as being affected by acids and alkalies.

Two groups of precious opals can be distinguished: those with a white or light basic color, known as white or milky opals (11–16), and the rarer black opals (4, 5 and 7–10). Their basic color is dark gray, dark blue, dark green or gray black. Deep black is rare.

Opal matrix (formerly known as opaline) is a banded or leafed inclusion of precious opal in the matrix rock. Cut as gemstones because of the good contrast with associated materials (1, 2, 6). See p. 152.

1 White opal in matrix	9 Black opal doublet, 16.90ct
2 Black opal in matrix	10 Black opal, 2 doublets
3 Opalized snail	11 White opal, 4 cabochons
4 Black opal, diverse shapes	12 White opal, rough, partly polished
5 Black opal, 86ct	13 White opal, cabochon, 10.39ct
6 Opal matrix, pendant	14 White opal, cabochon, 33.75ct
7 Black opal, 2 triplets	15 White opal, 2 cabochons, 7.78ct
8 Black opal, 4 cabochons	16 White opal, 4 cabochons, 14.21ct

About 20% smaller than original. Stones not numbered belong to no. 4.

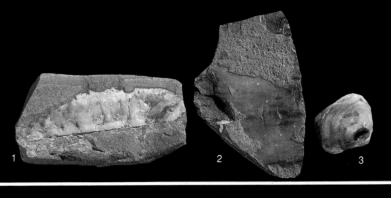

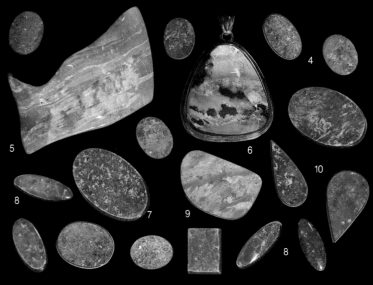

Precious Opal Continued from p. 150

Up to the turn of the century, the andesite lavas of Czechoslovakia supplied the best qualities. Then the Australian deposits were discovered. Famous deposits in New South Wales are at Lightning Ridge and White Cliffs; in South Australia at Coober Pedy and Andamooka; in Queensland at Bulla Creek and Burcoo River. Most of the 0.04–0.08in/1–2mm thin opal layers are bedded in sandstone. Further deposits are found in Brazil, Guatemala, Honduras, Japan and the U.S. (Nevada).

In Europe precious opal has been thought of as unlucky, but in the Orient it stands for loyalty and hope. The play of color is seen best if it is cut en cabochon. Very thin pieces of opal are sometimes mounted on a piece of common opal or onyx; this is the opal doublet. Triplets are also made with a protective top layer of rock crystal.

Fakes are prepared by coloring black or matrix opal in order to liven up the play of color; they are also made by impregnating porous opal with artificial resin. In 1970 white and black opal was synthesized in France.

FIRE OPAL (1–7)

Named after its orange color. It does not opalesce and is usually milky and turbid. The best qualities are clear and transparent (3, 4, 6). They are very sensitive to every stress. Important deposits are in Mexico (Hidalgo and Queretaro Provinces); also in Brazil, Guatemala, Honduras, U.S., Western Australia and Turkey (Simavopal). Glass imitations are found on the market.

Girasol: ("Sunflower") nearly colorless, transparent variety with slight bluish sheen and red play of color (opalescent p. 44). A name sometimes given to girasol or fire opal is sun opal.

Mexican Water Opal: variety from Mexico, colorless or slightly brown, transparent with unicolored schiller.

COMMON OPAL (8–14)

Mostly opaque, without play of color, it is quite common. Many names are used for it in trade such as: agate opal (agate with amorphous opal layers p. 132), hyalite (colorless, transparent), wood opal (agatized wood), honey opal (yellow, no. 8), milk opal (translucent, whitish, pearly luster; an opaque variety is called porcelain opal, if dendrites are included moss opal, no. 11), mother-of-pearl opal or cacholong (opaque to translucent, white or yellowish with mother-of-pearl luster), prase opal formerly called chrysopal (opaque, apple green, no. 10), wax opal (yellow brown with waxy luster, no. 12), and hydrophane (precious opal, turbid by loss of water, can temporarily become transparent and opalescent by absorption of water).

1 Fire opal, rough, Mexico	8 Honey opal, Western Australia
2 Fire opal, 5 cabochons, 11.80ct	9 Common opal, 3 stones, Mexico
3 Fire opal, 9 faceted stones, 11.95ct	10 Prase opal, Nevada
4 Fire opal, 4 faceted stones, 13.61ct	11 Moss opal, India
5 Fire opal, rough, Mexico	12 Wax opal, rough, Hungary
6 Fire opal, 3 faceted stones, 5.89ct	13 Dendrite opal, rough
7 Fire opal, cabochon and oval, 24.53ct	14 Liver opal or menilite, rough, Hungary

The illustrations are 20% smaller than the originals.

JADE

The name goes back to the time of the Spanish conquest of Central and South America and means *piedra de ijada*, i.e. hip stone, as it was seen as a protection against and cure for kidney diseases. This word was spread via Europe across the world. The corresponding Chinese word *yu* has not been generally accepted. In 1863 a Frenchman proved that two minerals were considered to be the same tough stone, a gemstone which had been known for 7,000 years. He named one jadeite and the other nephrite. In the trade, numerous green opaque stones have been falsely offered under the name "jade". Differentiation between jadeite and nephrite is very difficult, and this may be the reason why the word jade is used as a description of both.

In pre-historic times, jade was used in all parts of the world for arms and instruments because of its exceptional toughness. Therefore nephrite is sometimes called "axe stone". For over 2,000 years, jade was part of the religious cult in China and mystic figures and other symbols were carved from it. In pre-Columbian Central America, jade was more highly valued than gold. With the Spanish conquest, the high art of jade carving in America came to a sudden end. In China, however, this art was never interrupted. In former times only nephrite was worked in China, but for the last 150 years jadeite imported from Burma has also been used.

JADEITE (9–13) Augite group (pyroxene group)

Color: Brown, blackish, violet, green, also white, reddish, yellow
Color of streak: White
Mohs' hardness: $6\frac{1}{2}$–7
Specific gravity: 3.30–3.36
Cleavage: Imperfect
Fracture: Splintery, brittle
Crystal system: Monoclinic; inter-grown, grainy and fine fibrous aggregate
Chemical composition: $NaAl (Si_2O_6)$ sodium aluminium silicate

Transparency: Opaque, translucent
Refractive index: 1.654–1.667
Double refraction: $+0.013$, often none
Dispersion: None
Pleochroism: None
Absorption spectrum: Green: 6915, 6550, 6300, (4950), 4500, 4375, 4330
Fluorescence: Green: Very weak; gray blue

The name derives from jade. Because of its fibrous, felt-like structure, it is very tough and resistant. It occurs in all colors. Fractures are dull and when polished, greasy, sometimes even pearly in luster. Most valuable is the imperial jade, an emerald green translucent jadeite from Burma, with chrome as pigment. See also p. 156.

---

1 Nephrite, rough, partly polished
2 Nephrite, 2 stones, table cut
3 Nephrite, 6 cabochons
4 Nephrite, 2 navettes, together 7.68ct
5 Nephrite, 3 cabochons
6 Nephrite, cabochon
7 Nephrite, cabochon, Wyoming (U.S.)
8 Nephrite, octagon, cabochon

9 Jadeite, rough
10 Jadeite, flat table
11 Jadeite, 4 qualities
12 Jadeite, 2 drops
13 Jadeite, 3 different cuts
14 Nephrite, cat's eye
15 Chloromelanite, antique cut, 14.32ct
16 Chloromelanite, 4 different cuts

All illustrations are 20% smaller than the original

The most important jadeite deposits are in upper Burma, near Tawmav, interlayered in serpentinite, or in secondary deposits in conglomerates or in river gravels. The material found here is exported to China. Other deposits are in China, Guatemala, Japan, Mexico and the U.S. (California).

Chloromelanite (p. 155 nos 15, 16): green-black speckled variety of jadeite.

Jade-albite: composite of albite feldspar and jadeite from upper Burma, strong green with black spots.

NEPHRITE (p. 155 nos 1–8, 14) Actinolite group (Amphibole group)

Color: Green, also white, gray, yellowish, reddish, brown, often spotted	Chem. comp.: $Ca_2(Mg,Fe)_5 (Si_4O_{11})_2$ $(OH)_2$ calcium mag. iron silicate
Color of streak: White	Transparency: Opaque
Mohs' hardness: $6–6\frac{1}{2}$	Refractive index: 1.600–1.627
Specific gravity: 2.90–3.02	Double refraction: −0.027, often none
Cleavage: Lengthwise; perfect	Dispersion: None
Fracture: Splintery, sharp edged, brittle	Pleochroism: Weak; yellow to brown, green
Crystal system: Monoclinic; intergrown fine fibrous aggregate	Absorption spectrum: (6890), 5090, 4900, 4600
	Fluorescence: None

Nephrite (Greek – kidney) is even tougher than jade. Occurs in all colors, also striped and spotted. The most valuable color is green.

Nephrite is more common than jadeite. It is found in the west of Sinkiang (China), near Kashgar and Khutan in serpentinite and in river pebbles. On the west end of Baikal Lake, there is a spinach green variety (Russian jade). The large deposits on the south island of New Zealand are not very important on the world market, because exports of raw material have been prohibited. Further deposits are in Australia (Tasmania), Burma, Brazil, Canada (British Columbia), Mexico, New Guinea, Taiwan and in Poland.

Jadeite and nephrite are used for jewelry in ornamental and religious objects. It used to be cut with quartz sand; today carborundum or diamond powder is used. The main cutting centers are Canton, Peking and Hong Kong. There are many imitations on the market; also triplets of jade topped with a dull jade cabochon on top of which translucent jade is fixed. Green glue helps it to appear like imperial jade. It is also dyed to improve the color. For magnetite-jade, see p. 206. Can be confused with agalmatolite (p. 214), amazonite (p. 164), aventurine (p. 122), bowenite (p. 202), californite (p. 186), chrysoprase (p. 128), Connemara marble (p. 202), grossular (p. 106), plasma (p. 146), prase (p. 122), prehnite (p. 188), serpentine (p. 202), smithsonite (p. 198), verd-antique (p. 202) and williamsite (p. 202).

---

1 Jade, elephant, China	6 Jade, horse, China
2 Jade, necklace, China	7 Jade, 3 symbolic figures
3 Jade, cigarette holder	8 Jade, necklace, multi-colored
4 Jade, necklace, Burma	9 Jade, pendant
5 Jade, buddha, China	10 Chloromelanite, pendant

The illustrations are 20% smaller than the originals.

PERIDOT also called olivine, chrysolite

Color: Yellow-green, olive green, brownish
Color of streak: White
Mohs' hardness: $6\frac{1}{2}$–7
Specific gravity: 3.27–3.37
Cleavage: Imperfect
Fracture: Brittle, small conchoidal
Crystal system: Orthorhombic; short, compact prisms, vertically striated
Chemical composition: $(Mg, Fe)_2$ SiO_4 magnesium iron silicate

Transparency: Transparent
Refractive index: 1.654–1.690
Double refraction: +0.036
Dispersion: 0.020
Pleochroism: Very weak; colorless to pale green, lively green, olive green
Absorption spectrum: (6530), (5530), 5290, 4970, 4950, 4930, 4730, 4530
Fluorescence: None

The name derives from the Greek, but the meaning is uncertain. Perhaps it refers to the numerous crystal planes of the crystal. The name "chrysolite" (Greek – gold stone) was formerly applied not only to peridot but also to many similarly colored stones. The name commonly used in mineralogy is olivine (because of its olive green color).

It has a vitreous and greasy luster, and is not resistant to sulphuric acid. It tends to burst under great stress, therefore is sometimes metal-foiled. Dark stones can be lightened by burning. Rarities are peridot cat's eye and star peridot.

The most important deposits are in the Red Sea on the volcanic island of St. John, 188 miles/300km east of Asswan; they have been mined for 3500 years. Beautiful crystals can be found on the walls of cavities of weathering peridot rock. Good material can also be obtained from serpentine. There are also quarries in upper Burma (19 miles/30km northeast of Mogok). Less important finds have been in Australia (Queensland), Brazil (Minas Gerais), South Africa (together with diamond), the U.S. (Arizona, Hawaii, New Mexico) and Zaire. In Europe peridot is found in Norway, north of the Nord Fjord.

Peridot was brought to Europe by the crusaders in the Middle Ages and was often used for ecclesiastical purposes. It was very popular during the baroque period. It is not greatly desired by the trade because of its lower hardness. Used in table and emerald cuts, sometimes as brilliant. Usually set in gold.

The largest cut peridot weighs 310ct and was found on the island of St. John. It is at present in the Smithsonian Institution in Washington, D.C. In Russia there are some cut peridots which came out of a meteorite which fell in 1749 in east Siberia.

Can be confused with beryl (p. 96), chrysoberyl (p. 98), demantoid (p. 106), diopside (p. 190), moldavite (p. 212), prasiolite (p. 120), prehnite (p. 188), sinhalite (p. 186), emerald (p. 90), synthetic spinel (p. 66), tourmaline (p. 110) and idocrase (p. 186). The strong double refraction is an important distinguishing mark. In thick stones the doubling of the edges can be seen with the naked eye.

---

1 Peridot, 2 octagons, each 4.65ct
2 Peridot, 2 ovals, 5.67 and 6.38ct
3 Peridot, octagon, 4.14ct
4 Peridot, oval, 12.45ct
5 Peridot, 4 different cuts
6 Peridot, antique cut, 24.02ct
7 Peridot, 5 faceted stones
8 Peridot, 4 faceted stones
9 Peridot, 5 cabochons
10 Peridot, crystals, partly tumbled

The illustrations are 20% larger than the originals.

ZOISITE (12–14)

The mineral zoisite (named after the collector Zois) was first found in the Sau-Alp mountains of Austria in 1805. It was originally called saualpite, and has only recently been considered a gemstone.

In 1954 a green stone with black hornblende inclusions and large, mostly opaque, rubies was found in Tanzania. Because of its color contrast, this was a very effective gem and ornamental stone. In the native language it is called Masai anyolite (green). Scientifically it is zoisite or zoisite-amphibolite. Since 1967, sapphire-colored tanzanite has been found, and more recently other colored and colorless zoisites of gem quality. A dense reddish variety is called thulite (see below).

TANZANITE (1–11)

Color: Sapphire blue, amethyst, violet	Transparency: Transparent
Color of streak: White	Refractive index: 1.691–1.700
Mohs' hardness: $6\frac{1}{2}$–7	Double refraction: +0.009
Specific gravity: 3.35	Dispersion: 0.030
Cleavage: Perfect	Pleochroism: Very strong; violet blue, brown
Fracture: Uneven, brittle	
Crystal system: Orthorhombic; multi-faced prisms, mostly striated	Absorption spectrum: 7100, 6910, 5950, 5280, 4550
Chemical composition: Ca_2Al_3 $(O/OH/SiO_4/Si_2O_7)$ calcium aluminium silicate	Fluorescence: None

The name tanzanite (after the East African state of Tanzania) was introduced by the New York jewellers Tiffany & Co. It is accepted by the trade, although scientists do not encourage a multitude of names for gemstones and refer to it as blue zoisite. In good quality the color is ultramarine to sapphire blue; in artificial light, more amethyst violet. When heated to 752–932°F/400–500°C, the yellow and brown tints vanish, and the blue deepens. Tanzanite cat's eyes are also found. Some deposits in Tanzania near Arusha occur in veins or filling of fissures of gneisses.

There are glass imitations on the market; also doublets of glass with a tanzanite crown, or of two colorless synthetic spinels glued together with tanzanite-colored glue. Can be confused with sapphire (p. 86) and synthetic blue-violet corundum (p. 66).

THULITE (15, 16)

Dense red variety of zoisite. First found in Norway (near a place named Thule). Lately also found in Western Australia and South Africa. Used as cabochon and as an ornamental stone. Can be confused with rhodonite (p. 168).

1 Tanzanite, crystal	9 Tanzanite, cabochon, 8.5ct
2 Tanzanite in host rock	10 Tanzanite, five faceted stones
3 Tanzanite, 3 broken crystals	11 Tanzanite, 5 cabochons
4 Tanzanite, pear-shaped, 5.2ct	12 Zoisite-amphibolite with ruby
5 Tanzanite, antique cut, 24.4ct	13 Zoisite, 2 cabochons
6 Tanzanite, oval, 3.5ct	14 Zoisite-amphibolite with ruby
7 Tanzanite, brilliant cut, 6.8ct	15 Thulite, 2 pieces, rough
8 Tanzanite, oval, 3.1ct	16 Thulite, cabochon

HEMATITE (1–4) or bloodstone, specularite

Color: Black, black-gray, brown-red	Transparency: Opaque
Color of streak: Blood-red	Refractive index: 2.94–3.22
Mohs' hardness: $5\frac{1}{2}$–$6\frac{1}{2}$	Double refraction: -0.28
Specific gravity: 4.95–5.16	Dispersion: None
Cleavage: None	Pleochroism: None
Fracture: Conchoidal, uneven, fibrous	Absorption spectrum: (7000), (6400),
Crystal system: Hexagonal (trigonal);	(5950), (5700), (4800), (4500),
platy crystals	(4250), (4000)
Chemical composition: Fe_2O_3 iron	Fluorescence: None
oxide	

The name (Greek – blood) derives from the fact that, when cut, the coolant is colored red. Shiny hematite crystals are sometimes called specularite (Latin – mirror) as they were used as a mirror in ancient times.

When cut into thin plates, hematite is red and transparent; when polished, it is very shiny. Cuttable material comes from Cumberland (England), Saalfeld (Germany) and the island of Elba, as well as from Norway, Sweden, Spain, Brazil, New Zealand and the U.S. In antiquity, it was used as an amulet against bleeding. Formerly used as mourning jewelry, but today is mainly used for ring stones, bead-necklaces and intaglios (engravings). Can be confused with cassiterite (p. 184). Has been imitated by pressing and sintering hematite splinters.

PYRITE (5–10)

Color: Brass yellow, gray-yellow	Transparency: Opaque
Color of streak: Green-black	Refractive index: Over 1.81
Mohs' hardness: 6–$6\frac{1}{2}$	Double refraction: None
Specific gravity: 5.0–5.2	Dispersion: None
Cleavage: None	Pleochroism: None
Fracture: Conchoidal, uneven, brittle	Absorption spectrum: Not usable
Crystal system: Isometric; cubes,	Fluorescence: None
pentagonal dodecahedra, octahedra	
Chemical composition: FeS_2 iron	
sulphide or iron disulphide	

Pyrite (Greek – fire, as it produces sparks when knocked) is wrongly called marcasite in the trade. True marcasite is a mineral, in many ways similar to pyrite, but unsuitable for jewelry as it easily powders in air. Because of its similarity to gold, pyrite is often called fool's gold. Often found in well-formed crystals with a metallic luster. Found all over the world. There are important deposits in Elba and Italy. The Incas used pyrites as mirrors. Today they are cut as small roses or as small edging stones. Can be confused with gold (p. 208) and chalcopyrite (p. 206).

1 Hematite, radial aggregate	6 Pyrite cube, partly twinned
2 Hematite, 2 broken crystals	7 Pyrite crystals in matrix rock
3 Hematite, 5 cut stones	8 Pyrite, 4 different crystals
4 Hematite, table cut, truncated	9 Pyrite aggregate as brooch
corners	10 Pyrite octahedron crystal
5 Pyrite aggregate covered with	
crystals	

FELDSPAR

There are two main groups: potassium feldspar as orthoclase (varieties – adularia with moonstones, sanidine p. 204) and microcline (variety – amazonite); and calcium sodium feldspars (called plagioclase) with albite (variety – peristerite p. 204), oligoclase (variety – aventurine feldspar p. 166), andesine, labradorite (p. 166), bytownite (p. 204) and anorthite.

AMAZONITE (1–3) Feldspar group, also called amazon stone

Color: Green, blue-green	Transparency: Opaque
Color of streak: White	Refractive index: 1.522–1.530
Mohs' hardness: 6–6½	Double refraction: —0.008
Specific gravity: 2.56–2.58	Dispersion: 0.012
Cleavage: Perfect	Pleochroism: None
Fracture: Uneven	Absorption spectrum: Not usable
Crystal system: Triclinic; prismatic	Fluorescence: Weak; olive green
Chemical composition: K(AlSi$_3$O$_8$)	
potassium aluminium silicate	

The name derives from the Amazon. It is very sensitive to pressure. There are important deposits in Colorado, U.S.; also in Brazil, India, Malagasy Republic, Namibia and Russia. Usually cut flat or en cabochon, it is used for bead necklaces and ornamental objects. Can be confused with jade (p. 156) and turquoise (p. 170).

MOONSTONE (7–10) Feldspar group

Color: Colorless, yellow, pale sheen	Transparency: Turbid, transparent
Color of streak: White	Refractive index: 1.520–1.525
Mohs' hardness: 6–6½	Double refraction: —0.005
Specific gravity: 2.56–2.62	Dispersion: 0.012
Cleavage: Perfect	Pleochroism: None
Fracture: Uneven, conchoidal	Absorption spectrum: Not usable
Crystal system: Monoclinic; prismatic	Fluorescence: Weak; bluish, orange
Chemical composition: K(AlSi$_3$O$_8$)	
potassium aluminium silicate	

Named after its blue-white sheen which is caused by lamellar structure, this can also produce moonstone cat's eye. It is sensitive to pressure. There are important deposits in Sri Lanka, also in Australia, Burma, Brazil, India, Malagasy Republic, Tanzania and the U.S. Cut en cabochon. Can be confused with heat-treated amethyst (p. 118), chalcedony (p. 126), synthetic spinel (p. 66) and glass imitations. Also albite-moonstone, microcline-moonstone, labradorite-moonstone are well known.

ORTHOCLASE (4–6) Feldspar group

Champagne colored orthoclase variety is found in the Malagasy Republic and Upper Burma. Can be confused with several yellow stones.

1 Amazonite, broken crystal	6 Orthoclase, rough, Kenya
2 Amazonite, rough	7 Moonstone, rough, 2 pieces
3 Amazonite, 6 different cuts	8 Moonstone, 7 cabochons, India
4 Orthoclase, broken crystal	9 Moonstone, 2 cabochons, Sri Lanka
5 Orthoclase, 3 faceted stones	10 Moonstone, 3 cabochons, 13.23ct

The illustrations are 10% smaller than the originals.

LABRADORITE (1–4) Feldspar group

Color: Dark gray to gray-black with play of color
Color of streak: White
Mohs' hardness: 6–6½
Specific gravity: 2.69–2.70
Cleavage: Perfect
Fracture: Uneven, splintery
Crystal system: Triclinic; rare, platy prismatic, usually compact aggregates

Chemical composition: Na(AlSi$_3$O$_8$) Ca(Al$_2$Si$_2$O$_8$) sodium calcium aluminium silicate
Transparency: Opaque
Refractive index: 1.560–1.568
Double refraction: +0.008
Dispersion: None
Pleochroism: None
Absorption spectrum: Not usable
Fluorescence: Yellow striations

The name is derived from the Canadian peninsula of Labrador, where this stone was first found in 1770. It shows a play of color (labradorescence) in lustrous metallic tints, often blue and green, although specimens with the complete spectrum are most appreciated. It is probably caused by interferences of light on twinned lamellae. It is sensitive to pressure. There are deposits in Canada (Labrador, Newfoundland), also in the Malagasy Republic, Mexico, Russia and the U.S. At the beginning of the 1940s, labradorite deposits were discovered near Ylijärvi in Karelia (Finland) which exhibit the spectral color particularly well; they are offered in the trade as Spectrolite (2). Used for bead necklaces, brooches, rings and ornamental objects.

The Malagasy Republic produces a labradorite-moonstone with strong blue labradorescence. Lately also colorless and yellow-brown labradorites (3) have come from New South Wales (Australia). Suitable for faceting.

AVENTURINE FELDSPAR (5–8) also called sunstone, oligoclase

Color: Orange, red-brown, sparkling
Color of streak: White
Mohs' hardness: 6–6½
Specific gravity: 2.62–2.65
Cleavage: Perfect
Fracture: Grainy, splintery
Crystal system: Triclinic; very rare, usually compact aggregates
Chemical composition: Na(AlSi$_3$O$_8$) Ca(Al$_2$Si$_2$O$_8$) sodium calcium aluminium silicate

Transparency: Opaque
Refractive index: 1.532–1.542
Double refraction: +0.01
Dispersion: None
Pleochroism: Weak or none
Absorption spectrum: Not usable
Fluorescence: Dark brown-red

A type of glass, discovered by chance (Italian – *a ventura*), gave the name to the stone of similar appearance. It has a metallic glitter, which is red. Less often it is green or blue; and is caused by light interference on tiny hematite or goethite platelets. There are deposits in the U.S., India, Canada, South Norway and Russia. It is cut with flat surfaces or en cabochon. Can be confused with aventurine glass or aventurine quartz (p. 122).

1 Labradorite, rough, Canada
2 Spectrolite, rough, Finland
3 Labradorite, faceted, 4.08ct, U.S.
4 Labradorite, 13 cabochons

5 Aventurine feldspar, 2 rough pieces
6 Aventurine feldspar, 4 cabochons
7 Aventurine feldspar, faceted
8 Aventurine feldspar, cabochon

The illustrations are 10% smaller than the originals.

RHODOCHROSITE (1–5)

Color: Rose-red to white, striped
Color of streak: White
Mohs' hardness: 4
Specific gravity: 3.30–3.70
Cleavage: Perfect
Fracture: Uneven, conchoidal
Crystal system: Hexagonal (trigonal);
    rare, rhombohedra usually compact,
    longish aggregates
Chemical composition: $MnCO_3$

manganese carbonate
Transparency: Opaque to transparent
Refractive index: 1.600–1.820
Double refraction: −0.22
Dispersion: None
Pleochroism: None
Absorption spectrum: 5510, 4545,
    4100, 3910, 3830, 3780, 3630
Fluorescence: Weak; red

The name refers to the color (Greek – rose red). It has, on occasion, been called inca-rose because of the location of the main deposits. The aggregates are light-dark striped with the layers very notched. It has a vitreous luster; on cleavage faces, there is a pearly luster. Raspberry red is the most common color. The most important deposit is in Argentina, near San Luis, 144 miles/ 230km east of Mendoza. The rhodochrosite has formed as stalagmites in the silver mines of the Incas since they were abandoned in the 13th century. Further deposits are in Argentina and in the U.S. (Colorado).

Usually used in larger pieces, as then the marking is more distinct, for ornamental objects as well as for cabochons and bead necklaces. Can be confused with rhodonite (see below).

RHODONITE (6–12)

Color: Red, black inclusion
Color of streak: White
Mohs' hardness: $5\frac{1}{2}$–$6\frac{1}{2}$
Specific gravity: 3.40–3.70
Cleavage: Perfect
Fracture: Uneven, conchoidal
Crystal system: Triclinic; rarely in
    plates or long crystals, usually
    compact grainy aggregates
Chemical composition: $MnSiO_3$

manganese metasilicate
Transparency: Opaque-transparent
Refractive index: 1.733–1.744
Double refraction: +0.011
Dispersion: None
Pleochroism: Definite; yellow-red,
    rose-red, red-yellow
Absorption spectrum: 5480, 5030,
    4550, 4120, 4080
Fluorescence: None

The name comes from its color (Greek – rose). The black dendritic inclusions are of manganese oxide. When they are brownish or yellowish it is called fowlerite. Found once in the Urals, it now comes from Sweden (Wermland), Australia (transparent varieties), the U.S., the island of Vancouver in Canada; also from India, Malagasy Republic, Mexico and South Africa. It is cut with a table or en cabochon, for bead necklaces and ornamental objects. Can be confused with rhodochrosite (see above) and thulite (p. 160).

1 Rhodochrosite, baroque necklace
2 Rhodochrosite, 3 part polished pieces
3 Rhodochrosite, crystals
4 Rhodochrosite, 4 cabochons
5 Rhodochrosite, 3 cabochons
6 Rhodonite, high cabochon
7 Rhodonite, bead necklace
8 Rhodonite, flat cut
9 Rhodonite, unicolored cabochon
10 Rhodonite, 5 transparent stones
11 Rhodonite, rough, partly polished
12 Rhodonite, 5 cabochons
The illustrations are 40% smaller than the originals.

TURQUOISE sometimes called callais in U.S.

Color: Sky blue, blue-green, apple green
Color of streak: White, usually with brown or black spots
Mohs' hardness: 5–6
Specific gravity: 2.60–2.80
Cleavage: None
Fracture: Conchoidal, uneven
Crystal system: Triclinic; seldom small' usually grape- or kidney-shaped aggregate
Chem. comp.: $CuAl_6((OH)_2/PO_4)_4$.$4H_2O$; a copper containing basic aluminium phosphate
Transparency: Opaque
Refractive index: 1.61–1.65
Double refraction: +0.04
Dispersion: None
Pleochroism: Weak
Absorption spectrum: (4600), 4320, 4220
Fluorescence: Weak; green-yellow, light blue

The name means "Turkish stone" because the trade route that brought it to Europe used to come via Turkey. Up to 1911 when crystals were found in Virginia (U.S.), turquoise was thought to be amorphous. On fresh fractures it has a waxy or vitreous luster. The popular sky blue color changes at 482°F/250°C into a dull green (be careful when soldering). A negative change in color can also be brought about by the influence of light, perspiration, oils and cosmetics as well as loss of natural water content. Turquoise rings should be removed before hands are washed. Polishing makes the color more intense. The pores are closed by immersion in oil or paraffin or by using a plastic solution and so the stone hardens.

A pure, blue color is rare (9, 12), most pieces contain turquoise matrix, i.e. veins which may be brown (limonite), dark gray (sandstone) or black (jasper or psilomelane). It can also be intergrown with malachite (p. 176) and chrysocolla (p. 200).

Occurs in dense form, filling in fissures as grape-like masses and as nodules. Thickness of veins up to 0.8in/20mm. The best qualities are found in north east Iran (Persian turquoise) near Nischapur. Further deposits are in Afghanistan, eastern Australia, China (Tibet), Israel (north of Elat), Tanzania and in the southwest of the U.S.

The deposits in Sinai were already worked out by 4,000 BC. At that time the stone was used for jewelry, amulets and also in the preparation of cosmetics. In the early Victorian period, sky blue turquoise was most popular.

Because the stone is so porous, the color can be improved with aniline dyes and copper salts. It can be imitated with dyed chalcedony (p. 126) and dyed howlite (p. 208). Pulverized and broken turquoise pieces are reconstituted with paste as well as glass, ceramic and plastic. Synthetic imitations are offered as hamburger turquoise, neolite and neo-turquoise. Can be confused with amatrix (p. 196), amazonite (p. 164), chrysocolla (p. 200), hemimorphite (p. 198), lazulite (p. 192), odontolite (p. 218), serpentine (p. 202), smithsonite (p. 198) and variscite (p. 196).

---

1 Turquoise with matrix, 2 cabochons
2 Turquoise, Chinese figure
3 Turquoise, 3 cabochons, 25.89ct
4 Turquoise, rough
5 Turquoise, 9 cabochons, 26.10ct
6 Turquoise, 3 cabochons, octagon
7 Turquoise, bead necklace
8 Turquoise, 2 matrix cabochons
9 Turquoise, 7 cabochons, 14.30ct
10 Turquoise, baroque necklace
11 Turquoise, rough, partly polished
12 Turquoise, 2 cabochons, 38.53ct
13 Turquoise, 4 cabochons, 42.28ct
14 Turquoise, 3 cabochons

The illustrations are 40% smaller than the originals.

LAPIS LAZULI called lapis for short, sometimes lazurite

Color: Blue
Color of streak: Light blue
Mohs' hardness: 5–6
Specific gravity: 2.4–2.9
Cleavage: None
Fracture: Conchoidal, grainy
Crystal system: Isometric; crystals rare, mostly dense, grainy aggregate
Chemical composition: Na_8 $(Al_6Si_6O_{24})S_2$ sulphur containing sodium aluminium silicate

Transparency: Opaque
Refractive index: About 1.50
Double refraction: None
Dispersion: None
Pleochroism: None
Absorption spectrum: Not usable
Fluorescence: Strong; white

As lapis lazuli (arabic-latin – blue stone) is composed of several minerals – if only in small quantities (augite, calcite, diopside, mica, haüynite, hornblende, pyrite) – some experts consider it not to be a mineral, but a rock; the main ingredient being lazurite.

It is very sensitive to pressure and high temperatures, hot baths, acids, and alkalies. It has a vitreous to greasy luster. In the best quality the color is regularly distributed, but it is usually spotted or striped. In Chilean and Russian stones, the protruding white calcite diminishes the value. Well distributed fine pyrite is advantageous and is taken to show genuineness. Too much pyrite causes a dull, greenish tint.

Mineable deposits are rare. For centuries the most important deposit with the best qualities has been in the West Hindu Kush mountains of Afghanistan near the source of the river Amu-Darja. Lapis lazuli is mined under primitive conditions and in difficult terrain where it is present as an irregular occurrence in limestone. The Russian deposits are at the south west end of Baikal Lake. The matrix rock is white dolomitic marble. Chile supplies lower quality stones with many white spots of calcite. The deposits are north of Santiago in the Coquimbo Province.

Lapis was used for jewelry in antiquity. During the Middle Ages, it was also used as a pigment to produce aquamarine. Some castles have wallpanels and columns covered in lapis. Today it is used for ring stones and necklaces, Chilean lapis is used for carvings and ornamental objects.

The finely-grained, gray-brown jasper from Nunkirchen (p. 146) is colored with prussian blue and sold as an imitation under the name of "Swiss lapis." In 1954 a synthetic grainy spinel, colored with cobalt oxide, with a good lapis color made an appearance on the market. Inclusions of thin gold pieces simulated the pyrite and improved the character of the genuine stone.

Can be confused with azurite (p. 174), dumortierite (p. 182), lazulite (p. 192), sodalite (p. 174) and glass imitations.

---

1 Lapis lazuli, bowl, Chile
2 Lapis lazuli, rough, Afghanistan
3 Lapis lazuli, broken crystal
4 Lapis lazuli, Afghanistan, partly polished
5 Lapis lazuli, Buddha, Afghanistan
6 Lapis lazuli, bead necklace, Afghanistan
7 Lapis lazuli, cabochon, Afghanistan
8 Lapis lazuli, 3 cabochons, Afghanistan
9 Lapis lazuli ring stone, Russia
10 Lapis lazuli, 7 different cuts
11 Lapis lazuli, table cut, Chile
12 Lapis lazuli, rough, Russia
13 Lapis lazuli, rough, Afghanistan
14 Lapis lazuli, rough, Chile

The illustrations are 40% smaller than the originals.

SODALITE (1–4)

Color: Blue, gray	Transparency: Opaque, translucent
Color of streak: White	Refractive index: 1.48
Mohs' hardness: $5\frac{1}{2}$–6	Double refraction: None
Specific gravity: 2.13–2.29	Dispersion: None
Cleavage: Perfect	Pleochroism: None
Fracture: Uneven, conchoidal	Absorption spectrum: Not usable
Crystal system: Isometric; rhombic dodecahedra, grainy aggregates	Fluorescence: Strong; orange
Chemical composition: Na_8 $(Cl_2Al_6Si_6O_{24})$ chloric sodium aluminium silicate	

The name refers to the sodium content. All shades of blue are found partly interspersed with white calcite. It has a vitreous luster and on fractures, a greasy luster. The most important deposit is in Bahia, Brazil; there are others in Ontario (Canada), India, Namibia and the U.S. The dense aggregates are used for jewelry, cabochons, bead necklaces; but mainly for objets d'art. Can be confused with lapis lazuli (p. 172) especially as pyrite, a mark of genuineness in lapis, can also occur in sodalite. The safest method of differentiating is by the specific gravity. Can also be confused with azurite (see below), dumortierite (p. 182), haüynite (p. 204) and lazulite (p. 192).

AZURITE (5–8) sometimes called chessylite

Color: Dark blue	Transparency: Transparent to opaque
Color of streak: Sky blue	Refractive index: 1.730–1.838
Mohs' hardness: $3\frac{1}{2}$–4	Double refraction: +0.108
Specific gravity: 3.7–3.9	Dispersion: None
Cleavage: Perfect	Pleochroism: Definite; light blue, dark blue
Fracture: Conchoidal, uneven, brittle	Absorption spectrum: 5000
Crystal system: Monoclinic; short crystals, dense, earthy aggregates	Fluorescence: None
Chemical composition: $Cu_3((OH)_2/(CO_3)_2)$ basic copper carbonate	

Named after its azure-blue color. It has a vitreous luster. Occurs together with malachite in or near copper deposits, but also separately as spherical aggregates in Australia, Chile, Russia (Ural, Altai), the U.S. (Arizona, Pennsylvania) and in Chessy (hence chessylite) near Lyons, France. Formerly it was used for azure pigment. Because of its low hardness it is mainly used for ornamental objects. It is also cut by collectors en cabochon and even faceted. Can be confused with many blue stones, especially dumortierite (p. 182), haüynite (p. 204), lapis lazuli (p. 172), lazulite (p. 192) and sodalite (see above). Sometimes azurite and malachite (p. 176) have become intergrown to form a very effective azur-malachite (8 and p. 29).

---

1 Sodalite, rough, partly polished	5 Azurite, crystals
2 Sodalite, baroque necklace	6 Azurite, 5 differently cut stones
3 Sodalite, 4 flat cut pieces	7 Azurite, part of crystal
4 Sodalite, 2 cabochons	8 Azur-malachite, rough

The illustrations are 20% smaller than the originals.

MALACHITE

Color: Light green, emerald green, black-green
Color of streak: Light green
Mohs' hardness: $3\frac{1}{2}$–4
Specific gravity: 3.75–3.95
Cleavage: Perfect
Fracture: Splintery, scaly
Crystal system: Monoclinic; small, long prismatic crystals, aggregates with fine needles

Chemical composition: Cu_2 $((OH)_2CO_3)$ basic copper carbonate
Transparency: Opaque
Refractive index: 1.655–1.909
Double refraction: −0.254
Dispersion: None
Pleochroism: Very strong; colorless, green
Absorption spectrum: Not usable
Fluorescence: None

The name could be derived from its color (Greek *malache*=mallow), perhaps from its low hardness (Greek *malakos*, soft). When cut, it shows layers of lighter and darker concentric rings, parallel lines or other shapes caused by its shell-like formation. Large uni-colored pieces are rare. Sometimes intergrown with azurite which produces Azur-malachite (p. 175, no. 8 and p. 29) and with turquoise and chrysocolla to produce Eilat stone (p. 201, no. 8).

The malachite aggregates are formed from very small crystals. Larger crystals are very rare and in demand by collectors. There is a weak vitreous luster in rough pieces on fresh fractures; when polished the luster is silky. It is sensitive to heat and acids, ammonia and hot waters. Occurs in rounded nodules, grape shapes, stalactitic and, rarely, in encrusted slabs. Formed from copper-containing solutions in or near copper ore deposits. The most important deposit used to be in the Urals near Swerdlowsk (formerly Jekaterinenburg). From there the Russian Tsars obtained the malachite for decorating their castles, panelling the walls, and for beautiful inlaid works.

Today Zaire is the most important malachite producer as far as quality and quantity is concerned. Some of the stones are cut near the mine, some reach the world market as raw material. Further deposits are in Australia, Chile, Rhodesia (lighter quality), South Africa and the U.S. (Arizona).

Malachite was popular with the ancient Egyptians, Greeks and Romans for jewelry, amulets and as a powder for eye shadow. During the Middle Ages, it was thought to cure vomiting and to protect against witches and other dangers to small children. It is used as pigment for mountain green.

Although it is not very hard and not very resistant, malachite is popular for jewelry and ornaments. Used en cabochon and in slightly rounded table stones for necklaces and especially for objets d'art, such as plates, boxes, ashtrays and figures. The cutter must work the malachite so as to show the decorative marking to its best advantage. Concentric eye-like rings are most popular.

Not easily confused with other stones in larger pieces because of the striped character, but small unstriped stones can easily be confused with any opaque green stones.

1 Malachite, rough, partly polished
2 Malachite, bead necklace
3 Malachite, 2 cabochons
4 Malachite, cabochon, Rhodesia
5 Malachite, 7 various samples
6 Malachite, rough
The illustrations are 40% smaller than the originals.

GEMS FOR COLLECTORS

Mainly in demand by collectors, rarely worn in jewelry.

ANDALUSITE (2–3)

Color: Yellow, green, brown-red	Transparency: Transparent
Color of streak: White	Refractive index: 1.641–1.648
Mohs' hardness: $7\frac{1}{2}$	Double refraction: −0.007
Specific gravity: 3.12–3.18	Dispersion: 0.016
Cleavage: Imperfect	Pleochroism: Strong; yellow, olive,
Fracture: Uneven, brittle	red-brown to dark-red
Crystal system: Orthorhombic; thick, long crystals, elongated and grainy aggregates	Absorption spectrum: 5535, 5505, 5475, (5250), (5180), (5060), (4950), 4550, 4475, 4360
Chemical composition: Al(AlSiO$_5$) aluminium silicate	Fluorescence: Weak; green, yellow-green

Andalusite (after Andalusia in Spain) is of gemological interest because of its strong pleochroism. Large pieces of gem quality are rare. It has a vitreous luster. Occurs in schists, gneisses and in river gravel. Cuttable qualities come from Brazil and Sri Lanka, also from Canada (Quebec), Spain (Almeria/ Andalusia), Russia and the U.S. (Maine, Massachusetts). Confused with chrysoberyl (p. 98), smoky quartz (p. 116) and tourmaline (p. 110).

Chiastolite: variety of andalusite. Opaque, white, gray, yellowish: Mohs' hardness 5–5$\frac{1}{2}$. Occurs in long prisms which show a dark cross in cross-section, when viewed perpendicular to the prism axes, caused by carbonaceous inclusion. Deposits are found in southern Australia, Bolivia, Chile, France (Brittany), Spain (Galicia), Russia (Siberia) and the U.S. (California). Formerly worn as an amulet, it is now only of value to collectors. Cut en cabochon, flat or thin. Cannot be confused because of the typical markings. Sometimes called cross stone, but this usually refers to staurolite (p. 204).

EUCLASE (4–6)

Color: Colorless, sea green, light blue	Refractive index: 1.652–1.672
Color of streak: White	Double refraction: +0.020
Mohs' hardness: $7\frac{1}{2}$	Dispersion: 0.016
Specific gravity: 3.10	Pleochroism: Very weak; white-green, yellow-green, blue-green
Cleavage: Perfect	
Fracture: Conchoidal	Absorption spectrum: 7065, 7040, 6950, 6880, 6600, 6500, 6390, 4680, 4550
Crystal system: Monoclinic; prisms	
Chemical composition: BeAl(SiO$_4$)OH basic beryllium aluminium silicate	Fluorescence: None
Transparency: Transparent	

A very rare gem, which is difficult to cut because of its perfect cleavage (hence the name). It has a bright luster. Occurs in pegmatites, in secondary deposits and in geodes. There is an important deposit in the Ouri Preto district of Brazil, also in India, Rhodesia, Tanzania, Russia (Urals) and Zaire. Can be confused with aquamarine (p. 94), beryl (p. 96) and hiddenite (p. 114).

---

1 Chiastolite, 4 pieces, partly polished
2 Andalusite, 2 broken crystals
3 Andalusite, 4 faceted stones
4 Euclase, 2 colorless faceted stones
5 Euclase, light blue, faceted
6 Euclase, crystal in host rock

HAMBERGITE (1, 2)

Color: Colorless, very white	basic beryllium borate
Color of streak: White	Transparency: Transparent
Mohs' hardness: $7\frac{1}{2}$	Refractive index: 1.559–1.631
Specific gravity: 2.35	Double refraction: +0.072
Cleavage: Perfect	Dispersion: 0.015
Fracture: Brittle	Pleochroism: None
Crystal system: Orthorhombic; prisms	Absorption spectrum: Not usable
Chem. comp. $Be_2((OH, F) BO_3)$	Flourescence: None

Hambergite (after a Swedish mineralogist) is an extremely rare gemstone. Crystals are striated along the prisms. It has a vitreous luster and resembles glass when cut. Occurs in pegmatites and alluvial gem deposits. Found in India (Kashmir), the Malagasy Republic and Norway.

IOLITE (3–6) also called cordierite, dichroite and water sapphire

Color: Blue in various hues	Transparency: Transparent, translucent
Color of streak: White	Refractive index: 1.53–1.55
Mohs' hardness: $7–7\frac{1}{2}$	Double refraction: −0.008 to −0.012
Specific gravity: 2.58–2.66	Dispersion: 0.017
Cleavage: Imperfect	Pleochroism: Very strong; yellow,
Fracture: Conchoidal, uneven, brittle	dark blue-violet, pale blue
Crystal system: Orthorhombic; short	Absorption spectrum: 6450, 5930,
prisms	5850, 5350, <u>4920</u>, <u>4560</u>, 4360, 4260
Chem. comp. Mg_2Al_3 $(AlSi_5O_{18})$	Fluorescence: None
magnesium aluminium silicate	

The name comes from its violet color. The other names are derived from the French mineralogist, Cordier; from its multi-coloring (wrongly) dichroite; and from its similarity to sapphire. Greasy, vitreous luster; care must be taken when cutting because of the strong pleochroism. Stones must not be too thick. Main deposits are in Burma, Brazil, Sri Lanka, India and Malagasy Republic.

PHENACITE (7, 8)

Color: Colorless, wine-yellow, pink	beryllium silicate
Color of streak: White	Transparency: Transparent
Mohs' hardness: $7\frac{1}{2}$–8	Refractive index: 1.654–1.670
Specific gravity: 2.95–2.97	Double refraction: +0.016
Cleavage: Imperfect	Dispersion: 0.015
Fracture: Conchoidal	Pleochroism: Definite; colorless,
Crystal system: Hexagonal (trigonal);	orange-yellow
short prisms	Absorption spectrum: Not usable
Chemical composition: $Be_2(SiO_4)$	Fluorescence: None

Phenacite (Greek – deceiver) is rare. It has multiple faces on large crystals with vitreous luster. Found in Brazil (Minas Gerais), Sri Lanka, Mexico, Rhodesia, Namibia, Tanzania, Russia, the U.S. and Switzerland. Has been produced synthetically. Confused with rock crystal (p. 116) and topaz (p. 102).

---

1 Hambergite, 3 faceted stones	5 Iolite, 2 cut cubes
2 Hambergite, 2 broken crystals	6 Iolite, 3 ovals
3 Iolite, 6 faceted stones	7 Phenacite, rough 3 pieces
4 Iolite, 2 rough pieces	8 Phenacite, 2 faceted stones

DUMORTIERITE (1, 2)

Color: Dark blue, violet-blue, red-brown
Color of streak: Blue
Mohs' hardness: 7
Specific gravity: 3.26–3.41
Cleavage: Perfect
Fracture: Conchoidal
Crystal system: Orthorhombic; crystals rare, fibrous or radial aggregates

Chemical composition: $Al_7(O_3(BO_3)(SiO_4)_3)$ aluminium borate silicate
Transparency: Opaque
Refractive index: 1.686–1.723
Double refraction: —0.037
Dispersion: None
Pleochroism: Strong; black, red orange-brown
Absorption spectrum: Not usable
Fluorescence: Weak and variable

Named after a French palaeontologist, this mineral occurs in Brazil, Sri Lanka, Canada, Malagasy Republic, Namibia, the U.S., France and Poland. Confused with azurite (p. 174), lapis lazuli (p. 172) and sodalite (p. 174).
Dumortierite quartz is a compact quartz intergrown with dumortierite (1).

DANBURITE (3, 4)

Color: Colorless, wine-yellow, pink
Color of streak: White
Mohs' hardness: 7–7$\frac{1}{2}$
Specific gravity: 3.0
Cleavage: Imperfect
Fracture: Uneven, conchoidal
Crystal system: Orthorhombic; prismatic
Chemical composition: $Ca(B_2Si_2O_8)$ calcium boric silicate

Transparency: Transparent
Refractive index: 1.630–1.636
Double refraction: —0.006
Dispersion: 0.017
Pleochroism: Weak; light yellow
Absorption spectrum: 5900, 5860, 5845, 5840, 5830, 5820, 5805, 5780, 5760, 5730, 5710, 5680, 5665, 5645
Fluorescence: Sky blue

Named after the first find (Danbury, Conn., U.S.). It has a greasy to vitreous luster. There are deposits in upper Burma, Japan, Malagasy Republic, Mexico and the U.S. (Connecticut). Confused with citrine (p. 120) and topaz (p. 102).

AXINITE (5, 6)

Color: Brown, violet, blue
Color of streak: White
Mohs' hardness: 6$\frac{1}{2}$–7
Specific gravity: 3.27–3.29
Cleavage: Perfect
Fracture: Conchoidal, brittle
Crystal system: Triclinic; platy crystals
Chem. comp. $Ca_2(Fe, Mg, Mn)Al_2(BO_3/OH/Si_4O_{12})$ complicated borate silicate

Transparency: Translucent, transparent
Refractive index: 1.675–1.685
Double refraction: —0.010
Dispersion: None
Pleochroism: Strong; olive green, red-brown, yellow-brown
Absorption spectrum: 5320, 5120, 4920, 4660, 4400, 4150
Fluorescence: Usually none

Named after an axe because of its sharp edges. It has a strong vitreous luster, and is piezo-electric. Found in France (Dep. Isere), Mexico (Baja California) and the U.S. (California). Can be confused with smoky quartz (p. 116).

---

1 Dumortierite, quartz, California
2 Dumortierite, 2 cabochons
3 Danburite, 9 different cuts

4 Danburite, 3 broken crystals
5 Axinite, 5 different cuts
6 Axinite, rough

BENITOITE (1, 2)

Color: Light blue, dark blue
Color of streak: White
Mohs' hardness: 6–6½
Specific gravity: 3.65–3.68
Cleavage: None
Fracture: Conchoidal, brittle
Crystal system: Trigonal; bipyramidal
Chemical composition: $BaTi(Si_3O_9)$
  barium titanium silicate

Transparency: Transparent, translucent
Refractive index: 1.757–1.804
Double refraction: +0.047
Dispersion: 0.039 and 0.046
Pleochroism: Very strong; colorless,
  green to blue
Absorption spectrum: Not usable
Fluorescence: Strong; blue

Named after the only occurrence in San Benito county, California, U.S. Only very small crystals are found. Can be confused with sapphire (p. 86).

CASSITERITE (3–5)

Color: Various browns, colorless
Color of streak: White to light yellow
Mohs' hardness: 6–7
Specific gravity: 6.8–7.1
Cleavage: Imperfect
Fracture: Conchoidal, brittle
Crystal system: Tetragonal; short
  columnar crystals

Chem. comp. SnO_2 tin (IV) oxide
Transparency: Transparent, translucent
Refractive index: 1.997–2.093
Double refraction: +0.096
Dispersion: 0.071
Pleochroism: Definite
Absorption spectrum: Not usable
Fluorescence: None

Cassiterite (Greek – tin) has an adamantine luster. There are many deposits, but cuttable qualities are rare: Australia, Bolivia, Malaysia, Mexico, Namibia and England (Cornwall). Can be confused with colorless or yellow diamond (p. 70), hematite (p. 162), sphene (p. 194) and zircon (p. 108).

EPIDOTE (6–8) sometimes called pistacite

Color: Green, black-brown
Color of streak: Gray
Mohs' hardness: 6–7
Specific gravity: 3.4
Cleavage: Perfect
Fracture: Conchoidal, splintery
Crystal system: Monoclinic; prisms
Chemical composition: $Ca_2(Al,Fe)_3$
  $(Si_2O_7)(SiO_4)O(OH)$ calcium
  aluminium iron silicate

Transparency: Transparent, translucent
Refractive index: 1.733–1.768
Double refraction: +0.035
Dispersion: 0.030
Pleochroism: Strong; green, brown,
  yellow
Absorption spectrum: 4750, 4550,
  4350
Fluorescence: None

Named after the numerous crystal faces or its green color respectively. It has a bright vitreous luster. Found in cuttable qualities in Mexico, Mozambique, Norway, the U.S. (California) and Austria. Confused with idocrase (p. 186).
Clinozoisite: light green to green-brown variety with little iron content.
Piemontite: opaque, cherry-red. From Piemont in Italy, it contains manganese.

---

1 Benitoite, 2 crystal formations
2 Benitoite, 8 faceted stones
3 Cassiterite, crystals, Cornwall,
  England
4 Cassiterite, 3 stones from Malaysia

5 Cassiterite, crystal, Cornwall
6 Epidote, 3 faceted stones
7 Epidote, 2 broken crystals
8 Epidote, twinned aggregate

The illustrations are 30% larger than the originals.

IDOCRASE (1–4) also called vesuvianite

Color: Olive green, yellow-brown
Color of streak: White
Mohs' hardness: $6\frac{1}{2}$
Specific gravity: 3.32–3.42
Cleavage: Imperfect
Fracture: Uneven, splintery
Crystal system: Tetragonal; thick columnar crystals
Chem. comp.: $Ca_{10}(Mg,Fe)_2Al_4(OH)_4$ $/(SiO_4)_5/(Si_2O_7)_2$ complicated calcium aluminium silicate

Transparency: Transparent, translucent
Refractive index: 1.700–1.721
Double refraction: ±0.005
Dispersion: 0.019
Pleochroism: Weak; present color lighter and darker
Absorption spectrum: Green: 5300, 4870, 4610
Brown: 5910, 5880, 5845, 5820, 5775, 5745
Fluorescence: None

There are deposits in Canada, Russia, the U.S. and Italy. First found on Mount Vesuvius, hence other name. Confused with demantoid (p. 106), diopside (p. 190), epidote (p. 184), peridot (p. 158), smoky quartz (p. 116), tourmaline (p. 110) and zircon (p. 180).
Californite = green from California and Pakistan. **Cyprine:** blue from Norway. **Xanthite:** yellow from New York (U.S.). **Wiluite** = from Siberia, after a river.

SINHALITE (5, 6)

Color: Yellow-brown, green-brown
Color of streak: White
Mohs' hardness: $6\frac{1}{2}$
Specific gravity: 3.47–3.49
Cleavage: None
Fracture: Conchoidal
Crystal system: Orthorhombic; crystals rare
Chem. comp.: $Mg(Al,Fe)BO_4$ magnesium aluminium iron borate

Transparency: Transparent
Refractive index: 1.669–1.707
Double refraction: —0.038
Dispersion: 0.018
Pleochroism: Definite; green, light brown, dark brown
Absorption spectrum: 5260, 4925, 4760, 4630, 4520, 4355
Fluorescence: None

First recognized as an individual mineral in 1952. Occurs in Sri Lanka, upper Burma, Siberia (Russia) and New York state (U.S.). Can be confused with chrysoberyl (p. 98), peridot (p. 158) and zircon (p. 108).

KORNERUPINE (7, 8)

Color: Green, green-brown
Color of streak: White
Mohs' hardness: $6\frac{1}{2}$–7
Specific gravity: 3.28–3.35
Cleavage: Imperfect
Fracture: Conchoidal
Crystal system: Orthorhombic; long prisms
Chem. comp.: $Mg_4Al_6((O,OH)_2/BO_4$ $(SiO_4)_4)$ magnesium aluminium

borate silicate
Transparency: Transparent, translucent
Refractive index: 1.665–1.682
Double refraction: —0.013
Dispersion: 0.018
Pleochroism: Strong; green, yellow, brown
Absorption spectrum: 5400, 5030, 4630, 4460, 4300
Fluorescence: None

Named after the Greenland explorer. Occurs in Burma (sometimes as kornerupine cat's eye), Sri Lanka, Greenland, Canada, Malagasy Republic and South Africa. Confused with enstatite (p. 192) and tourmaline (p. 110).

---

1 Idocrase, crystal
2 Idocrase, 3 faceted stones, 6.25ct
3 Idocrase, cabochon, 4.19ct
4 Idocrase, 4 faceted stones

5 Sinhalite, rough
6 Sinhalite, 2 faceted stones
7 Kornerupine, 3 faceted stones
8 Kornerupine, aggregate, Sri Lanka

The illustrations are 20% larger than the originals.

PREHNITE (1–3)

Color: Yellow-green, brown-yellow	basic calcium aluminium silicate
Color of streak: White	Transparency: Transparent
Mohs' hardness: 6–6½	Refractive index: 1.61–1.64
Specific gravity: 2.87–2.93	Double refraction: +0.030
Cleavage: Perfect	Dispersion: None
Fracture: Uneven	Pleochroism: None
Crystal system: Orthorhombic; columnar, tabular crystals	Absorption spectrum: Not usable
	Fluorescence: None
Chem. comp.: $Ca_2Al_2((OH)_2/Si_3O_{10})$	

Crystals are very rare. It has a vitreous luster. It is sensitive to heat (careful when soldering). There are some prehnite cat's eyes. Occurs in Australia (New South Wales), China, Scotland, South Africa and the U.S. (New Jersey). Can be confused with chrysoprase (p. 128), jade (p. 154) and peridot (p. 158).

PETALITE (4–5)

Color: Colorless, pink	lithium sodium aluminium silicate
Color of streak: White	Transparency: Transparent, translucent
Mohs' hardness: 6–6½	Refractive index: 1.502–1.518
Specific gravity: 2.40	Double refraction: +0.016
Cleavage: Perfect	Dispersion: 0.014
Fracture: Conchoidal, brittle	Pleochroism: None
Crystal system: Monoclinic; thick tabular crystals	Absorption spectrum: (4540)
	Fluorescence: Weak; orange
Chem. comp.: $(Li,Na)(AlSi_4O_{10})$	

Vitreous luster; on cleavage planes, there is a pearly luster. There are some petalite cat's eyes. Occurs in Western Australia, Brazil (Minas Gerais), Elba, Sweden and Namibia. Confused with other colorless stones and glass.

SCAPOLITE (6–8) also called wernerite

Color: Yellow, pink, violet, colorless	Transparency: Transparent, translucent
Color of streak: White	Refractive index: 1.540–1.560
Mohs' hardness: 5–6½	Double refraction: −0.009 to −0.020
Specific gravity: 2.57–2.74	Dispersion: 0.017
Cleavage: Perfect	Pleochroism: Yellow: Definite; colorless–yellow
Fracture: Conchoidal, brittle	Pink: Definite; colorless–pink
Crystal system: Tetragonal; columnar	Absorption spectrum: Pinks: 6630, 6520
Chem. comp.: $Na_4(AlSi_3O_8)_3 Cl.nCa_4 (Al_2Si_2O_8)_3(SO_4,CO_3)$ complicated sodium calcium aluminium silicate	Fluorescence: Pink: orange, pink Yellow: violet, blue-red

Named after its crystal habit (Greek – stick stone). The other name refers to the German explorer. It has a vitreous luster. Often cut as pink or violet cat's eyes (7). Occurs in Burma, Brazil, Malagasy Republic and Tasmania. Confused with amblygonite (p. 192), chrysoberyl (p. 98) and golden beryl (p. 96).

---

1 Prehnite, 2 cabochons, 31.91ct	5 Petalite, 3 faceted stones
2 Prehnite, 2 faceted stones, Australia	6 Scapolite, 5 faceted stones
3 Prehnite, with apophyllite crystals	7 Scapolite cat's eye, 5 stones
4 Petalite, rough	8 Scapolite, 4 crystal pieces

DIOPSIDE (1–3) pyroxene group

Color: Light to dark green, bottle green, rarely yellow or colorless	Transparency: Transparent, translucent
Color of streak: White	Refractive index: 1.671–1.726
Mohs' hardness: 5–6	Double refraction: +0.028
Specific gravity: 3.27–3.31	Dispersion: None
Cleavage: Perfect	Pleochroism: Weak; yellow-green, grass green, olive green
Fracture: Rough	
Crystal system: Monoclinic; columnar crystals	Absorption spectrum: 5470, 5080, 5050, 4930, 4560
Chemical composition: $CaMg(Si_2O_6)$ calcium magnesium silicate	Chrome diopside: (6700), (6550), (6350), 5080, 5050, 4900
	Fluorescence: Strong; dark violet

There are well-known deposits in Burma, India, Malagasy Republic, South Africa, Finland (Outokumpu), Italy (Piemont) and Austria (Zillertal). Star diopside (3), diopside cat's eye, and emerald green diopside are much in demand. The violet variety from Piemont, Italy is called Violane. Confused with hiddenite (p. 114), peridot (p. 158), emerald (p. 90) and idocrase (p. 186).

BERYLLONITE (4)

Color: Colorless, white, weak yellow	sodium beryllium phosphate
Color of streak: White	Transparency: Transparent
Mohs' hardness: $5\frac{1}{2}$–6	Refractive index: 1.553–1.562
Specific gravity: 2.80–2.85	Double refraction: −0.009
Cleavage: Perfect	Dispersion: 0.010
Fracture: Conchoidal, brittle	Pleochroism: None
Crystals: Monoclinic; short prisms	Absorption spectrum: Not usable
Chemical composition: $NaBe(PO_4)$	Fluorescence: None

So named because of its beryllium content. It has a vitreous luster and is brittle (careful when cutting). Occurs in Maine (U.S.), also in Rhodesia and Finland. Can be confused with all colorless gemstones and glass.

BRAZILIANITE (5, 6)

Color: Yellow, green-yellow	phosphate
Color of streak: White	Transparency: Transparent, translucent
Mohs' hardness: $5\frac{1}{2}$	Refractive index: 1.603–1.623
Specific gravity: 2.98–2.99	Double refraction: +0.020
Cleavage: Perfect	Dispersion: 0.014
Fracture: Small conchoidal, brittle	Pleochroism: Very weak
Crystals: Monoclinic; short prisms	Absorption spectrum: Not usable
Chemical composition: $NaAl_3(PO_4)_2 (OH)_4$ basic sodium aluminium	Fluorescence: None

Has a vitreous luster. The only important deposits are in Minas Gerais and Espirito Santo, Brazil; also in New Hampshire (U.S.). Confused with amblygonite (p. 192), beryl (p. 96), chrysoberyl (p. 98) and topaz (p. 102).

---

1 Diopside, 10 different cuts
2 Diopside, 2 broken crystals
3 Diopside, 4-rayed asterism
4 Beryllonite, 3 faceted stones
5 Brazilianite, rough
6 Brazilianite, 5 faceted stones

The illustrations are 15% larger than the originals.

AMBLYGONITE (1, 2)

Color: Golden-yellow to colorless	basic lithium aluminium phosphate
Color of streak: White	Transparency: Transparent
Mohs' hardness: 6	Refractive index: 1.611–1.637
Specific gravity: 3.01–3.03	Double refraction: +0.026
Cleavage: Perfect	Pleochroism: None
Fracture: Uneven, brittle	Absorption spectrum: Not usable
Crystals: Triclinic; rarely well formed	Fluorescence: Very weak; green
Chem. comp.: $LiAl(PO_4)$ (F/OH)	

Has a vitreous luster and on cleavage faces, a pearly luster. Can be polished but is sensitive to acids and heat. Cuttable qualities are found in Brazil (Minas Gerais, Sao Paulo) and the U.S. (California). A light purple variety is found in Namibia. Can be confused with brazilianite (p. 190) and scapolite (p. 188).

ENSTATITE (3, 4) pyroxene group

Color: Brown-green, green, gray, yellowish	Transparency: Transparent to opaque
	Refractive index: 1.663–1.673
Color of streak: White	Double refraction: +0.010
Mohs' hardness: $5\frac{1}{2}$	Dispersion: None
Specific gravity: 3.26–3.28	Pleochroism: Definite; green, yellow-green
Cleavage: Perfect	Absorption spectrum: <u>5475</u>, 5090,
Fracture: Lamellar or scaly	<u>5058</u>, 5025, 4830, 4720, 4590, 4490,
Crystal system: Orthorhombic; prismatic	4250
Chemical composition: $Mg_2(Si_2O_6)$ magnesium silicate	Chrome enstatite: 6880, 6690, 5060
	Fluorescence: None

Very difficult to melt (Greek – resistor). Has a vitreous luster. Green-gray enstatite cat's eyes come from Sri Lanka, star enstatite from India. Further occurrences in South Africa and Burma. Confused with kornerupine (p. 186). The metallic-green-brown variety has high iron content and is called bronzite.

LAZULITE (5–6)

Color: Dark blue to blue-white	phosphate
Color of streak: White	Transparency: Opaque, transparent
Mohs' hardness: 5–6	Refractive index: 1.615–1.645
Specific gravity: 3.1–3.2	Double refraction: −0.030 '
Cleavage: Perfect	Dispersion: None
Fracture: Uneven, splintery, brittle	Pleochroism: Strong; colorless, dark blue
Crystal system: Monoclinic; pointed pyramids	Absorption spectrum: Not usable
Chem. comp.: $(Mg,Fe)Al_2(PO_4)_2(OH)_2$ basic magnesium iron aluminium	Fluorescence: None

Crystals are rare. It has a vitreous luster. Occurs in Brazil (Minas Gerais), India, Malagasy Republic, the U.S. (North Carolina, Maine, California), Austria (Salzburg, Steiermark) and Sweden (Wermland). Confused with azurite (p. 174), lapis lazuli (p. 172), sodalite (p. 174) and turquoise (p. 170).

---

1 Amblygonite, 2 rough pieces	4 Enstatite, 3 rough pieces
2 Amblygonite, 6 different cuts	5 Lazulite, 9 different cuts
3 Enstatite, 2 faceted stones and Star enstatite	6 Lazulite, rough

The illustrations are 20% larger than the originals.

DIOPTASE (1, 2)

Color: Emerald green	hydrous copper silicate
Color of streak: Green	Transparency: Transparent
Mohs' hardness: 5	Refractive index: 1.644–1.709
Specific gravity: 3.28–3.35	Double refraction: +0.053
Cleavage: Perfect	Dispersion: 0.022
Fracture: Conchoidal, brittle	Pleochroism: Weak; emerald green
Crystal system: Hexagonal (trigonal);	Absorption spectrum: 5700, 5600,
short columnar crystals	4650–4000
Chem. comp.: $Cu_6(Si_6O_{18})$. $6H_2O$	Fluorescence: None

Crystals are small with a vitreous luster. Occurs in Chile, Namibia, Russia (Kirgisistan), the U.S. (Arizona) and Zaire. Confused with emerald (p. 90).

APATITE (3–6)

Color: Colorless, pink, yellow, green, blue, violet	Refractive index: 1.632–1.646
	Double refraction: −0.002 to −0.004
Color of streak: White to yellow-gray	Dispersion: 0.016
Mohs' hardness: 5	Pleochroism: Green: weak; yellow, green
Specific gravity: 3.17–3.23	Blue: very strong; blue, colorless
Cleavage: Poor	Absorption spectrum: Yellow-green:
Fracture: Conchoidal, brittle	6053, 6025, 5975, 5855, 5772, 5742,
Crystal system: Hexagonal; short and long columns, thick tabular with numerous faces	5335, 5295, 5270, 5250, 5210, 5140, 4690, 4425
	Blue: 6310, 6220, 5250, 5120,
Chem. comp.: $Ca_5(F,Cl,OH)(PO_4)_3$ calcium fluoro- and chloro- phosphate	5070, 4910, 4640
	Fluorescence: Very variable
Transparency: Transparent	

Has a vitreous luster and is sensitive to acids. It is found in upper Burma, Brazil, Sri Lanka, Czechoslovakia, India, Malagasy Republic, Mexico and the U.S. Green variety called asparagus-stone. Apatite cat's eye is found in Burma and Brazil. Confused with beryl (p. 96), topaz (p. 102), tourmaline (p. 110).

SPHENE (7, 8) also called titanite

Color: Yellow, brown, green	Transparency: Transparent
Color of streak: White	Refractive index: 1.885–2.050
Mohs' hardness: 5–5½	Double refraction: +0.105 to +0.135
Specific gravity: 3.52–3.54	Dispersion: 0.051
Cleavage: Perfect	Pleochroism: Green: colorless, green
Fracture: Conchoidal, brittle	Yellow: strong; colorless, yellow, reddish
Crystal system: Monoclinic; wedge-shaped crystals	Absorption spectrum: 5900, 5860,
Chemical composition: $CaTi_9(O/SiO_4)$ calcium titanium silicate	5820, 5800, 5750, 5340, 5300, 5280
	Fluorescence: None

Very intense fire, it has an adamantine luster as well. Found in Mexico and Brazil. Can be confused with many gems.

---

1 Dioptase, 2 crystals	5 Apatite, 8 different cuts
2 Dioptase, 12 faceted stones	6 Apatite, 3 crystals
3 Apatite, crystal	7 Sphene, 8 different cuts
4 Apatite cat's eye, Brazil	8 Sphene, rough

KYANITE (1–3) also called disthene

Color: Blue to colorless, blue-green
Color of streak: White
Mohs' hardness: Along axes $4\frac{1}{2}$, across 6 and 7
Specific gravity: 3.65–3.69
Cleavage: Perfect
Fracture: Fibrous, brittle
Crystals: Triclinic; long, flat prisms
Chemical composition: $Al_2O(SiO_4)$ aluminium silicate

Transparency: Transparent, translucent
Refractive index: 1.715–1.732
Double refraction: −0.017
Dispersion: 0.020
Pleochroism: Strong; light blue to colorless, light blue, dark blue
Absorption spectrum: (7060), (6890), (6710), (6520), 4460, 4330
Fluorescence: Blue-green: strong; red

The color is often in irregular streaks. Has a vitreous luster. The crystals are difficult to cut because of their variable hardness and cleavage. Occurs in Burma, Brazil, Kenya, the U.S. (North Carolina), Austria (Tyrol) and Switzerland. Confused with aquamarine (p. 94) and sapphire (p. 86).

SCHEELITE (4, 5)

Color: Yellow, brown, orange, colorless
Color of streak: White
Mohs' hardness: $4\frac{1}{2}$–5
Specific gravity: 5.1–6.1
Cleavage: Perfect
Fracture: Conchoidal, splintery, brittle
Crystals: Tetragonal; dipyramids
Chem. comp.: $CaWO_4$ calcium tungstate

Transparency: Transparent, translucent
Refractive index: 1.918–1.934
Double refraction: +0.016
Dispersion: 0.026
Pleochroism: Definite
Absorption spectrum: 5840
Fluorescence: Blue, whitish or yellow

Cuttable qualities are found in Mexico and the U.S. (Arizona, California). Scheelite was synthesized in the U.S. in 1963. When dyed it can be confused with many gemstones.

VARISCITE (6–8) also called utahlite

Color: Yellow-green, bluish
Color of streak: White
Mohs' hardness: 4–5
Specific gravity: 2.4–2.6
Cleavage: Perfect
Fracture: Conchoidal, brittle
Crystal system: Orthorhombic; short needles
Chemical composition: $AlPO_4.2H_2O$ hydrous aluminium phosphate

Transparency: Translucent to opaque
Refractive index: 1.55–1.59
Double refraction: −·0.010
Dispersion: None
Pleochroism: None
Absorption spectrum: 6880, (6500)
Fluorescence: None

Sometimes utahlite is looked upon as a separate mineral and not as a synonym for variscite. Found in Utah and Nevada (U.S.), and in Queensland (Australia). Can be confused with chrysocolla (p. 200), chrysoprase (p. 128) and turquoise (p. 170). "Amatrix" (American matrix), sometimes also called variscite quartz, is variscite intergrown with quartz or chalcedony from Utah.

1 Kyanite, 3 broken crystals	5 Scheelite, 3 faceted stones
2 Kyanite, 5 different cuts	6 Variscite, 3 cabochons
3 Kyanite, crystal	7 Variscite in host rock, 2 pieces
4 Scheelite, broken crystal	8 Variscite with host rock, cabochon

FLUORITE (1–3) also called fluorspar

Color: Colorless, red, orange, yellow, green, blue, violet, nearly black
Color of streak: White
Mohs' hardness: 4
Specific gravity: 3.18
Cleavage: Perfect
Fracture: Even to conchoidal, brittle
Crystal system: Isometric; cubes, octahedra
Chem. comp.: CaF_2 calcium fluoride
Transparency: Transparent, translucent

Refractive index: 1.434
Double refraction: None
Dispersion: 0.007
Pleochroism: None
Absorption spectrum: Green: 6400, 6006, 5850, 5700, 5530, 5500, 4520, 4350
Yellow: 5450, 5150, 4900, 4700, 4520
Fluorescence: Usually strong; blue-violet

Has a zonal or spotty distribution of color, which can be changed by radiation, also a vitreous luster. There are deposits in West Germany (Wolsendorf/ Oberpfalz) and England (Cumberland, Derbyshire, where the blue-layered "Blue John" is found). Can be synthesized; confused with many gemstones.

HEMIMORPHITE (4–6) also called calamine

Color: Blue, green, colorless
Color of streak: White
Mohs' hardness: 5
Specific gravity: 3.4–3.5
Cleavage: Perfect
Fracture: Conchoidal, uneven, brittle
Crystal system: Orthorhombic; tabular
Chem. comp.: $Zn_4((OH)_2/Si_2O_7).H_2O$

hydrous basic zinc silicate
Transparency: Transparent to opaque
Refractive index: 1.614–1.636
Double refraction: +0.022
Dispersion: None
Pleochroism: None
Absorption spectrum: Not usable
Fluorescence: Weak; not characteristic

Often found in blue-white layers, also with dark matrix (5). Deposits are in Algeria, Italy, Greece, Mexico and Namibia. Can be confused with smith-sonite (see below) and turquoise (p. 170).

SMITHSONITE (7, 8) also called bonamite

Color: Light green, light blue, pink
Color of streak: White
Mohs' hardness: 5
Specific gravity: 4.3–4.5
Cleavage: Perfect
Fracture: Uneven, brittle
Crystal system: Hexagonal (trigonal); rhombohedral, usually in compact grape-like masses

Chemical composition: $ZnCO_3$ zinc carbonate
Transparency: Translucent, opaque
Refractive index: 1.621–1.849
Double refraction: –0.228
Dispersion: 0.014 and 0.031
Pleochroism: None
Absorption spectrum: Not usable
Fluorescence: None

Often found in soft white layers; has a pearly luster. Deposits in Greece (Attica), Mexico (Cananea), Spain, Namibia (Tsumeb) and the U.S. (Arkansas, Colorado, New Mexico, Utah). Can be confused with chrysoprase (p. 128), hemimorphite (see above), jade (p. 156) and turquoise (p. 170).

---

1 Fluorite, 2 cleaved octahedrons
2 Fluorite, 2 rough pieces
3 Fluorite, 9 different cuts
4 Hemimorphite, crystal and stones

5 Hemimorphite, 3 cabochons
6 Hemimorphite, radial aggregate
7 Smithsonite, 2 aggregates
8 Smithsonite, 3 cabochons

SPHALERITE (1–3) also called zinc blende

Color: Yellow, green, colorless	Transparency: Transparent, translucent
Color of streak: Yellow to light brown	Refractive index: 2.368–2.371
Mohs' hardness: $3\frac{1}{2}$–4	Double refraction: None
Specific gravity: 4.08–4.10	Dispersion: 0.156
Cleavage: Perfect	Pleochroism: None
Fracture: Uneven, brittle	Absorption spectrum: 6900, 6650,
Crystal system: Cubic; tetrahedral	6510
Chemical composition: ZnS zinc	Fluorescence: Usually yellow-orange,
sulphide	also red, sometimes none

Has a non-metallic resinous luster. The amber colored variety is called "honey blende" and the red variety is misnamed "ruby blende". Difficult to cut because of its perfect cleavage. Cuttable qualities found in Spain (near Santander) and Mexico. Confused with yellowish stones and colorless diamond.

CERUSSITE (4–5)

Color: Colorless, gray, brown	Chem. comp.: $PbCO_3$ lead carbonate
Color of streak: White to gray	Transparency: Transparent
Mohs' hardness: $3\frac{1}{2}$	Refractive index: 1.804–2.078
Specific gravity: 6.46–6.57	Double refraction: -0.274
Cleavage: Perfect	Dispersion: 0.051
Fracture: Conchoidal, uneven, very	Pleochroism: None
brittle	Absorption spectrum: Not usable
Crystal system: Orthorhombic;	Fluorescence: Usually yellow, rarely
tabular, columnar	pink, whitish, green or none

Often found as twin crystal formations. Has an adamantine luster. Cuttable crystals are found in Czechoslovakia, Sardinia, Austria (Bleiberg), Scotland, Namibia (Tsumeb) and the U.S. (southern Rocky Mountains and Pennsylvania). Confused with diamond (p. 70) and other colorless or brownish stones.

CHRYSOCOLLA (6–8)

Color: Green, blue	Transparency: Opaque, sometimes
Color of streak: Green-white	just translucent
Mohs' hardness: 2–4	Refractive index: About 1.50
Specific gravity: 2.00–2.40	Double refraction: None
Cleavage: None	Dispersion: None
Fracture: Conchoidal	Pleochroism: Weak
Crystal system: Amorphous; compact	Absorption spectrum: Not usable
grape-like aggregates	Fluorescence: None
Chemical composition: $CuSiO_3.2H_2O$	
hydrous copper silicate	

Has a greasy, vitreous luster. Deposits are in Chile, Russia (Ural), the U.S. (Arizona, Nevada) and Zaire (Katanga). Can be confused with (blue) dyed chalcedony (p. 126), turquoise (p. 170) and variscite (p. 196). Chrysocolla quartz is quartz intergrown with chrysocolla. Eilat stone (8) is chrysocolla intergrown with turquoise and malachite; found north of Eilat (Israel).

---

1 Sphalerite, 3 rough pieces	5 Cerussite, 5 faceted stones
2 Sphalerite, faceted, 47.97ct	6 Chrysocolla, 4 cabochons
3 Sphalerite, 3 faceted stones	7 Chrysocolla, 2 rough pieces
4 Cerussite, twinned crystal	8 Eilat stone, 2 cabochons

SERPENTINE (1, 2)

Color: All hues of green	Transparency: Usually opaque,
Color of streak: White	sometimes translucent or
Mohs' hardness: 2–5½	transparent
Specific gravity: 2.4–2.8	Refractive index: 1.560–1.571
Cleavage: None	Double refraction: None
Fracture: Conchoidal, splintery, tough	Dispersion: None
Crystal system: Usually monoclinic;	Pleochroism: None
only microcrystalline aggregates	Absorption spectrum: 4970, 4640
Chemical composition: $Mg_6((OH)_8/$	Fluorescence: Partly yellow
$Si_4O_{10})$ basic magnesium silicate	

A mineral with variable appearance, variable chemical properties and numerous names. Science differentiates between antigorite (leafy serpentine) and chrysotile (fibrous serpentine). Asbestos is a very finely fibrous variety. Two types used for jewelry are the apple-green Bowenite with irregular little spots, and the rarer transparent Williamsite (3) with black inclusions. Various green marbled rocks, combinations of serpentine with marble (such as Connemara, Verd-antique) are designated as serpentines in the trade and are used for ornaments. It is found in many countries. Can be confused with jade (p. 154), onyx marble (p. 210) and turquoise (p. 170).

Stichtite (4) Rose-red to purple. Decomposition product of chrome-containing serpentine. Found in Algeria, South Africa and Tasmania.

Bastite Pseudomorphs of serpentine after bronzite (p. 192) with a silky sheen.

ULEXITE (5, 6) also called television stone

Color: White	Transparency: Transparent, translucent
Color of streak: White	Refractive index: 1.491–1.520
Mohs' hardness: 2	Double refraction: +0.029
Specific gravity: 1.9–2.0	Dispersion: None
Cleavage: Perfect	Pleochroism: None
Fracture: Fibrous	Absorption spectrum: Not usable
Crystal system: Triclinic; fibrous	Fluorescence: Green-yellow, blue
aggregates	
Chemical comp.: $NaCaB_5O_9 \cdot 6H_2O$	
hydrous sodium calcium borate	

Shows a cat's eye effect because of its fibrous structure (5), has a silky sheen. A piece of writing placed underneath the stone appears on the surface (therefore also called "TV stone"). Occurs in Argentina, Chile, Canada and the U.S. (California, Nevada).

TIGER'S EYE MATRIX (7, 8)

This quartz-lignite aggregate has gold-yellow highlights and sometimes scenic markings (p. 124).

1 Serpentine, rough	6 Ulexite, 3 rough pieces
2 Serpentine-asbestos, 2 cabochons	7 Tiger's eye matrix, 2 pieces partly
3 Williamsite, 2 faceted stones	polished
4 Stichtite, rough and cabochon	8 Tiger's eye matrix, rough
5 Ulexite, 3 cabochons	

RARITIES FOR GEM COLLECTORS

1 **Gahnite** (Zinc Spinel) Transparent, various intensities of blue, red-violet, green. Mohs' hardness $7\frac{1}{2}$–8. Specific gravity 3.58–3.98. Isometric. $ZnAl_2O_4$. Since 1937 has been found to be of gem quality. For other spinels, see p. 100.

2 **Binghamite** Quartz (p. 116) with geothite inclusions. Shimmers when cut en cabochon. Minnesota (U.S.).

3 **Sanidine** (Three faceted stones) Transparent, light gray to light brown orthoclase variety (p. 164). Mohs' hardness 6, strong vitreous luster.

4 **Tantalite** (Two faceted stones) Transparent, red-brown. Mohs' hardness 5–6. Specific gravity 5.18–8.20. Orthorhombic, $(Fe,Mn)(Ta_2O_6)$. Mixed series with niobium.

5 **Rutile** (Three faceted stones) Transparent, red-brown. Mohs' hardness 6–$6\frac{1}{2}$. Specific gravity 4.20–4.30. Tetragonal. TiO_2. Strong, nearly metallic luster.

6 **Peristerite** (Four cabochons) Opaque albite variety (p. 164) with bluish iridescence on white or brown base. Mohs' hardness $6\frac{1}{2}$.

7 **Haüynite** (Three faceted stones) Transparent, lazuli-blue. Mohs' hardness $5\frac{1}{2}$–6. Specific gravity 2.4. Isometric. $(Na,Ca)_{8-4}((SO_4)_{2-1}(AlSiO_4)_6)$. Constituent of lapis lazuli (p. 172).

8 **Tugtupite** (Three cabochons) Usually opaque, dark red with a violet tint, spotty appearance caused by mineral inclusions. Mohs' hardness 6. Specific gravity 2.36–2.57. Tetragonal. $Na_2Al_2Be_2Si_8O_{24}$. Found in 1960 simultaneously in South Greenland and on the Kola Peninsula in Russia.

9 **Willemite** (Three cabochons) Transparent, yellow, greenish, red-brown. Mohs' hardness $5\frac{1}{2}$. Specific gravity 3.89–4.18. Tetragonal. $Zn_2(SiO_4)$. Crystals rare. Resinous luster. Strong green fluorescence.

10 **Natrolite** (Three faceted stones) Transparent, white, yellowish. Mohs' hardness $5\frac{1}{2}$. Specific gravity 2.20–2.25. Orthorhombic. $Na_2(Al_2SiO_3O_{10})$. $2H_2O$.

11 **Smaragdite** (Two cabochons) Transparent, grass to emerald green. Mohs' hardness $6\frac{1}{2}$. Specific gravity 3.25. Monoclinic. $Ca_2(Mg,Fe)_5$ $(Si_4O_{11})_2(OH)_2$. A variety of actinolite, not related to emerald. Sometimes imitations from artistically fused masses are called smaragdite.

12 **Leucite** Transparent, colorless, white. Mohs' hardness $5\frac{1}{2}$. Specific gravity 2.45–2.50. Isometric and tetragonal. $K(AlSi_2O_6)$.

13 **Actinolite** Transparent, green. Mohs' hardness $5\frac{1}{2}$–6. Specific gravity 3.03–3.07. Monoclinic. $Ca_2(Mg,Fe)_5(Si_4O_{11})_2(OH)_2$.

14 **Hypersthene** (Three faceted stones) Transparent, black-green, black-brown. Mohs' hardness 5–6. Specific gravity 3.4–3.5. Orthorhombic. $(Fe,Mg)_2(Si_2O_6)$. Partly copper-red iridescence.

15 **Datolite** (Three faceted stones) Transparent, colorless, greenish. Mohs' hardness 5–$5\frac{1}{2}$. Specific gravity 2.90–3.00. Monoclinic. $CaB(OH/SiO_4)$.

Rarities of similar hardness not illustrated: anatase (brown, $5\frac{1}{2}$–6), bytownite (reddish, pale yellow, 6), ekanite (green, light brown, 6–$6\frac{1}{2}$), elaeolite (blue-green, brown-red, $5\frac{1}{2}$–6), painite (red, $7\frac{1}{2}$–8), rhodizite (pink, light yellow, greenish, 8), saussurite (whitish, light green, $6\frac{1}{2}$), fibrolite (or sillimanite, blue, 6–$7\frac{1}{2}$), staurolite (reddish-brown, 7–$7\frac{1}{2}$), taaffeite (red-blue, 8) and tremolite (green, $5\frac{1}{2}$–$6\frac{1}{2}$). Further data in tables.

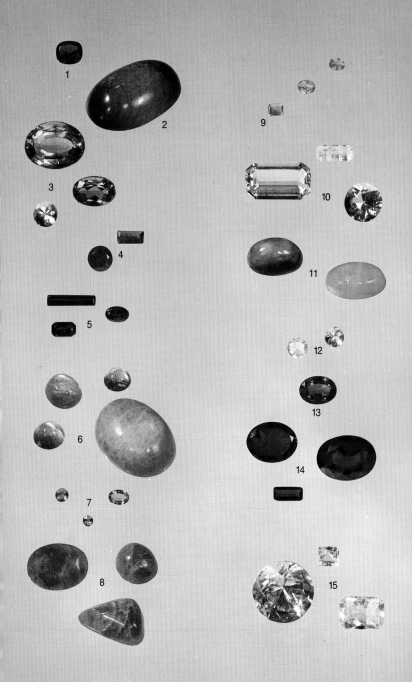

1 **Periclase** (Cabochon, and two faceted stones) Transparent, colorless, yellowish, gray-green. Mohs' hardness $5\frac{1}{2}$–6. Specific gravity 3.7–3.9. Isometric. MgO. Vitreous luster. Synthetic (lavernite) used as imitation of spinel.

2 **Purpurite** Transparent, purple, deep pink, dark brown. Mohs' hardness 4–$4\frac{1}{2}$. Specific gravity 3.2–3.4. Orthorhombic. $MnFe(PO_4)$. Metallic luster. Brittle.

3 **Apophyllite** Transparent, colorless or weakly red, yellowish, greenish, bluish. Mohs' hardness $4\frac{1}{2}$–5. Specific gravity 2.30–2.50. Tetragonal. $KCa_4(Si_8O_{20})(OH,F).8H_2O$. Mother-of-pearl luster and characteristic light sheen, also called Fish-eye stone. See illustration p. 189, no. 3.

4 **Zincite** (Three faceted stones) Transparent, red to orange-red. Mohs' hardness $4\frac{1}{2}$–5. Specific gravity 5.66. Hexagonal. ZnO. Adamantine luster. Only cuttable material found in now abandoned mine in Franklin, New Jersey, U.S.

5 **Kurnakovite** (Two faceted stones) Transparent, colorless, pink. Mohs' hardness $4\frac{1}{2}$. Specific gravity 1.86. Triclinic. $Mg_2B_6O_{11}.15H_2O$.

6 **Chalybite** (Two faceted stones) Transparent, gold-brown, red-brown. Mohs' hardness $3\frac{1}{2}$–$4\frac{1}{2}$. Specific gravity 3.85. Hexagonal (trigonal), $FeCO_3$. Very difficult to cut. Also globular chalybite (sphere shaped aggregate) cut by collectors. Also called Siderite, which is another name for Blue Quartz as well.

7 **Colemanite** (Three faceted stones) Translucent, watery appearance. Mohs' hardness $4\frac{1}{2}$. Specific gravity 2.42. Monoclinic. $Ca_2(B_6O_{11}).5H_2O$. Strong vitreous luster.

8 **Cuprite** Transparent, carmine red. Mohs' hardness $4\frac{1}{2}$. Specific gravity 5.85–6.15. Isometric. Cu_2O. Metallic luster. Very high refractive index. There are various types of stone offered in the trade as cuprite, which are colored red by copper content.

9 **Barite** (Five faceted stones) Transparent, colorless, brown, yellow, also red, green, blue. Mohs' hardness 3. Specific gravity 4–5. Orthorhombic. $BaSO_4$. Vitreous luster. On cleavage planes, mother-of-pearl luster, brittle. Also called Barytes.

10 **Dolomite** (Three faceted stones) Transparent, colorless, pastel colors. Mohs' hardness $3\frac{1}{2}$–$4\frac{1}{2}$. Specific gravity 2.85–2.95. Hexagonal (trigonal). $CaMg(CO_3)_2$. Vitreous luster. Also called Pearl Spar.

11 **Chalcopyrite** Opaque, brass yellow, gold-yellow with a green tint. Mohs' hardness $3\frac{1}{2}$–4. Specific gravity 4.1–4.3. Tetragonal. $CuFeS_2$. Metallic luster. Also called Copper Pyrite.

12 **Witherite** (Two faceted stones) Transparent, yellow white to colorless. Mohs' hardness $3\frac{1}{2}$. Specific gravity 4.27–4.35. Orthorhombic. $BaCO_3$. Waxy luster; on fractures, greasy luster. Witherite dust is poisonous.

13 **Anhydrite** Transparent, colorless, bluish also red-violet. Mohs' hardness $3\frac{1}{2}$. Specific gravity 2.90–2.99. Orthorhombic. $CaSO_4$. Bright luster.

14 **Magnetite-jade** Opaque black jade, electrolytically plated with gold originally, also black magnetite inclusions. Mohs' hardness $5\frac{1}{2}$–7. Specific gravity depends on magnetite content 3.4–4.4. Rough stones rare. Some finds in California (U.S.). First cut by hobby collectors, has been done commercially in Europe since 1970.
Further data in tables.

1 **Calcite** (Three faceted stones) Transparent, colorless and in various colors. Mohs' hardness 3. Specific gravity 2.71. Hexagonal (trigonal). $CaCO_2$. Common. Rough crystals sometimes set in jewelry.

2 **Howlite** Opaque, but also transparent, snow white, sometimes with black or brown veins, rarely colorless. Mohs' hardness $3\frac{1}{2}$. Specific gravity 2.53–2.59. Monoclinic? $Ca_2((BOOH)_5/SiO_4)$. Easily dyed as it is very porous. See no. 16.

3 **Cobalt-calcite** (Cabochon and faceted) Calcite, colored violet-red with cobalt (see 1). Cuttable material from Spain.

4 **Barytocalcite** Transparent, yellow-white. Mohs' hardness 4. Specific gravity 3.66. Monoclinic. $BaCa(CO_3)_2$. Vitreous luster, brittle.

5 **Celestine or Celestite** (Three faceted stones) Transparent, bluish-white colorless, Mohs' hardness $3–3\frac{1}{2}$. Specific gravity 3.97–4.00. Orthorhombic. $SrSO_4$. Vitreous luster; on cleavage planes pearly luster, brittle.

6 **Wulfenite** Transparent to translucent, honey-yellow, orange, red. Mohs' hardness 3. Specific gravity 6.7–7.0. Tetragonal. $PbMoO_4$. Adamantine luster, greasy luster in fractures, brittle. Because of its high luster, the rough crystals are sometimes set in jewelry.

7 **Aragonite** (Two faceted stones) Transparent, colorless or in various colors. Mohs' hardness $3\frac{1}{2}–4$. Specific gravity 2.94. Orthorhombic. $CaCO_3$. Vitreous luster.

8 **Crocoite** (Three faceted stones) Transparent, red-orange. Mohs' hardness $2\frac{1}{2}–3$. Specific gravity 5.9–6.1. Monoclinic. $PbCrO_4$. Adamantine luster.

9 **Gaylussite** Transparent, colorless, white. Mohs' hardness $2\frac{1}{2}$. Specific gravity 1.99. Monoclinic. $Na_2Ca(CO_3)_2.5H_2O$. Dull vitreous luster.

10 **Phosgenite** (Four faceted stones) Transparent, colorless, white, yellow-white, greenish. Mohs' hardness $2\frac{1}{2}–3$. Specific gravity 6.13. Tetragonal. $Pb_2(Cl_2/CO_3)$. Greasy adamantine luster.

11 **Silver** Dendritic inclusion in quartz. Opaque, black. Mohs' hardness $2\frac{1}{2}–3$. Specific gravity 9.6–12.0. Isometric. Ag.

12 **Gold** Inclusions in quartz. Opaque, yellow gold. Mohs' hardness $2\frac{1}{2}–3$· Specific gravity 15.5–19.3. Isometric. Au.

13 **Vivianite** Transparent, colorless, blue-green, dark blue. Mohs' hardness $1\frac{1}{2}–2$. Specific gravity 2.6–2.7. Monoclinic. $Fe_3(PO_4)_2.8H_2O$. Vitreous to pearly luster.

14 **Sulphur** Translucent, yellow. Mohs' hardness $1\frac{1}{2}–2$. Specific gravity 2.05–2.08. Orthorhombic. S. Adamantine luster. On fracture surfaces there is a greasy luster.

15 **Proustite** Translucent, ruby red. Mohs' hardness $2\frac{1}{2}$. Specific gravity 5.57–5.64. Hexagonal (trigonal). Ag_3AsS_3. Tarnishes when left in light after a few months and thus darkens. Also called Ruby Silver Ore.

16 **Howlite** When colored, used to imitate turquoise (p. 170), (see also no. 2).

Rarities of similar hardness not illustrated: augelite (colorless, 5), cancrinite (yellow, orange, 5–6), chromite (iron black, $5\frac{1}{2}$), garnierite (emerald green, light green, $2\frac{1}{2}$), ilmenite (black, 5–6), magnesite (colorless, 4), pseudophite (Styrian Jade, green, pink, $2\frac{1}{2}$), psilomelane (dull black, $5\frac{1}{2}–6$), thomsonite (reddish-white, green, $5–5\frac{1}{2}$) and wardite (light bluish-green, 5).

Further data in tables.

ROCKS AS ORNAMENTAL MATERIAL

ONYX MARBLE (1–4) also called oriental alabaster

Color: Yellow green, white, brown, striped	Specific gravity: 2.7
Color of streak: According to color of stone	Composition: Calcite or aragonite
	Transparency: Translucent to opaque
	Refractive index: 1.486–1.658
Mohs' hardness: 3	Double refraction: —0.172

The rock called onyx marble (onyx=Greek – fingernail, because of its translucency) in the trade is a limestone formed by the minerals calcite or aragonite. It must not be confused with chalcedony-onyx (p. 142). It is incorrect to name this rock onyx without the addition of the word "marble", and in some countries, even this is unacceptable.

It is formed by the layered deposits (therefore always banded) of hydrated calcium carbonate from a warm spring, or as stalactites or stalagmites in caves. Occurs in North Africa, Argentina, Mexico and the U.S. It is used for ornamental objects, such as pendants and brooches. Can be confused with the mineral serpentine as well as with various serpentine-like rocks, especially with the green-white spotted Connemara from Connaught in Ireland, or the green Ricolite found in New Mexico (U.S.), or Verd-antique (*verde antico*), a white stone with green spots from Italy and Greece.

TUFA (5–7) also called aragonite

Color: White, yellow, brown, reddish	Composition: Aragonite
Color of streak: According to color of stone	Transparency: Opaque
Mohs' hardness: 3½–4	Refractive index: Aragonite 1.530–1.685
Specific gravity: 2.95	Double refraction: Aragonite —0.155

This is the calcium carbonate deposit from hot springs in the form of encrustations or stalactites, often with wavy layers. The best known occurrence is at Karlsbad (Karlovy Vary) in Czechoslovakia. Goethe spoke of the Karlsbad stone as "a type of gem". In some forms, also known as Travertine.

LANDSCAPE MARBLE (8)

This is also called ruin marble and is a fine grained limestone, where the layers have been fractured, displaced and again solidified. Because of the intense coloring of the individual layers, images are formed which convey the impression of a landscape. The landscape marble illustrated could make one think of skyscrapers in a metropolis with low, thundery clouds above. Found in Tuscany (Italy). A decorative rock, sometimes cut en cabochon for pendants and brooches.

---

1 Onyx marble, bowl	5 Tufa 2 pieces from Karlsbad
2 Onyx marble, partly polished	6 Tufa brooch and pendant
3 Onyx marble, 2 pendants	7 Tufa, New Mexico, U.S.
4 Onyx marble, figurine	8 Landscape marble, Tuscany, Italy

The illustrations are 50% smaller than the originals.

ORBICULAR DIORITE (1, 2)

Rock composed of feldspar, hornblende, biotite and quartz. Formed by rhythmic crystallization which produces a separation of light and dark materials into spherical shapes. Used for decorative purposes and cut en cabochon for pendants and brooches (2). Other rocks (such as granite, syenite and its variety kakortokite) are popular because of their structure or color and are sometimes used as decorative stones or for costume jewelry.

OBSIDIAN (3–7)

Color: Black, gray, brown, green	Transparency: Opaque, translucent
Color of streak: White	Refractive index: 1.48–1.51
Mohs' hardness: 5–5½	Double refraction: None
Specific gravity: 2.3–2.6	Dispersion: 0.010
Cleavage: None	Pleochroism: None
Fracture: Large conchoidal, sharp edged	Absorption spectrum: Green: 6800, 6700, 6600, 6500, 6350, 5950, 5550, 5000
Composition: Volcanic, amorphous, siliceous glassy rock	Fluorescence: None

Named after a Roman (Obsius), it was used in antiquity because of its sharp edges and high vitreous luster. Varieties show golden (4) or silver (5) sheen caused by inclusions. Flowering obsidian (6, 7) with gray-white inclusions of radial (spherulitic) structure comes from Utah (U.S.).

MOLDAVITE (10–12) tektite group

Color: Bottle green to brown-green	Transparency: Translucent to transparent
Color of streak: White	Refractive index: 1.48–1.50
Mohs' hardness: 5½	Double refraction: None
Specific gravity: 2.32–2.38	Disperson: None
Cleavage: None	Pleochroism: None
Fracture: Conchoidal	Absorption spectrum: Not usable
Crystal system: Amorphous	Fluorescence: None
Chem. comp.: $SiO_2(+Al_2O_3)$ silicon dioxide + (aluminium oxide)	

Moldavite belongs to the Tektite group. Possibly the tektites are formed from rock which has melted after being hit by a meteorite. They have scarred surfaces, a vitreous luster, are often brown to black in color and are rarely found larger than 1.2in/3cm. Usually named after a particular occurrence: i.e. Moldavite (Moldau, Czechoslovakia), Australite (Australia), Georgiaite (Georgia, U.S.).

---

1 Orbicular diorite, partly polished, Corsica
2 Orbicular diorite, cabochon, Corsica
3 Obsidian, rough, Mexico
4 Golden obsidian, Mexico
5 Silver obsidian, Mexico
6 Flowering obsidian, 2 cabochons
7 Flowering obsidian, part polished

8 Tektite, rough, Thailand
9 Tektite, 2 faceted stones, Thailand
10 Moldavite, 4 rough pieces, Czechoslovakia
11 Moldavite, 6 faceted stones, Czechoslovakia
12 Moldavite, cabochon, Czechoslovakia

The illustrations are 40% smaller than the originals.

ALABASTER (1, 2)

Color: White, pink, brownish
Color of streak: White
Mohs' hardness: 2
Specific gravity: 2.30–2.33
Chemical comp.: $CaSO_4.2H_2O$
hydrous calcium sulphate

Transparency: Opaque, translucent at edges
Refractive index: 1.520–1.530
Double refraction: +0.010
Dispersion: None

Alabaster is the fine grained variety of gypsum. In former times the name also referred to microcrystalline limestone. The name (Greek) was probably derived from the small cosmetic pots which were carved from alabaster. Used for ornamental objects, rarely as jewelry. Can easily be dyed because of its porosity. Well known deposits are near Volterra in Tuscany (Italy).

Agalmatolite Dense variety of the mineral pyrophyllite, which looks very much like alabaster, and used to be used for sculptures. The green variety is sometimes used instead of jade (p. 154). When heat treated, the very soft stone (Mohs' hardness 1–1½) hardens considerably.

Steatite (Soapstone) A dense, white or greenish variety of talc, in recent times worked into costume jewelry in Mediterranean countries.

MEERSCHAUM (3–5) also called sepiolite

Color: White, also yellowish, gray, reddish
Color of streak: White
Mohs' hardness: 2–2½
Specific gravity: 2.0
Cleavage: None
Fracture: Flat conchoidal, earthy
Crystal system: Orthorhombic; microcrystalline

Chem. comp.: $Mg_4(OH)_2/Si_6O_{15}.6H_2O$
hydrous magnesium silicate
Transparency: Opaque
Refractive index: 1.53
Double refraction: None
Dispersion: None
Pleochroism: None
Absorption spectrum: Not usable
Fluorescence: None

Because of its high porosity, meerschaum (German – sea foam) can float. It is very porous; has a dull greasy luster. Formed as the decomposition product of serpentine. The only important occurrence is in Eskischehir, Anatolia (Turkey). Worked into bowls for pipes and cigarette holders which, because of the smoke, gradually become yellowish (5). Recently made into costume jewelry in Turkey. Becomes lustrous when impregnated with grease.

FOSSILS (6–9)

Petrified wood pieces (p. 148) have long been used for adornment, but only lately have fossils (petrified animals or parts of animal) been worked into jewelry. It may be the shape which make the pieces so attractive, or that they are millions of years old.

1 Alabaster, 2 pieces dyed red
2 Alabaster ashtray, dyed blue
3 Meerschaum, rough
4 Meerschaum, costume jewelry
5 Meerschaum, cigarette holder

6 Ammonite, shell replaced by pyrite
7 Ammonite, shell replaced by pyrite
8 Trilobite, primeval crab in shale
9 Actaeonella, a sea snail, Austria

The illustrations are 20% smaller than the originals.

ORGANIC GEM MATERIALS

CORAL

Color: Red, pink, white (black, blue)	Transparency: Opaque
Color of streak: White	Refractive index: 1.486–1.658
Mohs' hardness: 3–4	Double refraction: −0.172
Specific gravity: 2.6–2.7	Dispersion: None
Cleavage: None	Pleochroism: None
Fracture: Irregular, splintery	Absorption spectrum: Not usable
Crystal system: Hexagonal; microcrystalline	Fluorescence: Weak
Chemical composition: $CaCO_3$ calcium carbonate (+magnesia +organic substance)	

Coral (Greek – meaning unknown) have built reefs and atolls with their branching trunks. Only their calcified skeletons are used in jewelry. They are formed by tiny polyps which sit within the cavities secreting a calcite substance through their bases.

The most valued type of coral is the noble red coral (*Corallicum rubrum*). The color is uniform throughout the branch, from soft pink to dark red, sometimes white or pink spotted (11). White, black and blue coral are also used; white coral as well as red is composed of calcium carbonate; the black and blue are composed of an organic horn substance (specific gravity 1.34–1.46). Black coral grows to a height of 10ft/3m.

Unworked coral is dull; when polished it has a vitreous luster. Sensitive to heat, acids and hot solutions; the color can fade when worn.

Found on the coasts of the Western Mediterranean, Bay of Biscay, Canary Isles, Malaysian Archipelago and Japan. Black coral is found in the Malaysian Archipelago, northern Australia and in the Red Sea.

Coral is to be found at depths of 10–1020ft/3–300m and is harvested in a weighted, wide-meshed net dredged across the sea bed. Because the coral grows with its broad base on the rocky seabed, this method destroys much valuable material. When it is brought to the surface, the soft parts are rubbed away and the material is sorted as to quality. The main trade center is Torre del Greco, south of Naples (Italy). Recently corals have also been imported from Japan, Australia and Hawaii.

Coral is worked with saw, knife, file and drill, rarely cut and polished. Used for beads in necklaces and bracelets; little stick-like rods are drilled and strung as spiky necklaces. Cabochons, ornamental objects and sculptures are also produced.

There are many imitations made from glass, horn, rubber, bone and plastics.

1 Noble coral, 3 beads, together 23.77ct	8 White coral, 2 engraved beads
2 Noble coral, branch, Sicily	9 Noble coral, engraved, Italy
3 Noble coral, 2 figurines, Japan	10 Noble coral, branch, Japan
4 Noble coral, 5 cabochons	11 Noble coral, 3 cabochons, 14.05ct
5 Noble coral, 2 necklaces	12 Noble coral, figurine, Italy
6 Noble coral, figurine, Japan	13 White coral, spiky necklace
7 White coral, branches, Japan	14 Black coral, branch, Australia

The illustrations are 50% smaller than the originals.

JET (7, 8)

Color: Black, dark brown	Transparency: Opaque
Color of streak: Black-brown	Refractive index: 1.64–1.68
Mohs' hardness: 2½–4	Double refraction: None
Specific gravity: 1.30–1.35	Dispersion: None
Cleavage: None	Pleochroism: None
Fracture: Conchoidal	Absorption spectrum: Not usable
Chemical composition: Lignite	Fluorescence: None

Jet is an organic product, a bituminous coal which can be polished. Has a velvety waxy luster, sometimes with pyrite inclusions and, when rubbed, becomes electrically charged. Much was found in England (Whitby, Yorks, but today it comes from Spain (Asturias), France (Dep. Aude) and the U.S. (Utah, Colorado). It is worked on a lathe. Used for mourning jewelry, rosaries, ornamental objects and cameos. Imitated by other types of coal (anthracite, cannel coal), glass, vulcanized rubber and onyx.

Cannel Coal (6) is used as an imitation of jet. The name means "candle" and refers to the wax which was extracted from these coals to make candles. Cannel coal is formed predominantly from plant spores and pollen by a coalification process into carbonaceous layers rich in combustible, volatile constituents. Due to its homogeneity and density, it can be worked on common carpenters' tools such as a lathe; high luster can be achieved through polishing.

IVORY (1–5, 9)

Color: White, creamy	Transparency: Translucent, opaque
Color of streak: White	Refractive index: 1.54
Mohs' hardness: 2–3	Double refraction: None
Specific gravity: 1.7–2.0	Dispersion: None
Cleavage: None	Pleochroism: None
Fracture: Fibrous	Absorption spectrum: Not usable
Chemical composition: Calcium phosphate	Fluorescence: Various blues

Ivory, originally, only referred to the material of the elephant's tusk. Today it is also the teeth of hippopotamus, narwhal, sea lion, wild boar, and fossilized mammoth. Most comes from Africa, some from Burma, India and Sumatra. Worked with tools and file, it can be dyed. Used for ornamental objects, pendants and costume jewelry. Imitated by all bones (10).

Odontolite Fossilized tooth or bone substance from extinct prehistoric animals (mammoth, mastodon, dinosaurs). Dyed turquoise blue with vivianite (p. 208), it is used as an imitation of turquoise (p. 170). Found in Siberia and the south of France. Has become very rare.

---

1 Ivory, concentric spheres, China	7 Jet, 3 faceted pieces
2 Ivory, figurine and bowl	8 Jet, 2 cabochons
3 Ivory, rough, Congo	9 Ivory, brooch, China
4 Ivory, necklace, China	10 Bone, dyed, Israel
5 Ivory, bracelet and figurine	
6 Cannel coal, rough and partly polished	

The illustrations are 50% smaller than the originals.

AMBER

Color: Light yellow to brown, red, nearly colorless, milky white, blue, black, greenish
Color of streak: White
Mohs' hardness: $2-2\frac{1}{2}$
Specific gravity: Usually 1.05–1.09, maximum 1.30
Cleavage: None
Fracture: Conchoidal, brittle
Crystal system: Amorphous
Chemical composition: Approx. $C_{10}H_{16}O$, mixture of various resins

Transparency: Transparent to opaque
Refractive index: 1.54
Double refraction: None
Dispersion: None
Pleochroism: None
Absorption spectrum: Not usable
Fluorescence: Bluish-white to yellow-green
Burmite: blue

Amber is the fossilized, hardened resin of the pine tree, *Pinus succinifera*, formed in the Eocene period about 50 million years ago. Mostly amber is drop or nodular shaped with a homogeneous structure, or has a shell-like formation, often with a weathered crust. Pieces the size of a head, weighing over 22lb/10kg, have been found. It is sometimes found with inclusions of insects (see p. 47), parts of plants, or sometimes pyrites. It is often turbid because of numerous blisters, hair lines or tension fissures. It is possible to clear air bubbles and enclosed liquids from the material by boiling in rapeseed oil, thus improving the quality.

Reaction to chemicals and hot solutions varies with origin. Can be ignited by a match. When rubbed with a cloth, amber becomes electrically charged and can attract small particles. Takes polish well, and has a resinous luster. The largest deposit in the world is in Samland near Palmnicken, west of Konigsberg, formerly eastern Prussia, and now Poland. Under 100ft/30m of sand is a 30ft/9m layer of amber-containing clay, the so-called blue earth. Mined from the surface, the amber is picked and washed out. Only about 15% is suitable for jewelry. The remainder is used for pressed amber or melted for technical purposes.

There are large reserves on the seabed of the Baltic. After heavy storms, amber is found on the beaches and in shallow waters of bordering countries, after the surf has stirred up the seabed. This sea amber is especially solid and used to be regularly fished for by fishermen. Further but less important suppliers are Sicily (named Simetite), Rumania (Rumanite), Burma (Burmite), Canada, some Atlantic states of the U.S. and the Dominican Republic.

It has been used since prehistoric times for jewelry and religious objects, accessories for smokers, also as a cure for various illnesses. Amber, the "gold of the North", is the earliest-used gem material of all. Used today for ornamental objects, ring stones, pendants, brooches and necklaces. Smaller pieces and remains are welded at 284–482°F/140–250°C and 3000 atmospheres into Ambroid, a natural-looking pressed amber. Imitated by new resins (copal), synthetic resins and yellow glass.

1 Amber, rough
2 Amber, partly polished
3 Amber, 3 cabochons
4 Amber, 2 bead necklaces

5 Amber, 2 baroque necklaces
6 Amber, various colors
7 Amber, with insect inclusion
8 Amber, with bubble inclusion

PEARL

Color: Pink, silver, cream, golden, green, blue, black
Color of streak: White
Mohs' hardness: 3–4
Specific gravity: 2.60–2.78
Cleavage: None
Fracture: Conchoidal or scaly
Crystal system: Microcrystalline
Chemical composition: 84–92% calcium-carbonate, 4–13% organic substances, 3–4% water

Transparency: Translucent to opaque
Refractive index: 1.52–1.66
  Black: 1.53–1.69
Double refraction: Weak or none
Dispersion: None
Pleochroism: None
Absorption spectrum: Not usable
Fluorescence: Weak; not usable.
  Natural black: red-reddish

The derivation of the name is uncertain but may be from a type of shell (Latin – *perna*) or from its spherical shape (Latin – *sphaerula*). Pearls are produced by molluscs, rarely by snails. They consist of mother-of-pearl, which is mainly calcium carbonate (in the form of aragonite), and an organic horn substance (conchiolin) which are formed concentrically around microcrystals. Although the Mohs' hardness is only 3 to 4, pearls are extraordinarily compact and it is difficult to crush them.

The size can vary between a pin head and a pigeon's egg. The largest pearl ever found weighs 450cts (1800 grains); it is in the South Kensington Geological Museum in London.

The typical pearly luster also called "orient" is produced by the overlapping platelets of aragonite and skins of conchiolin nearer to the pearl surface. This formation also causes the refraction of light and the resulting colors of the spectrum which can be observed on the pearl surface. The color of the pearl varies with the type of mollusc and the water, and is dependent on the color of the upper conchiolin layer. If the conchiolin is irregularly distributed, the pearl becomes spotty.

As conchiolin is an organic substance it tends to change, especially when dehydrated. This can lead to an "ageing" of the pearl and to a shortening of its life. Firstly such a pearl becomes dull, then cracks and finally peels. There is no assuredness of a definite length of life for a pearl. The average estimate is about 100–150 years. There are some pearls which are known to be several hundred years old and are of good appearance. Certainly care can help to preserve pearls. Dryness, as well as humidity, are detrimental. Pearls are very sensitive to acids, perspiration, cosmetics and hair spray. See also p. 224.

1 Mother-of-pearl shell with cultured pearl
2 Pearl necklace, Biwaco cultivation, baroque
3 Pearl necklace, 3 chokers silver white
4 Pearl necklace, baroque
5 Pearl necklace, Biwaco cultivation, graduated
6 4 baroque pearls
7 Pearl, Mabe cultivation, silver white, 20mm
8 Pearl, Mabe cultivation, gray, oval
9 6 baroque pearls, 35.71cts
10 10 baroque pearls, Biwaco cultivation
11 Mother-of-pearl, 2 cut pieces
12 Pearl necklace, gray
13 3 pearls, Biwaco cultivation, 29.67cts
14 4 cultured pearls, 16.16cts
15 Pearl necklace, choker, gray
16 6 black baroque pearls
17 Pearl necklace, black baroque
18 6 gray pearls, 17.28cts

The illustrations are 60% smaller than the originals.

Pearl continued from p. 222

Pearls are formed by oyster-type shelled sea molluscs, some fresh water mussels, and rarely by some snails. They are formed as a reaction against a foreign body which has intruded between the shell and mantle or into the interior of the mantle. The outer skin of the mantle – the ectoderm – forms the shell by secretion of mother-of-pearl (nacre) and also encrusts all foreign bodies within its reach. Such an encrustation forms a pearl. If the pearl is formed as a wart-like growth on the inside of the shell, it must be separated from the shell when it is collected. Its shape is therefore semi-spherical so that it is called a blister pearl. In the trade they sometimes complement these with mother-of-pearl pieces shaped to form complete spheres.

When a foreign body enters the inner part of the mantle, the mussel forms a non-attached, rounded pearl as a type of immunity defense. The process is shown in the diagram below. The ectodermal skin tissue, which has been drawn into the mantle together with the foreign body, forms a pearl sac around the intruder and isolates it by secretion of nacre. As we know now, the nacre can also produce a pearl without any foreign body. It is sufficient that a part of the ectoderm (for instance by an injury from the outside) is drawn into the cell lining of the mantle.

Pearl-producing sea molluscs live in long stretches of banks near the coast at a depth of about 50ft/15m. The pearl oysters are roughly 3in/8cm in diameter, their life span is about 13 years. The most important occurrences yielding best qualities (rose and creamy white) are in the Persian Gulf, which was fished for pearls in antiquity. Because of this occurrence, all natural sea-water pearls, wherever they came from, were called "oriental pearls" in the trade. Mostly small pearls (called seed pearls) were fished in grounds (pinky red and soft yellow) in the Gulf of Manaar between India and Sri Lanka. Other economically important occurrences are on the coasts of Central America and North Australia.

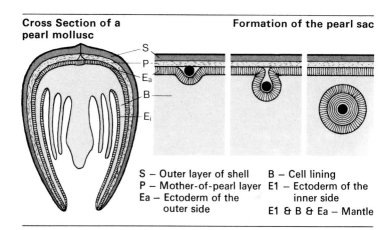

Cross Section of a pearl mollusc

Formation of the pearl sac

S – Outer layer of shell
P – Mother-of-pearl layer
Ea – Ectoderm of the outer side
B – Cell lining
E1 – Ectoderm of the inner side
E1 & B & Ea – Mantle

Pearls are harvested by divers, mainly women. Only every 30th or 40th oyster contains a pearl. In Sri Lanka in 1958, dragnets were experimentally used, the result was catastrophic as the next growth was completely destroyed.

Some snails (notably *Strombus gigas*) can produce pearls (called conch or pink pearl) with a silky sheen which are like porcelain. Commercially they are not important. Also of no great commercial importance are the river pearls. They are rarely of good quality. Fresh-water pearl-producing mussels are found in moderate climates. In Scandinavia they have been placed under a nature conservation law. During the Middle Ages, fishing for pearl in the rivers of central Europe was of some importance. Because of pollution of the water, the pearl mussel has not survived well.

CULTURED PEARLS

The increased demand for pearls has led to their cultivation in large quantities. Such cultured pearls are not imitation, but a natural product which has been produced with man's help. Today cultured pearls amount to 90% of the total pearl trade.

The principle behind pearl culturing is simple. Man causes the mollusc to produce a pearl by insertion of a foreign body (see Formation of the pearl, p. 224). In China as early as the 13th century, small leaden figures of Buddha were fixed to the inner wall of a mollusc shell so that they would be covered with pearl material. Round pearls were first produced by the Swedish naturalist, Carl V. Linne, in 1761. In 1893 the Japanese, K. Mikimoto, managed to produce semi-spherical pearls.

Modern cultivation of round pearls is based on the experimental work of the German, F. Alverdes, as well as the Japanese, T. Nishikawa, T. Mise and K. Mikimoto between 1910 and 1920. To stimulate the molluscs to produce pearls, rounded mother-of-pearl beads from the shell of the North American fresh-water mussel, along with a piece of tissue from the mantle of a pearl mollusc (*Pinetada martensi*), are inserted by a complicated operation into the cell lining of the mantle of another pearl mollusc. The inserted tissue grows around the bead and has the effect of a pearl sac in which pearl material is secreted. The most important element in the production of a pearl is the tissue, not the foreign body. Theoretically one can do without the bead, but then the process would not normally be economical because the culture of a large pearl would take too much time. By inserting a bead, the "working time" of the mollusc is shortened. Only one layer of nacre is necessary for the bead to receive a typical pearl luster.

The insertion of the bead into the mollusc requires clever hands, women being most suitable for this job. They operate on 300 to 1000 oysters a day. The normal size of bead (0.24–0.27in/6–7mm) requires a three-year-old mollusc. For smaller beads, younger molluscs can be used. When the bead is above 0.35in/9mm, the mortality rate of the oysters is 80%.

See also p. 227.

Pearl farm in Japan. Wire baskets or plastic cages containing the cultivated mussels are suspended from large wooden or bamboo floats

Modern cultivated pearl farm. Mussel cages are hung from ropes which are fixed to buoys

Cages must always be supervised and several times a year cleaned of unwanted deposits

Prepared molluscs are kept under water in the bay in wire cages or, preferably nowadays, plastic cages which are suspended at a depth of 6½–20ft/ 2–6m and hung from bamboo floats or ropes which are fixed to buoys. Several times a year the molluscs and their cages must be cleaned and freed from seaweed and other deposits. Their natural enemies are fishes, crabs, polyps and various parasites, mainly a zooplankton which appears in large quantities like a "red flood" and endangers a whole cultivation farm because it consumes large quantities of oxygen. The temperature of the water has a great influence on the growth of the molluscs, the Japanese variety dies at 51°F/ 11°C. If the temperature suddenly falls before the winter, the floats with the submerged burden must be dragged from northern farms to warmer waters.

The yearly growth rate of the pearl layer surrounding the bead in Japan used to be 0.09mm; it has now reached 0.3mm and is said to be 1.5mm in southern seas. Experiments are being made to transfer the farms from the bays to the open sea, as it is thought that the water current would activate the molluscs to produce faster, with better shapes. At the same time, the bays with their innumerable floats would be less crowded and conditions improved for other pearl-molluscs.

The molluscs remain in the water for 3 to 4 years; by then the layers around the bead are of about 0.8–1.2mm. If they remain longer in the water, there is a danger that they will become ill, die or mar the shape of the pearl. No mother-of-pearl is secreted after the 7th year. Cultured pearls with a thin pearl covering are considered inferior.

Insertion of the bead into the mollusc

The best times for harvesting in Japan are the dry winter months, as the secretion of the mother-of-pearl is halted and a specially good luster is present. The pearls are taken from the molluscs, washed, dried and sorted according to color, size and quality. The whole production yields roughly 10% for good quality jewelry, 15–20% are rejected.

The first Japanese farms were founded in southern Honshu, today there are also some on Shikoku and Kyushu. Since 1956 pearls of good quality have been grown in coastal waters of north and west Australia, also blister pearls (called Mabe cultured pearls) with a diameter of 0.6–1in/15–25mm from the black-shelled mabe pearl oyster. Recently a number of experimental farms have been started in several states in South East Asia.

Since the 1950s there has been a fresh water pearl farm in the Biwa Lake (Japanese—Biwa co), north of Kyoto on Honshu. Pieces of tissue measuring 4×4mm, usually without solid beads, are inserted into the fresh water mussels (*Hyriopsis schlegeli*). As these mussels are very large (8×4.3in/ 20×11cm), ten insertions can be made into each half and, sometimes an additional one with a mother-of-pearl bead. For each insertion a sac with pearl is formed. After one to two years the pearls are 0.24–0.28in/6–8mm large, but rarely round. They are taken out of the mussel, covered with new tissue and inserted into another mussel of the same type to improve the shape. The life of a fresh water mussel is 13 years, but after the operation it produces mother-of-pearl only for 3 more years. Many mussels can be harvested three times.

Biwaco cultured pearls reach a diameter of 0.5in/12mm, but rarely have a perfect round shape. The natural colors of white-pink, orange, gold-yellow, brown and blue are often bleached.

Cultivation methods are the same as for the sea molluscs. The cages are hung on a bamboo frame at about 3–6½ft/1–2m depth. The success rate is about 60% higher than in sea water, probably because there are fewer dangers in Biwa Lake.

Use and valuation of pearls

Pearls have been regarded as one of the most valuable gem materials. They have been used for adornment for 6000 years. In 2500 BC, there was a substantial pearl trade in China. Pearls are also popular because they do not require any processing. In their natural state they show their full gloss, the desired luster.

70% of all pearls are strung and worn as necklaces. The usual length is about 15½in/40cm. Double lengths are called sautoirs. Pearls are either matched for size to make a necklace or are graduated in size with the biggest in the middle and smallest at the ends. The careful selection of the pearls for a necklace or collar is done by eye.

A point on the pearl, which either has a mark or is less perfect, is chosen for drilling a hole, thus eliminating the mark. The diameter of the drill hole according to international agreement should be 0.3mm. To fix the pin for earrings, needles and rings a drill hole to the depth of $\frac{2}{3}$ or $\frac{3}{4}$ of the pearl's diameter should suffice. Blue pearls should never be drilled, as they may change color when air reaches the drill hole.

Spotted or damaged pearls can be peeled; i.e. the outer layer can be removed. Badly damaged parts can be cut away; the remaining part is traded as half or three-quarter pearl (not to be confused with blister pearls). They are used mainly for earrings and brooches. The luster of pearls, lost by wear or wrong storage, can usually be revived by the expert.

The pearl is valued according to shape, color, size and luster. The most valuable is the spherical shape. Half-spherical pearls, or those flattened on one side are called bouton or button pearls, irregular pearls are baroque pearls. Pearls worn down in a necklace become barrel shaped.

Fair-skinned women in Europe and the U.S. prefer rose color; brunettes and dark-haired southern ladies prefer cream-colored pearls. Dull colors are often bleached or dyed.

Pearls are weighed in grains (1 grain 0.05g=0.25ct, i.e. $\frac{1}{4}$ carat) and today often in carats; the Japanese weight of *momme* (=3.75g=18.75ct) is becoming rarer in European trade circles. The pearl is evaluated as follows: the weight is multiplied by itself which is called "once the weight". This is then multiplied by a base price which takes account of quality and all other factors. It can be 1, but can also be 40. For necklaces and collars where a large number of matched pearls are required, the base price tends to be very high.

The word "pearl" without addition should only be used for natural pearls. Cultured pearls must be designated as such.

Recognizing pearls

There is little difference in the appearance of natural and cultured pearls. To differentiate between them is difficult. The specific gravity can help, as it is greater than 2.73 in the case of most (but not all!) cultured pearls, while the specific gravity of natural pearls is usually (but not always) lower. Under ultra-violet light, the cultured pearls have a yellow luminescence, and under x-rays a green one.

A reliable method of differentiating between cultured and natural pearls is by examining the inner structure. Natural pearls have a concentrically layered structure, while the inner structure of the cultured pearl varies according to the type of bead. Formerly experts used a special instrument to help check the structure of drilled pearls. The method commonly employed today is the use of x-ray radiography (Lauegrams). This can be applied to drilled and undrilled pearls. As in the case of all valuable gems there are numerous imitations of pearls. Among these one has to include the Australian blister pearl; this is not a cultured pearl in the trade sense. It consists of a thin mother-of-pearl layer and some other artificial part. A clay or resin bead is fixed to the inner part of a shell and is then covered with a thin pearl layer. After the harvest the bead is removed and replaced by a mother-of-pearl half-bead. The product is begun in Australia, but finished in Japan.

A fine imitation is the fish-scale imitation pearl. It consists of glass coated with *essence d'orient* which is produced from the scales of certain fish. In other imitations, part of a sea snail (antilles pearls), mussels (takara pearls from Japan) or teeth (of the sea cow – dugong pearls) are used. There are also plastic products on the market.

The operculum (Chinese cat's eye) has a similar structure as a half-pearl, with a porcelain-type coloring, but is actually the slightly arched lid of a sea snail found in the Australasian islands area, where it is used for adornment. It is not well known in Europe.

MOTHER-OF-PEARL (p.223 nos 1, 11)

The inner nacreous layer of a mollusc shell which has an iridescent play of color is called mother-of-pearl. In the jewelry industry it is used for ornamental purposes, costume jewelry or for inlaid work (for instance in the handles of knives and pistols). For structure and formation, see p. 222 and 224.

Structure of a natural pearl

Structure of a cultured pearl

Diamond Production

Total carat production per year

1913	6,580,000	1957	26,045,000
1920	3,580,000	1958	28,041,000
1930	7,457,000	1959	26,655,000
1940	14,300,000	1960	27,300,000
1945	14,384,000	1961	33,213,000
1946	10,127,000	1962	34,006,000
1947	9,754,000	1963	36,661,000
1948	10,335,000	1964	37,815,000
1949	14,264,000	1965	37,030,000
1950	15,517,000	1966	39,955,000
1951	16,947,000	1967	42,685,000
1952	18,741,000	1968	46,362,000
1953	20,163,000	1969	48,883,500
1954	20,521,000	1970	50,056,021
1955	21,377,000	1971	49,559,524
1956	23,718,000	1973	43,067,000

World Production by countries (1,000 carat)

Country	1974			1975†		
	Gem	Industrial	Total	Gem	Industrial	Total
Angola	1,470	490	1,960	345	115	*460
Botswana	408	2,310	2,718	362	2,052	2,414
Central African Republic	220	118	338	220	119	339
Ghana	257	2,315	2,572	233	2,095	2,328
Guinea*	25	55	80	25	55	80
Ivory Coast	112	167	279	84	125	209
Lesotho	2	9	11	1	2	3
Liberia	377	259	636	241	165	406
Sierra Leone	670	1,000	*1,670	600	900	*1,500
Republic of South Africa	3,440	4,070	7,510	3,435	3,860	7,295
Namibia	1,491	79	1,570	1,660	88	1,748
Tanzania	249	249	498	224	224	448
Zaire	1,143	12,468	13,611	1,076	11,734	12,810
Brazil	127	127	254	135	135	*270
Guyana	12	18	30	8	13	21
India	18	3	21	17	3	20
Indonesia*	12	3	15	12	3	15
U.S.S.R.*	1,900	7,600	9,500	1,950	7,750	9,700
Venezuela	279	970	1,249	239	821	1,060
Total	12,212	32,310	44,522	10,867	30,259	41,126

*Estimate   †Preliminary figures

STONES AS SYMBOLS (see p. 8)

Stones of the Planets

Sun	Chrysoberyl, diamond
Moon	Moonstone, pearl, emerald
Mars	Red garnet, ruby
Mercury	Yellow sapphire, topaz
Jupiter	Amethyst, lapis lazuli, blue sapphire
Saturn	Aquamarine, blue spinel
Venus	Orange-yellow sapphire (padparadschah)
	Yellow-red zircon (Hyacinth)

Stones of the Zodiac

Sign	Dates	Stone
Aquarius	21.1 –18.2	Hawk's eye, turquoise
Pisces	19.2 –20.3	Amethyst, amethyst quartz
Aries	21.3 –20.4	Red jasper, red cornelian
Taurus	21.4 –20.5	Orange cornelian, rose quartz
Gemini	21.5 –20.6	Citrine, tiger's eye
Cancer	21.6 –20.7	Green aventurine, chrysoprase
Leo	21.7 –22.8	Rock crystal, golden quartz
Virgo	23.8 –22.9	Yellow agate, yellow citrine
Libra	23.9 –22.10	Orange citrine, smoky quartz
Scorpio	23.10–22.11	Blood-red cornelian, sard
Sagittarius	22.11–21.12	Blue quartz, chalcedony
Capricorn	22.12–20.1	Onyx, quartz cat's eye

Stones of the Month

Month	In English-speaking countries	In German-speaking countries
January	Garnet	Garnet, rose quartz
February	Amethyst	Amethyst, onyx
March	Aquamarine	Aquamarine, red jasper
April	Diamond	Rock crystal, diamond
May	Emerald	Chrysoprase, emerald
June	Pearl	Moonstone, pearl
July	Ruby	Cornelian, ruby
August	Peridot	Aventurine, peridot
September	Sapphire	Lapis lazuli, sapphire
October	Opal	Opal, tourmaline
November	Topaz	Tiger's eye, topaz
December	Turquoise	Turquoise, zircon

Tables of Constants

How to use the tables

These tables have been compiled to aid both the professional and the amateur to identify individual gemstones. They are designed to be used in conjunction with the standard gemological tests. They are not totally comprehensive but they should enable the tester to eliminate some possibilities and perhaps suggest some, if he or she is faced with one of the more unusual examples.

Suppose that you have an unknown yellow gemstone to identify, using the Tables of Constants this is how you go about identifying it:

1 Turn to pages 238–239 which cover yellow, orange and brown stones.

2 Test for specific gravity (p. 23–5); this gives you a weight of 3.65.

3 Test the refractive index (p. 31–3); this gives a reading of 1.738.

4 Run down the 1.700–1.799 column and across the 3.50–3.99 line until they meet. This gives you several possibilities.

5 Test for double refraction (p. 34). If there is none, the field is narrowed to periclase or one of the three members of the garnet group.

6 If feasible (see p. 20), make a scratch test using the No. 6 tester. If this makes no mark, the stone is a garnet.

7 Turning to the garnet section in the main text, the tester will observe that the absorption spectra of grossular, pyrope and hessonite are very different. Using the spectroscope (p. 36–9), you can easily identify the class of garnet from which the specimen stone comes.

Illustration Acknowledgements

Photos: Dr H. Bank, Idar-Oberstein: 56 top right; G. Becker, Idar-Oberstein: 89; E. A. Bunzel, Idar-Oberstein: 56 top left and below, 57 top and below left, 60 below, 61 below; Chudoba-Guebelin, Edelsteinkundliches Handbuch, Wilhelm Stolifuss Verlag, Bonn: 39; De Beers Consolidated Mines Ltd, Johannesburg, South Africa: 40, 50, 53 59, 60 top, 72 left, 73, 75; H. Eisenbeiss, Munich: 34; Dr E. Geubelin Lucerne: 52 below, 57 below right, 85, 93; K. Hartmann, Sobernheim: all gemstone plates as well as 29, 43, 47, 67; Her Majesty's Stationary Office, London: 9; Jain Cultured Pearls, *see* Heim/Bergstrasse: 61, 226, 227, 228; E. Pauly, Veitsrudt: 144; J. Petsch jr., Idar-Oberstein: 52 top; A. Ruppenthal KG Idar-Oberstein: 138, 140.

Drawings: H. Hoffmann, Munich all diagrams apart from 16 and 17; W. Schumann: das Grusse Buch der Erde (The large book of the Earth), Deutscher Buercherbund, Stuttgart: 16, 17.

Chart: R. Webster: The Gemmologists' Compendium, N.A.G. Press Ltd, London.

Refr. Index	1.400–1.499	1.500–1.599	1.600–1.699
Spec. Grav. 1.00–1.99	Ulexite (2) 0.029 Opal ($5\frac{1}{2}$–$6\frac{1}{2}$) –	Ulexite (2) 0.029 Amber (2–$2\frac{1}{2}$) – Ivory (2–3) – Gaylussite ($2\frac{1}{2}$) –	
2.00–2.49	Ulexite (2) 0.029 Natrolite ($5\frac{1}{2}$) 0.013 Sodalite ($5\frac{1}{2}$–6) – Opal ($5\frac{1}{2}$–$6\frac{1}{2}$) –	Ulexite (2) 0.029 Meerschaum (2–$2\frac{1}{2}$) – Ivory (2–3) – Colemanite ($4\frac{1}{2}$) 0.028 Thomsonite (5–$5\frac{1}{2}$) 0.028 Leucite ($5\frac{1}{2}$) 0.001 Petalite (6–$6\frac{1}{2}$) 0.016 Hambergite ($7\frac{1}{2}$) 0.072	Colemanite ($4\frac{1}{2}$) 0.028 Hambergite ($7\frac{1}{2}$) 0.072
2.50–2.99	Calcite (3) 0.172 Coral (3–4) 0.172	Vivianite ($1\frac{1}{2}$–2) 0.047 Calcite (3) 0.172 Anhydrite (3–$3\frac{1}{2}$) 0.043 Coral (3–4) 0.172 Pearl (3–4) – Howlite ($3\frac{1}{2}$) 0.019 Aragonite ($3\frac{1}{2}$–4) 0.155 Dolomite ($3\frac{1}{2}$–$4\frac{1}{2}$) 0.179 Augelite (5) 0.014 Scapolite (5–$6\frac{1}{2}$) 0.009 Leucite ($5\frac{1}{2}$) 0.001 Beryllonite ($5\frac{1}{2}$–6) 0.009 Sanidine (6) 0.006 Labradorite (6–$6\frac{1}{2}$) 0.008 Moonstone (6–$6\frac{1}{2}$) 0.005 Chalcedony ($6\frac{1}{2}$–7) 0.006 Jasper ($6\frac{1}{2}$–7) – Rock crystal (7) 0.009 Smoky quartz (7) 0.009 Beryl ($7\frac{1}{2}$–8) 0.006	Vivianite ($1\frac{1}{2}$–2) 0.047 Calcite (3) 0.172 Anhydrite (3–$3\frac{1}{2}$) 0.043 Coral (3–4) 0.172 Pearl (3–4) – Howlite ($3\frac{1}{2}$) 0.019 Aragonite ($3\frac{1}{2}$–4) 0.155 Dolomite ($3\frac{1}{2}$–$4\frac{1}{2}$) 0.179 Datolite (5–$5\frac{1}{2}$) 0.044 Nephrite (6–$6\frac{1}{2}$) 0.027 Beryl ($7\frac{1}{2}$–8) 0.006 Phenacite ($7\frac{1}{2}$–8) 0.016
3.00–3.49	Fluorite (4) –	Magnesite (4) 0.202	Magnesite (4) 0.202 Apatite (5) 0.002 Hemimorphite (5) 0.022 Datolite (5–$5\frac{1}{2}$) 0.044 Enstatite ($5\frac{1}{2}$) 0.010 Amblygonite (6) 0.026 Nephrite (6–$6\frac{1}{2}$) 0.027 Jadeite ($6\frac{1}{2}$–7) 0.013 Danburite (7–$7\frac{1}{2}$) 0.006 Tourmaline (7–$7\frac{1}{2}$) 0.014 Euclase ($7\frac{1}{2}$) 0.020
3.50–3.99			Celestite (3–$3\frac{1}{2}$) 0.009 Barytocalcite (4) – Hemimorphite (5) 0.022 Topaz (8) 0.008
4.00–4.99		Witherite ($3\frac{1}{2}$) 0.148	Barite (3) 0.012 Celestite (3–$3\frac{1}{2}$) 0.009 Witherite ($3\frac{1}{2}$) 0.148

Refr. Index	1.700–1.799	1.800–1.899	1.900 and higher
Spec. Grav. 1.00–1.99			
2.00–2.49			
2.50–2.99			
3.00–3.49	Magnesite (4) 0.202		Diamond (10) –
3.50–3.99	Kyanite ($4\frac{1}{2}$–7) 0.017 Periclase ($5\frac{1}{2}$–6) – Zircon ($6\frac{1}{2}$–$7\frac{1}{2}$) 0.059 Sapphire (9) 0.008	Zircon ($6\frac{1}{2}$–$7\frac{1}{2}$) 0.059	Zircon ($6\frac{1}{2}$–$7\frac{1}{2}$) 0.059 Diamond (10) –
4.00–4.99	Zircon ($6\frac{1}{2}$–$7\frac{1}{2}$) 0.059 Sapphire (9) 0.008	Zircon ($6\frac{1}{2}$–$7\frac{1}{2}$) 0.059 YAG (8) –	Sphalerite ($3\frac{1}{2}$–4) – Hematite ($5\frac{1}{2}$–$6\frac{1}{2}$) 0.28 Zircon ($6\frac{1}{2}$–$7\frac{1}{2}$) 0.059
5.00–5.99			Scheelite ($4\frac{1}{2}$–5) 0.016 Hematite ($5\frac{1}{2}$–$6\frac{1}{2}$) 0.28 Strontium titanate (6–$6\frac{1}{2}$)–
6.00–6.99		Cerussite ($3\frac{1}{2}$) 0.274	Phosgenite ($2\frac{1}{2}$–3) 0.028 Cerussite ($3\frac{1}{2}$) 0.274 Scheelite ($4\frac{1}{2}$–5) 0.016 Cassiterite (6–7) 0.096
7.00 and higher			Cassiterite (6–7) 0.096

Refr. Index	1.400–1.499	1.500–1.599	1.600–1.699
Spec. Grav.			
1.00–1.99	Opal $(5\frac{1}{2}–6\frac{1}{2})$ –	Amber $(2–2\frac{1}{2})$ –	
2.00–2.49	Cancrinite (5–6) 0.023 Opal $(5\frac{1}{2}–6\frac{1}{2})$ – Tugtupite (6) 0.006	Stichtite $(1\frac{1}{2}–2\frac{1}{2})$ 0.027 Alabaster (2) 0.010 Meerschaum $(2–2\frac{1}{2})$ – Apophyllite $(4\frac{1}{2}–5)$ 0.002 Thomsonite $(5–5\frac{1}{2})$ 0.028 Cancrinite (5–6) 0.023 Tugtupite (6) 0.006 Petalite $(6–6\frac{1}{2})$ 0.016	
2.50–2.99	Calcite (3) 0.172 Coral (3–4) 0.172 Cancrinite (5–6) 0.023 Tugtupite (6) 0.006	Calcite (3) 0.172 Anhydrite $(3–3\frac{1}{2})$ 0.043 Coral (3–4) 0.172 Pearl (3–4) – Aragonite $(3\frac{1}{2}–4)$ 0.155 Dolomite $(3\frac{1}{2}–4\frac{1}{2})$ 0.179 Apophyllite $(4\frac{1}{2}–5)$ 0.002 Cancrinite (5–6) 0.023 Scapolite $(5–6\frac{1}{2})$ 0.009 Elaeolite $(5\frac{1}{2}–6)$ 0.004 Bytownite (6) 0.009 Tugtupite (6) 0.006 Aventurine Feldspar $(6–6\frac{1}{2})$ 0.01 Fossilized wood $(6\frac{1}{2}–7)$ – Jasper $(6\frac{1}{2}–7)$ – Rose quartz (7) 0.009 Beryl $(7\frac{1}{2}–8)$ 0.006	Calcite (3) 0.172 Anhydrite $(3–3\frac{1}{2})$ 0.043 Coral (3–4) 0.172 Pearl (3–4) – Aragonite $(3\frac{1}{2}–4)$ 0.155 Dolomite $(3\frac{1}{2}–4\frac{1}{2})$ 0.179 Nephrite $(6–6\frac{1}{2})$ 0.027 Beryl $(7\frac{1}{2}–8)$ 0.006 Phenacite $(7\frac{1}{2}–8)$ 0.016
3.00–3.49	Fluorite (4) –		Rhodochrosite (4) 0.22 Apatite (5) 0.002 Nephrite $(6–6\frac{1}{2})$ 0.027 Kunzite (6–7) 0.015 Jadeite $(6\frac{1}{2}–7)$ 0.013 Danburite $(7–7\frac{1}{2})$ 0.006 Tourmaline $(7–7\frac{1}{2})$ 0.014 Andalusite $(7\frac{1}{2})$ 0.007 Rhodizite (8) –
3.50–3.99			Chalybite $(3\frac{1}{2}–4\frac{1}{2})$ 0.24 Rhodochrosite (4) 0.22 Willemite $(5\frac{1}{2})$ 0.028 Topaz (8) 0.008
4.00–4.99			Barite (3) 0.012 Smithsonite (5) 0.228 Willemite $(5\frac{1}{2})$ 0.028
5.00–5.99			
6.00–6.99			
7.00 and higher			

Refr. Index	1.700–1.799	1.800–1.899	1.900 and higher
Spec. Grav. .00–1.99			
.00–2.49			
.50–2.99			
.00–3.49	Rhodochrosite (4) 0.22 Rhodonite $(5\frac{1}{2}$–$6\frac{1}{2})$ 0.011	Rhodochrosite (4) 0.22 Purpurite $(4$–$4\frac{1}{2})$ 0.08	Purpurite $(4$–$4\frac{1}{2})$ 0.08
.50–3.99	Chalybite $(3\frac{1}{2}$–$4\frac{1}{2})$ 0.24 Rhodochrosite (4) 0.22 Willemite $(5\frac{1}{2})$ 0.028 Rhodonite $(5\frac{1}{2}$–$6\frac{1}{2})$ 0.011 Zircon $(6\frac{1}{2}$–$7\frac{1}{2})$ 0.059 Pyrope $(7$–$7\frac{1}{2})$ – Rhodolite $(7$–$7\frac{1}{2})$ – Almandine $(7\frac{1}{2})$ – Hessonite $(7\frac{1}{2})$ – Gahnite $(7\frac{1}{2}$–8) – Spinel (8) – Taaffeite (8) 0.004 Alexandrite $(8\frac{1}{2})$ 0.010 Ruby (9) 0.008 Sapphire (9) 0.008	Chalybite $(3\frac{1}{2}$–$4\frac{1}{2})$ 0.24 Rhodochrosite (4) 0.22 Zircon $(6\frac{1}{2}$–$7\frac{1}{2})$ 0.059 Almandine $(7\frac{1}{2})$ –	Zircon $(6\frac{1}{2}$–$7\frac{1}{2})$ 0.059
.00–4.99	Smithsonite (5) 0.228 Willemite $(5\frac{1}{2})$ 0.028 Zircon $(6\frac{1}{2}$–$7\frac{1}{2})$ 0.059 Spessartite $(7$–$7\frac{1}{2})$ – Almandine $(7\frac{1}{2})$ – Painite $(7\frac{1}{2}$–8) 0.029 Ruby (9) 0.008 Sapphire (9) 0.008	Smithsonite (5) 0.228 Zircon $(6\frac{1}{2}$–$7\frac{1}{2})$ 0.059 Spessartite $(7$–$7\frac{1}{2})$ – Almandine $(7\frac{1}{2})$ – Painite $(7\frac{1}{2}$–8) 0.029	Sphalerite $(3\frac{1}{2}$–4) – Hematite $(5\frac{1}{2}$–$6\frac{1}{2})$ 0.28 Rutile $(6$–$6\frac{1}{2})$ 0.28 Zircon $(6\frac{1}{2}$–$7\frac{1}{2})$ 0.059
.00–5.99			Crocoite $(2\frac{1}{2})$ 0.35 Proustite $(2\frac{1}{2})$ 0.296 Cuprite $(3\frac{1}{2}$–4) – Scheelite $(4\frac{1}{2}$–5) 0.016 Zincite $(4\frac{1}{2}$–5) 0.016 Tantalite (5–6) 0.17 Hematite $(5\frac{1}{2}$–$6\frac{1}{2})$ 0.28
.00–6.99			Crocoite $(2\frac{1}{2})$ 0.35 Wulfenite (3) 0.10 Cuprite $(3\frac{1}{2}$–4) – Scheelite $(4\frac{1}{2}$–5) 0.016 Tantalite (5–6) 0.17
.00 nd higher			Wulfenite (3) 0.10 Tantalite (5–6) 0.17

Refr. Index	1.400–1.499	1.500–1.599	1.600–1.699
Spec. Grav.			
1.00–1.99	Opal ($5\frac{1}{2}$–$6\frac{1}{2}$) –	Amber (2–$2\frac{1}{2}$) – Ivory (2–3) –	Jet ($2\frac{1}{2}$–4) –
2.00–2.49	Cancrinite (5–6) 0.023 Natrolite ($5\frac{1}{2}$) 0.013 Opal ($5\frac{1}{2}$–$6\frac{1}{2}$) –	Ivory (2–3) – Apophyllite ($4\frac{1}{2}$–5) 0.002 Cancrinite (5–6) 0.023	
2.50–2.99	Calcite (3) 0.172 Onyx Marble (3) 0.172 Cancrinite (5–6) 0.023	Calcite (3) 0.172 Onyx Marble (3) 0.172 Pearl (3–4) – Aragonite ($3\frac{1}{2}$–4) 0.155 Dolomite ($3\frac{1}{2}$–$4\frac{1}{2}$) 0.179 Apophyllite ($4\frac{1}{2}$–5) 0.002 Cancrinite (5–6) 0.023 Scapolite (5–$6\frac{1}{2}$) 0.009 Beryllonite ($5\frac{1}{2}$–6) 0.009 Elaeolite ($5\frac{1}{2}$–6) 0.004 Bytownite (6) 0.009 Sanidine (6) 0.006 Aventurine Feldspar (6–$6\frac{1}{2}$) 0.01 Moonstone (6–$6\frac{1}{2}$) 0.005 Orthoclase (6–$6\frac{1}{2}$) 0.006 Jasper ($6\frac{1}{2}$–7) – Aventurine (7) 0.009 Citrine (7) 0.009 Smoky quartz (7) 0.009 Tiger's eye (7) 0.009 Beryl ($7\frac{1}{2}$–8) 0.006	Calcite (3) 0.172 Onyx Marble (3) 0.172 Pearl (3–4) – Aragonite ($3\frac{1}{2}$–4) 0.155 Dolomite ($3\frac{1}{2}$–$4\frac{1}{2}$) 0.179 Brazilianite ($5\frac{1}{2}$) 0.020 Nephrite (6–$6\frac{1}{2}$) 0.027 Prehnite (6–$6\frac{1}{2}$) 0.030 Beryl ($7\frac{1}{2}$–8) 0.006 Phenacite ($7\frac{1}{2}$–8) 0.016
3.00–3.49	Fluorite (4) –		Apatite (5) 0.002 Hypersthene (5–6) 0.014 Amblygonite (6) 0.026 Ekanite (6–$6\frac{1}{2}$) – Nephrite (6–$6\frac{1}{2}$) 0.027 Hiddenite (6–7) 0.015 Sinhalite ($6\frac{1}{2}$) 0.038 Axinite ($6\frac{1}{2}$–7) 0.010 Jadeite ($6\frac{1}{2}$–7) 0.013 Kornerupine ($6\frac{1}{2}$–7) 0.01 Peridot ($6\frac{1}{2}$–7) 0.036 Dumortierite (7) 0.037 Danburite (7–$7\frac{1}{2}$) 0.006 Tourmaline (7–$7\frac{1}{2}$) 0.014 Andalusite ($7\frac{1}{2}$) 0.007 Rhodozite (8) –
3.50–3.99			Chalybite ($3\frac{1}{2}$–$4\frac{1}{2}$) 0.24 Barytocalcite (4) – Hypersthene (5–6) 0.014 Willemite ($5\frac{1}{2}$) 0.028 Topaz (8) 0.008
4.00–4.99		Witherite ($3\frac{1}{2}$) 0.148	Barite (3) 0.012 Witherite ($3\frac{1}{2}$) 0.148 Willemite ($5\frac{1}{2}$) 0.028

Refr. Index Spec. Grav.	1.700–1.799	1.800–1.899	1.900 and higher
2.00–1.99			
2.00–2.49			Sulphur $(1\frac{1}{2}–2)$ 0.288
2.50–2.99			
3.00–3.49	Hypersthene (5–6) 0.014 Epidote (6–7) 0.035 Clinozoisite (6–7) 0.010 Sinhalite $(6\frac{1}{2})$ 0.038 Idocrase $(6\frac{1}{2})$ 0.005 Dumortierite (7) 0.037	Purpurite $(4–4\frac{1}{2})$ 0.08	Purpurite $(4–4\frac{1}{2})$ 0.08 Diamond (10) –
3.50–3.99	Chalybite $(3\frac{1}{2}–4\frac{1}{2})$ 0.24 Hypersthene (5–6) 0.014 Willemite $(5\frac{1}{2})$ 0.028 Periclase $(5\frac{1}{2}–6)$ – Zircon $(6\frac{1}{2}–7\frac{1}{2})$ 0.059 Grossular $(7–7\frac{1}{2})$ – Pyrope $(7–7\frac{1}{2})$ – Staurolite $(7–7\frac{1}{2})$ 0.015 Hessonite $(7\frac{1}{2})$ – Chrysoberyl $(8\frac{1}{2})$ 0.011 Sapphire (9) 0.008	Chalybite $(3\frac{1}{2}–4\frac{1}{2})$ 0.24 Sphene $(5–5\frac{1}{2})$ 0.105 Zircon $(6\frac{1}{2}–7\frac{1}{2})$ 0.059	Sphene $(5–5\frac{1}{2})$ 0.105 Anatase $(5\frac{1}{2}–6)$ 0.06 Zircon $(6\frac{1}{2}–7\frac{1}{2})$ 0.059 Diamond (10) –
4.00–4.99	Willemite $(5\frac{1}{2})$ 0.028 Zircon $(6\frac{1}{2}–7\frac{1}{2})$ 0.059 Spessartite $(7–7\frac{1}{2})$ – Sapphire (9) 0.008	Zircon $(6\frac{1}{2}–7\frac{1}{2})$ 0.059 Spessartite $(7–7\frac{1}{2})$ –	Sphalerite $(3\frac{1}{2}–4)$ – Hematite $(5\frac{1}{2}–6\frac{1}{2})$ 0.28 Rutile $(6–6\frac{1}{2})$ 0.28 Zircon $(6\frac{1}{2}–7\frac{1}{2})$ 0.059
5.00–5.99		Pyrite $(6–6\frac{1}{2})$ –	Crocoite $(2\frac{1}{2})$ 0.35 Scheelite $(4\frac{1}{2}–5)$ 0.016 Zincite $(4\frac{1}{2}–5)$ 0.016 Tantalite (5–6) 0.17 Hematite $(5\frac{1}{2}–6\frac{1}{2})$ 0.28
6.00–6.99		Cerussite $(3\frac{1}{2})$ 0.274	Crocoite $(2\frac{1}{2})$ 0.35 Phosgenite $(2\frac{1}{2}–3)$ 0.028 Wulfenite (3) 0.10 Cerussite $(3\frac{1}{2})$ 0.274 Scheelite $(4\frac{1}{2}–5)$ 0.016 Tantalite (5–6) 0.17 Cassiterite (6–7) 0.096
7.00 and higher			Wulfenite (3) 0.10 Tantalite (5–6) 0.17 Cassiterite (6–7) 0.096

GEM COLOR
Green+Yellow-green+Blue-green

Refr. Index	1.400–1.499	1.500–1.599	1.600–1.699
Spec. Grav. 1.00–1.99	Opal ($5\frac{1}{2}$–$6\frac{1}{2}$) –	Amber (2–$2\frac{1}{2}$) –	
2.00–2.49	Chrysocolla (2–4) – Moldavite ($5\frac{1}{2}$) – Sodalite ($5\frac{1}{2}$–6) – Opal ($5\frac{1}{2}$–$6\frac{1}{2}$) –	Chrysocolla (2–4) – Serpentine (2–$5\frac{1}{2}$) – Variscite (4–5) 0.010 Apophyllite ($4\frac{1}{2}$–5) 0.002 Thomsonite (5–$5\frac{1}{2}$) 0.028 Moldavite ($5\frac{1}{2}$) –	
2.50–2.99	Onyx Marble (3) 0.172	Vivianite ($1\frac{1}{2}$–2) 0.047 Serpentine (2–$5\frac{1}{2}$) – Onyx Marble (3) 0.172 Variscite (4–5) 0.010 Apophyllite ($4\frac{1}{2}$–5) 0.002 Wardite (5) 0.009 Elaeolite ($5\frac{1}{2}$–6) 0.004 Amazonite (6–$6\frac{1}{2}$) 0.008 Chrysoprase ($6\frac{1}{2}$–7) 0.004 Aventurine (7) 0.009 Prasiolite (7) 0.009 Iolite (7–$7\frac{1}{2}$) 0.008 Aquamarine ($7\frac{1}{2}$–8) 0.006 Beryl ($7\frac{1}{2}$–8) 0.006 Emerald($7\frac{1}{2}$–8) 0.006	Vivianite ($1\frac{1}{2}$–2) 0.047 Onyx Marble (3) 0.172 Datolite (5–$5\frac{1}{2}$) 0.044 Turquoise (5–6) 0.04 Brazilianite ($5\frac{1}{2}$) 0.020 Tremolite ($5\frac{1}{2}$–$6\frac{1}{2}$) 0.02 Nephrite (6–$6\frac{1}{2}$) 0.027 Prehnite (6–$6\frac{1}{2}$) 0.030 Beryl ($7\frac{1}{2}$–8) 0.006
3.00–3.49	Fluorite (4) –		Apatite (5) 0.002 Dioptase (5) 0.053 Hemimorphite (5) 0.022 Datolite (5–$5\frac{1}{2}$) 0.044 Diopside (5–6) 0.028 Hypersthene (5–6) 0.014 Enstatite ($5\frac{1}{2}$) 0.010 Actinolite ($5\frac{1}{2}$–6) 0.023 Tremolite ($5\frac{1}{2}$–$6\frac{1}{2}$) 0.02 Amblygonite (6) 0.026 Ekanite (6–$6\frac{1}{2}$) – Nephrite (6–$6\frac{1}{2}$) 0.027 Hiddenite (6–7) 0.015 Smaragdite ($6\frac{1}{2}$) 0.022 Jadeite ($6\frac{1}{2}$–7) 0.013 Kornerupine ($6\frac{1}{2}$–7) 0.01 Peridot ($6\frac{1}{2}$–7) 0.036 Tourmaline (7–$7\frac{1}{2}$) 0.01 Andalusite ($7\frac{1}{2}$) 0.007 Euclase ($7\frac{1}{2}$) 0.020
3.50–3.99			Malachite ($3\frac{1}{2}$–4) 0.254 Hemimorphite (5) 0.022 Hypersthene (5–6) 0.01 Willemite ($5\frac{1}{2}$) 0.028 Topaz (8) 0.008
4.00–4.99			Barite (3) 0.012 Smithsonite (5) 0.228 Willemite ($5\frac{1}{2}$) 0.028

ohs' hardness) and double refraction		Green + Yellow-green + Blue-green
fr. Index 1.700–1.799	1.800–1.899	1.900 and higher

ec. Grav.	1.700–1.799	1.800–1.899	1.900 and higher
00–1.99			
00–2.49			Sulphur $(1\frac{1}{2}–2)$ 0.288
50–2.99			
00–3.49	Dioptase (5) 0.053 Diopside (5–6) 0.028 Epidote (6–7) 0.035 Clinozoisite (6–7) 0.010 Sinhalite $(6\frac{1}{2})$ 0.038 Idocrase $(6\frac{1}{2})$ 0.005		Diamond (10) –
00–3.99	Malachite $(3\frac{1}{2}–4)$ 0.254 Kyanite $(4\frac{1}{2}–7)$ 0.017 Hypersthene (5–6) 0.014 Willemite $(5\frac{1}{2})$ 0.028 Periclase $(5\frac{1}{2}–6)$ – Zircon $(6\frac{1}{2}–7\frac{1}{2})$ 0.059 Grossular $(7–7\frac{1}{2})$ – Ceylonite (8) – Spinel (8) – Alexandrite $(8\frac{1}{2})$ 0.010 Chrysoberyl $(8\frac{1}{2})$ 0.011 Sapphire (9) 0.008	Malachite $(3\frac{1}{2}–4)$ 0.254 Sphene $(5–5\frac{1}{2})$ 0.105 Demantoid $(6\frac{1}{2}–7)$ – Zircon $(6\frac{1}{2}–7\frac{1}{2})$ 0.059 Uvarovite $(7\frac{1}{2})$ – Ceylonite (8) –	Malachite $(3\frac{1}{2}–4)$ 0.254 Sphene $(5–5\frac{1}{2})$ 0.105 Zircon $(6\frac{1}{2}–7\frac{1}{2})$ 0.059 Diamond (10) –
00–4.99	Smithsonite (5) 0.228 Willemite $(5\frac{1}{2})$ 0.028 Zircon $(6\frac{1}{2}–7\frac{1}{2})$ 0.059 Sapphire (9) 0.008	Smithsonite (5) 0.228 Zircon $(6\frac{1}{2}–7\frac{1}{2})$ 0.059	Sphalerite $(3\frac{1}{2}–4)$ – Zircon $(6\frac{1}{2}–7\frac{1}{2})$ 0.059
00–5.99		Pyrite $(6–6\frac{1}{2})$ –	Scheelite $(4\frac{1}{2}–5)$ 0.016
00–6.99			Phosgenite $(2\frac{1}{2}–3)$ 0.028 Scheelite $(4\frac{1}{2}–5)$ 0.016
00 d her			

The numbers after the gem names refer

Refr. Index	1.400–1.499	1.500–1.599	1.600–1.699
Spec. Grav. 1.00–1.99	Opal $(5\frac{1}{2}-6\frac{1}{2})$ –	Amber $(2-2\frac{1}{2})$ –	
2.00–2.49	Chrysocolla (2–4) – Lapis lazuli (5–6) – Sodalite $(5\frac{1}{2}-6)$ – Opal $(5\frac{1}{2}-6\frac{1}{2})$ –	Chrysocolla (2–4) – Variscite (4–5) 0.010 Apophyllite $(4\frac{1}{2}-5)$ 0.002 Lapis lazuli (5–6) – Haüynite $(5\frac{1}{2}-6)$ –	
2.50–2.99	Coral (3–4) 0.172 Lapis lazuli (5–6) –	Vivianite $(1\frac{1}{2}-2)$ 0.047 Anhydrite $(3-3\frac{1}{2})$ 0.043 Coral (3–4) 0.172 Pearl (3–4) – Variscite (4–5) 0.010 Apophyllite $(4\frac{1}{2}-5)$ 0.002 Wardite (5) 0.009 Lapis lazuli (5–6) – Elaeolite $(5\frac{1}{2}-6)$ 0.004 Amazonite $(6-6\frac{1}{2})$ 0.008 Chalcedony $(6\frac{1}{2}-7)$ 0.006 Chrysoprase $(6\frac{1}{2}-7)$ 0.004 Jasper $(6\frac{1}{2}-7)$ – Aventurine (7) 0.009 Prasiolite (7) 0.009 Iolite $(7-7\frac{1}{2})$ 0.008 Aquamarine $(7\frac{1}{2}-8)$ 0.006 Emerald $(7\frac{1}{2}-8)$ 0.006	Vivianite $(1\frac{1}{2}-2)$ 0.047 Anhydrite $(3-3\frac{1}{2})$ 0.043 Coral (3–4) 0.172 Pearl (3–4) – Turquoise (5–6) 0.04 Brazilianite $(5\frac{1}{2})$ 0.020 Nephrite $(6-6\frac{1}{2})$ 0.027
3.00–3.49	Fluorite (4) –		Apatite (5) 0.002 Dioptase (5) 0.053 Hemimorphite (5) 0.022 Diopside (5–6) 0.028 Lazulite (5–6) 0.030 Nephrite $(6-6\frac{1}{2})$ 0.027 Hiddenite (6–7) 0.015 Sillimanite $(6-7\frac{1}{2})$ 0.02 Sinhalite $(6\frac{1}{2})$ 0.038 Smaragdite $(6\frac{1}{2})$ 0.022 Axinite $(6\frac{1}{2}-7)$ 0.010 Jadeite $(6\frac{1}{2}-7)$ 0.013 Kornerupine $(6\frac{1}{2}-7)$ 0.0 Tanzanite $(6\frac{1}{2}-7)$ 0.009 Dumortierite (7) 0.037 Tourmaline $(7-7\frac{1}{2})$ 0.01 Euclase $(7\frac{1}{2})$ 0.020
3.50–3.99			Celestite $(3-3\frac{1}{2})$ 0.009 Malachite $(3\frac{1}{2}-4)$ 0.254 Hemimorphite (5) 0.022 Willemite $(5\frac{1}{2})$ 0.028 Topaz (8) 0.008
4.00–4.99			Barite (3) 0.012 Celestite $(3-3\frac{1}{2})$ 0.009 Smithsonite (5) 0.228 Willemite $(5\frac{1}{2})$ 0.028

Mohs' hardness) and double refraction

efr. Index	1.700–1.799	1.800–1.899	1.900 and higher
ɔec. Grav. ̣00–1.99			
̣00–2.49			
̣50–2.99			
̣00–3.49	Dioptase (5) 0.053 Diopside (5–6) 0.028 Epidote (6–7) 0.035 Sinhalite (6½) 0.038 Tanzanite (6½–7) 0.009 Dumortierite (7) 0.037	Purpurite (4–4½) 0.08	Purpurite (4–4½) 0.08 Diamond (10) –
̣50–3.99	Azurite (3½–4) 0.108 Malachite (3½–4) 0.254 Kyanite (4½–7) 0.017 Willemite (5½) 0.028 Benitoite (6–6½) 0.047 Zircon (6½–7½) 0.059 Gahnite (7½–8) – Spinel (8) – Taaffeite (8) 0.004 Ruby (9) 0.008 Sapphire (9) 0.008	Azurite (3½–4) 0.108 Malachite (3½–4) 0.254 Sphene (5–5½) 0.105 Benitoite (6–6½) 0.047 Demantoid (6½–7) – Zircon (6½–7½) 0.059 Uvarovite (7½) –	Malachite (3½–4) 0.254 Sphene (5–5½) 0.105 Zircon (6½–7½) 0.059 Diamond (10) –
̣00–4.99	Smithsonite (5) 0.228 Willemite (5½) 0.028 Zircon (6½–7½) 0.059 Ruby (9) 0.008 Sapphire (9) 0.008	Smithsonite (5) 0.228 Zircon (6½–7½) 0.059	Sphalerite (3½–4) – Zircon (6½–7½)
̣00–5.99			Zincite (4½–5) 0.016

Refr. Index	1.400–1.499	1.500–1.599	1.600–1.699
Spec. Grav. 1.00–1.99	Opal ($5\frac{1}{2}$–$6\frac{1}{2}$) –	Amber (2–$2\frac{1}{2}$) –	
2.00–2.49	Opal ($5\frac{1}{2}$–$6\frac{1}{2}$) – Tugtupite (6) 0.006	Stichtite ($1\frac{1}{2}$–$2\frac{1}{2}$) 0.027 Tugtupite (6) 0.006	
2.50–2.99	Calcite (3) 0.172 Coral (3–4) 0.172 Tugtupite (6) 0.006	Calcite (3) 0.172 Anhydrite (3–$3\frac{1}{2}$) 0.043 Coral (3–4) 0.172 Scapolite (5–$6\frac{1}{2}$) 0.009 Tugtupite (6) 0.006 Chalcedony ($6\frac{1}{2}$–7) 0.006 Fossilized wood ($6\frac{1}{2}$–7) – Jasper ($6\frac{1}{2}$–7) – Amethyst (7) 0.009 Rose quartz (7) 0.009 Iolite (7–$7\frac{1}{2}$) 0.008	Calcite (3) 0.172 Anhydrite (3–$3\frac{1}{2}$) 0.043 Coral (3–4) 0.172 Nephrite (6–$6\frac{1}{2}$) 0.027
3.00–3.49	Fluorite (4) –		Apatite (5) 0.002 Hemimorphite (5) 0.022 Nephrite (6–$6\frac{1}{2}$) 0.027 Kunzite (6–7) 0.015 Axinite ($6\frac{1}{2}$–7) 0.010 Jadeite ($6\frac{1}{2}$–7) 0.013 Tanzanite ($6\frac{1}{2}$–7) 0.009 Dumortierite (7) 0.037 Tourmaline (7–$7\frac{1}{8}$) 0.014
3.50–3.99			Chalybite ($3\frac{1}{2}$–$4\frac{1}{2}$) 0.24 Hemimorphite (5) 0.022
4.00–4.99			Barite (3) 0.012 Smithsonite (5) 0.228
5.00–5.99			
6.00–6.99			
7.00 and higher			

Refr. Index	1.700–1.799	1.800–1.899	1.900 and higher
Spec. Grav.			
1.00–1.99			
2.00–2.49			
2.50–2.99			
3.00–3.49	Tanzanite ($6\frac{1}{2}$–7) 0.009 Dumortierite (7) 0.037	Purpurite (4–$4\frac{1}{2}$) 0.08	Purpurite (4–$4\frac{1}{2}$) 0.08
3.50–3.99	Chalybite ($3\frac{1}{2}$–$4\frac{1}{2}$) 0.24 Zircon ($6\frac{1}{2}$–$7\frac{1}{2}$) 0.059 Almandine ($7\frac{1}{2}$) – Gahnite ($7\frac{1}{2}$–8) – Spinel (8) – Taaffeite (8) 0.004 Ruby (9) 0.008 Sapphire (9) 0.008	Chalybite ($3\frac{1}{2}$–$4\frac{1}{2}$) 0.24 Zircon ($6\frac{1}{2}$–$7\frac{1}{2}$) 0.059 Almandine ($7\frac{1}{2}$) –	Zircon ($6\frac{1}{2}$–$7\frac{1}{2}$) 0.059
4.00–4.99	Smithsonite (5) 0.228 Zircon ($6\frac{1}{2}$–$7\frac{1}{2}$) 0.059 Almandine ($7\frac{1}{2}$) – Ruby (9) 0.008 Sapphire (9) 0.008	Smithsonite (5) 0.228 Zircon ($6\frac{1}{2}$–$7\frac{1}{2}$) 0.059 Almandine ($7\frac{1}{2}$) –	Zircon ($6\frac{1}{2}$–$7\frac{1}{2}$) 0.059
5.00–5.99			Proustite ($2\frac{1}{2}$) 0.296 Cuprite ($3\frac{1}{2}$–4) – Zincite ($4\frac{1}{2}$–5) 0.016 Tantalite (5–6) 0.17
6.00–6.99			Cuprite ($3\frac{1}{2}$–4) – Tantalite (5–6) 0.17
7.00 and higher			Tantalite (5–6) 0.17

The numbers after the gem names refer

Refr. Index	1.400–1.499	1.500–1.599	1.600–1.699
Spec. Grav.			
1.00–1.99	Coral (3–4) 0.172 Opal $(5\frac{1}{2}-6\frac{1}{2})$ –	Amber $(2-2\frac{1}{2})$ – Coral (3–4) 0.172	Jet $(2\frac{1}{2}-4)$ – Coral (3–4) 0.172
2.00–2.49	Obsidian $(5-5\frac{1}{2})$ – Sodalite $(5\frac{1}{2}-6)$ – Opal $(5\frac{1}{2}-6\frac{1}{2})$ –	Meerschaum $(2-2\frac{1}{2})$ – Obsidian $(5-5\frac{1}{2})$ – Hambergite $(7\frac{1}{2})$ 0.072	Hambergite $(7\frac{1}{2})$ 0.072
2.50–2.99 ·	Obsidian $(5-5\frac{1}{2})$ –	Pearl (3–4) – Aragonite $(3\frac{1}{2}-4)$ 0.155 Obsidian $(5-5\frac{1}{2})$ – Sanidine (6) 0.006 Labradorite $(6-6\frac{1}{2})$ 0.008 Chalcedony $(6\frac{1}{2}-7)$ 0.006 Fossilized wood $(6\frac{1}{2}-7)$ – Jasper $(6\frac{1}{2}-7)$ – Smoky quartz (7) 0.009	Pearl (3–4) – Aragonite $(3\frac{1}{2}-4)$ 0.155 Nephrite $(6-6\frac{1}{2})$ 0.027
3.00–3.49	Fluorite (4) –		Hypersthene (5–6) 0.014 Enstatite $(5\frac{1}{2})$ 0.010 Nephrite $(6-6\frac{1}{2})$ 0.027 Jadeite $(6\frac{1}{2}-7)$ 0.013 Tourmaline $(7-7\frac{1}{2})$ 0.014
3.50–3.99			Hypersthene (5–6) 0.014
4.00–4.99			
5.00–5.99			
6.00–6.99			
7.00 and higher			

Refr. Index	1.700–1.799	1.800–1.899	1.900 and higher
Spec. Grav.			
2.00–1.99			
2.00–2.49			
2.50–2.99			
3.00–3.49	Hypersthene (5–6) 0.014 Epidote (6–7) 0.035		Diamond (10) –
3.50–3.99	Hypersthene (5–6) 0.014 Ceylonite (8) – Spinel (8) – Sapphire (9) 0.008		Diamond (10) –
4.00–4.99	Sapphire (9) 0.008		Chromite ($5\frac{1}{2}$) – Hematite ($5\frac{1}{2}$–$6\frac{1}{2}$) 0.28
5.00–5.99			Hematite ($5\frac{1}{2}$–$6\frac{1}{2}$) 0.28
6.00–6.99		Cerussite ($3\frac{1}{2}$) 0.274	Cerussite ($3\frac{1}{2}$) 0.274
7.00 and higher			

Refr. Index	1.400–1.499	1.500–1.599	1.600–1.699
Spec. Grav. 1.00–1.99	Opal ($5\frac{1}{2}$–$6\frac{1}{2}$) –		
2.00–2.49	Lapis lazuli (5–6) – Opal ($5\frac{1}{2}$–$6\frac{1}{2}$) – Tugtupite (6) 0.006	Lapis lazuli (5–6) – Tugtupite (6) 0.006	
2.50–2.99	Onyx Marble (3) 0.172 Lapis lazuli (5–6) – Tugtupite (6) 0.006	Onyx Marble (3) 0.172 Howlite ($3\frac{1}{2}$) 0.019 Aragonite ($3\frac{1}{2}$–4) 0.155 Lapis lazuli (5–6) – Jade-albite (6) 0.015 Tugtupite (6) 0.006 Aventurine Feldspar (6–$6\frac{1}{2}$) 0.01 Labradorite (6–$6\frac{1}{2}$) 0.008 Moonstone (6–$6\frac{1}{2}$) 0.005 Peristerite (6–$6\frac{1}{2}$) 0.011 Agate ($6\frac{1}{2}$–7) 0.009 Chalcedony ($6\frac{1}{2}$–7) 0.006 Fossilized wood ($6\frac{1}{2}$–7) – Jasper ($6\frac{1}{2}$–7) – Moss agate ($6\frac{1}{2}$–7) 0.006 Amethyst quartz (7) 0.009 Aventurine (7) 0.009 Tiger's eye (7) 0.009	Onyx Marble (3) 0.172 Howlite ($3\frac{1}{2}$) 0.019 Aragonite ($3\frac{1}{2}$–4) 0.155 Turquoise (5–6) 0.04 Nephrite (6–$6\frac{1}{2}$) 0.027
3.00–3.49			Rhodochrosite (4) 0.22 Nephrite (6–$6\frac{1}{2}$) 0.027 Jadeite ($6\frac{1}{2}$–7) 0.013 Tourmaline (7–$7\frac{1}{2}$) 0.014
3.50–3.99			Malachite ($3\frac{1}{2}$–4) 0.254 Rhodochrosite (4) 0.22
4.00–4.99			
5.00–5.99			
6.00–6.99			
7.00 and higher			

Refr. Index	1.700–1.799	1.800–1.899	1.900 and higher
Spec. Grav. 2.00–1.99			
2.00–2.49			
2.50–2.99			
3.00–3.49	Rhodochrosite (4) 0.22 Rhodonite $(5\frac{1}{2}-6\frac{1}{2})$ 0.011	Rhodochrosite (4) 0.22	
3.50–3.99	Malachite $(3\frac{1}{2}-4)$ 0.254 Rhodochrosite (4) 0.22 Rhodonite $(5\frac{1}{2}-6\frac{1}{2})$ 0.011 Alexandrite $(8\frac{1}{2})$ 0.010	Malachite $(3\frac{1}{2}-4)$ 0.254 Rhodochrosite (4) 0.22	Malachite $(3\frac{1}{2}-4)$ 0.254
4.00–4.99			
5.00–5.99			
6.00–6.99			
7.00 and higher			

Bibliography

Anderson, B. W., 1971: *Gem Testing*. London.

Betechtin, A. G., 1971: *Lehrbuch der speziellen Mineralogie*. Leipzig, East Germany.

Bruton, E., 1977: *Diamonds*. 2nd Edition, Northwood, London.

Chudoba, K. F. & E. J., 1974: *Edelsteinkundliches Handbuch*. Bonn, West Germany.

CIBJO, 1975: *Bestimmungen zur Benennung und Beschreibung von Edelsteinen, Perlen, Kulturperlen, Synthesen, Imitationen*. Bern, Switzerland.

Copeland, L. L., 1960: *The Diamond Dictionary*. Los Angeles, U.S.

Dake, H. C., 1950: *Northwest Gem Trails*. Portland, Oregon, U.S.

Eppler, W. F., 1973: *Praktische Gemmologie*. Stuttgart, West Germany.

Fisher, P. J., 1966: *The Science of Gems*. Scribner's Sons, New York.

Gubelin, E., 1974: *Innenwelt der Edelsteine*. Dusseldorf, West Germany.

Henry, D. J., 1952: *Gem Trail Journal*. Long Beach, California, U.S.

Jahns, R. H., 1975: "Gem Materials" (pp 271–326), *Industrial Minerals and Rocks*. 4th Edition, A.I.M.E., New York.

Kraus, E. H. & C. B. Slawson, 1947: *Gems and Gem Materials*. McGraw-Hill, New York.

Lewis, D., 1977: *Practical Gem Testing*. Northwood, London.

Lenzen, G., 1966: *Produktions-und-Handlegeschicte des Diamanten*. Berlin.

Lenzen, G., 1973: *Kurzgefasste Diamantenkunde*. Kirschweiler.

Liddicoat, R. T., Jr., 1962: *Handbook of Gem Identification*. Los Angeles, U.S.

McIver, J. R., 1967: *Gems, Minerals, and Rocks in Southern Africa*. Elsevier (U.S.), New York.

Pagel-Theisen, V., 1972: *Diamanten-Fibel*. Frankfurt, West Germany.

Ramdohr, P. & H. Strunz, 1967: *Klockmann's Lehrbuch der Mineralogie*. Stuttgart, West Germany.

Schlossmacher, K., 1969: *Edelsteine und Perlen*. Stuttgart, West Germany.

Schumann, W., 1975: *Steine und Mineralien*. Munich, West Germany.

Shaub, B. M., 1975: *Treasures from the Earth*. Crown Publishers, New York.

Shipley, R. M., 1945: *Dictionary of Gems and Gemology*. Los Angeles, U.S.

Sinkankas, J., 1959: *Gemstones of North America*. D. Van Nostrand, Princeton,.N.J., U.S.

Sinkankas, J., 1972: *Gemstone and Mineral Data Book*. New York.

Smith, G. F. H. & F. C. Phillips, 1962: *Gemstones*. 13th edition, Methuen & Co., London.

Strunz, H., 1970: *Mineralogische Tabellen*. Leipzig, East Germany.

Walton, J.: *Tabellen zur Edelstein-Bestimmung*, 2. Auflage, Stuttgart, West Germany.

Webster, R., 1970: *The Gemmologist's Compendium*. 5th edition, Northwood, London.

Webster, R., 1975: *Gems in Jewellery*. Northwood, London.

Webster, R., 1975: *Gem Identification*. Sterling Publishing Co., New York.

Webster, R., 1976: *Practical Gemmology*. 6th edition, Northwood, London.

Journal of the German Gemmological Association, Idar-Oberstein.

Gems and Gemology, Gemological Institute of America, Los Angeles, U.S.

Gems and Minerals, Mentone, California, U.S.

Journal of Gemmology, Gemmological Institute of Great Britain, London.

Lapidary Journal, San Diego, California, U.S.

Schweizer Strahler, Journal of the Swiss Association of Mineral Collectors and Polishers.

Index

The numbers with asterisks refer to pages opposite the appropriate color plate. Pages with the most important information are mentioned first.

252